Community Power
& Democratic Theory

CONSULTING EDITOR:

Douglas Rae
Yale University

RANDOM HOUSE, New York

Community Power & Democratic Theory

THE LOGIC OF POLITICAL ANALYSIS

David M. Ricci
Pennsylvania State University

Library of Congress Catalog Card Number: 79–134870

Manufactured in the United States of America. Composed by H. Wolff Book Mfg. Co., Inc., New York
Printed and bound by Halliday Lithograph Corp., West Hanover, Mass.

Design by Karin Batten

First Edition

9 8 7 6 5 4 3 2 1

To Iry, Ronit, and Anat

Acknowledgments

I have received a great deal of assistance, directly or indirectly, while writing this book. I am therefore especially grateful to my professional colleagues, Edward Keynes and Miss Ruth C. Silva, who read parts of my work when it was in manuscript form. In addition, I wish to thank Miss Susan Rothstein of Random House for her unrelenting efforts to improve the quality of my writing. And finally, the Pennsylvania State University deserves credit, along with the Beit Berl Institute for Education, Culture, and Research (Tsofit, Israel), for generously making time available for me to write. To all I extend my appreciation.

D.M.R.

Contents

Community Power
& Democratic Theory

Introduction

Every reader should be aware of what the volume before him contains and why; he should also be forewarned as to what it does not contain and why. This book was written with several presumptions in mind, and they collectively determined its contents. From the outset, it seemed clear that both community power and democracy are matters of widespread concern; scholars, journalists, university students, and general readers alike, as alert citizens, are all troubled by the problems America faces today. The Vietnam war, racial discrimination, ecological imbalance, urban decay, and many other affairs are constantly discussed and debated, and, in fact, weigh upon our consciousness like living nightmares. Their common moving force is community power—that is, they are the result of, or they will be alleviated by, the exercise of social, economic, and political power in our national and local communities. Their common ideological reference point is democracy—that is, what kind of democratic society is it that has managed to produce such results? Or could it be we have no democracy at all? Our discourse may be scholarly or commonplace, and we may talk about these great problems with colleagues or neighbors, but our concern is the same. In view of the problems that we confront, it can be presumed that few Americans are entirely indifferent to, or ignorant of, community power and democracy.

It may further be presumed, however, that most people do not think very clearly about either of these two broad subjects. Precise thinking in these areas eludes us for two reasons. On the one hand, community power and democracy both pertain to the sum total of politics—to "our lives, our fortunes, and our sacred honor," as the Declaration of Independence put it—and therefore we cannot consider them as dispassionately and as analytically as we might view insects set in orderly entomological array. We tend instead to think of politics in terms of vague and misleading stereotypes like "the knee-jerk liberal," "the foreign policy hawk," "the party of fiscal responsibility," and "the wily Oriental." Thus in regard to politics, we usually justify our preconceptions rather than employ our intelligence; we are, after all, only human.

On the other hand, even if we were capable of calm and deliberate political calculation, precise thinking would still elude us because power, the key to our understanding of what happens in politics, is intangible. Some men lead, and other men follow; some command, others obey. Here is power, but it is a relationship that cannot be measured and weighed, that cannot be placed under a microscope, that cannot be tested by chemicals and electrodes. It is a relationship among men, an immaterial reflection of often inscrutable motivations and impulses. And so it is doubly difficult to think clearly about community power and democracy, first because we the thinkers are human, and second because our subject matter is itself a manifestation of human nature, a force only imperfectly understood and so subtle as to defy exact description.

It may be presumed, then, that most Americans are concerned about community power and democracy, yet their thinking about both subjects is likely to be muddled. In light of this, the selection of material for inclusion in *Community Power and Democratic Theory* was determined; the book was designed to discuss various scholarly works dealing with the two subjects, and to explain concepts and categories of conceptualization which have been rigorously and systematically applied to both. In short, it is about the logic of community power analysis and the relationship of that logic to different perspectives of American democracy. Because scholars are themselves only human, it should not be surprising to discover that the net effect of scholarly thought on community power and democracy is inconclusive, that well-known and highly respected students of American politics disagree with each other on many fundamental points. Nevertheless, the reader can profit from their agreements and disagreements by using their carefully conceived ideas to clarify and sharpen his own thinking. In the end, he will be better equipped to arrive at realistic conclusions concerning the problems we face if he appreciates the analytical strengths and weaknesses of academic concepts such as "actual power," "potential power," "slack power," "direct influence," "indirect influence," "decisions," "nondecisions," "inertia," "noncumulative resources," and "potential groups."

As the positive content of this book was the outcome of two presumptions, so also the "negative content"—that is, what was omitted—was presumptively determined. *Community Power and Democratic Theory* does *not* include much detailed information about America's greatest contemporary problems because it was presumed that such data could not be covered adequately in a short book devoted mainly to the logical intricacies of power analysis. It was further presumed, however, that no one who is aware of the communications media and the quality of life around him can fail to recognize the broad outlines of problems such as poverty, racial tension, planned obsolescence, and the deterioration of our environment. Even though it was not possible to present here *many* of the facts concerning such situations, this book outlines the logic of community power analysis with repeated references to a *few* of the facts. These few are couched in terms broad enough to be easily understood, and they are intended to maintain the reader's sense of what is important and relevant even when rather abstract concepts and seemingly narrow scholarly controversies are being examined. For some readers, no doubt, the smattering of facts will serve also to maintain a sense of indignation, urgency, and even anger.

A great many facts that bear on our major problems are readily available, of course. In order to compensate for their absence here, Appendix B: Selected Readings on Contemporary American Problems has been provided. As a supplement to what does not appear in the text itself, Appendix B affords the reader two opportunities: (1) the books it cites all deal at length and in considerable detail with great social, economic, and political problems, and may be read with an eye toward better understanding the relationship between those problems, community power, and democracy; and (2) the same books, while they offer a wealth of facts, give us some indication of whether or not scholars especially concerned with the analysis of community power have paid sufficient attention to the most pressing matters confronting American democracy. On this second point, more will be said in Chapter 12.

Three Views of Democracy:
Liberalism, Conservatism, and Socialism

Anyone who seeks to appreciate the ultimate significance of community power studies, and their relation to democratic thought, must begin with the unquestionable fact that for some time America has endured adverse political conditions that justify grave concern about the manner in which power is exercised in our local and national communities. Newspaper headlines chronicle the latest episodes of acute crises: the war in Vietnam, racial strife, poverty, crime, air and water pollution, urban sprawl and decay, unsafe commodities, depletion of natural resources, and others too numerous to mention. Books portray the same crises more systematically, even in their very titles. For example, consider these volumes: Theodore Lowi, *The End of Liberalism: Ideology, Policy, and the Crisis of Public Authority*,[1] Charles Silberman, *Crisis in Black and White*,[2] Seymour Melman, *Our Depleted Society*,[3] and Paul Jacobs, *Prelude to Riot: A View of America from the Bottom*.[4] If the Devil were to respond now to Daniel Webster's query—"How goes the Union?"—his answer surely would be, "Not well."

In the realm of political studies, American democracy has long been a source of anxiety. Of course scholars are disposed to view society more analytically than laymen. Their apprehensions, far-reaching and profound, are likely to be directed more to fundamental causes than to immediate symptoms. In any event, in

7

viewing the practical difficulties of the day as manifestations of persistent political problems, serious students of politics have long questioned the validity of certain principles and practices that are part and parcel of American democracy. It is imperative that we pay some attention to our intellectual heritage and its influence on political thought today. What we find is that democratic Liberalism in America has been severely challenged by nondemocratic Conservatism and Socialism, and that the latter two raise provocative questions about the manner in which, and by whom, power is exercised in our communities, as against how and where it should be brought to bear instead.

AN HISTORICAL TYPOLOGY

Recent scholarship tends to speak of America as a fundamentally Liberal society,[5] even though the assertion is not consistent with our everyday use of political labels. The common practice is to reserve the term "liberal" for politicians such as Hubert Humphrey, because they espouse certain political principles. In opposition to the liberals stand the "conservatives," such as Barry Goldwater, who argue the merits of certain alternative principles. It is thus the fashion to mark as liberals those who encourage government to deal directly with social problems, whereas conservatives are distinguished by their faith that the relatively unhampered exchange mechanism of a private marketplace can alone resolve the same problems. To many contemporary Americans this system of identifying competing political factions seems both natural and universally applicable. In reality, however, the two labels as we use them are quite parochial and are suitable only for specific issues in American political experience.[6] If other issues are discussed—for example, the war in Vietnam—we immediately perceive the impossibility of accurately classifying our leaders and their policies by the use of such categories.

In the larger historical context the term "Liberal" is best reserved for the great political ideas and policies formulated by the middle class of the Western world since about 1650, and especially since the American and French revolutions. If Liberalism is thus generally defined, Conservatism can be seen by contrast to have embraced mainly the thoughts and programs of the Western aristocracy in the same era, and Socialism may be viewed as an ideology and set of social propositions then advanced by or on behalf of the Western working class. Liberalism, middle class; Conservatism, upper class; Socialism, lower class: here is the most common typology used to explain the general features of political thought in the modern world.

Within this typology, America stands as almost purely Liberal. Its political culture—with constitutional moderation, limited government by consent, frequent elections, competitive political parties, basic political rights—has always, in its totality, been heavily weighted with middle-class values. As the Founding Fathers intended and as immigration assured, America never suffered an entrenched upper-class Conservatism of the type found in Europe, which had tenacious hereditary roots in a feudal society. Moreover, at the other extreme, due to the combination of democratic government and bourgeois capitalism, many workingmen were permitted to rise above their original station in life. Socialism therefore never had a sufficient accumulation of lower-class discontent upon which to flourish.

If the terms "Liberalism," "Conservatism," and "Socialism" are applied loosely in historical context, they have only limited utility for intellectual history, and they fail to account for political movements whose origins are complex and whose support extended across class lines. They are useless, therefore, in unraveling the subtleties of Romanticism, Nationalism, Imperialism, and Fascism. Furthermore, they tell us nothing about how one Conservative differs from another, and they blur distinctions among Liberals and among Socialists, even though such variances are important in political analysis. For example, in the sense that both Humphrey and Goldwater serve and cherish a Liberal form of government, they are Liberals; but there is a notable difference between the programs each recommends to that same government, a difference so significant that we need labels to distinguish them. Similarly, members of the British Labour party are far more acceptable to most Americans than are the Russian Communists, although both could fairly, albeit misleadingly, be called Socialists.

Despite its limitations, the simple typology, which crudely

links each of the three historical classes with a typical outlook, enjoys the virtue of drawing attention to an immensely important confrontation in the history of political thought. By and large, Liberalism has created, sustained, and revered democracy, while Conservatism and certain forms of Socialism have done , exactly the reverse. Indeed, in their purest forms, there exists a long-lasting and deep-seated antipathy between the first school of thought and the other two. And this antipathy may be defined in terms of consistent and irreconcilable differences of belief in how power is to be distributed and exercised in our political communities.

LIBERALISM

To begin with, what were historically the basic tenets of Liberalism, and how did they contrast with those of Conservatism? The answer to this question will always be imprecise, since the remarkable variety of men and political movements encompassed by both terms invites interminable academic quibbling rather than useful generalizations, and since even the most knowledgeable scholars are careful to hedge their remarks. Harold Laski, for instance, cautioned that the evolution of Liberalism "was never direct and rarely conscious. The pedigree of ideas is never straightforward." Moreover, he observed that Liberalism is "not easy to describe, much less define, for it is hardly less a habit of mind than a body of doctrine."[7] Quite apart from the elusive nature of Liberalism, it is no less difficult to ascertain how widely it has been pursued as a way of life, for, as another historian has warned us, "no man and no generation has entertained it in its entirety."[8]

Conceding the hazards of oversimplification, then, let us presume that America is predominantly a Liberal society with its intellectual origins in England. The conclusions of some of the best-known Liberal political thinkers in the Anglo-American tradition as to the nature of citizenship and an ideal polity rested upon three fundamental convictions: (1) most men are rational; (2) the individual rather than the group is politically important; and, (3) the interests of men can best be represented directly in government through a democratic electoral system.

The first Liberal tenet, that most men do possess and can use a reasoning faculty, is well known to all Americans if only because of the Declaration of Independence, which expounded a theory of "self-evident" inalienable rights to "life, liberty, and the pursuit of happiness."[9] What this meant, of course, was that if government does not interfere, people are capable of intelligently handling their own affairs, of determining the desirability of certain goals for themselves, and of calculating the most efficacious and painless means necessary to achieve those goals. In the most general terms, this process of deliberation may be viewed as a propensity pervading all social behavior; thus, regardless of the sphere of his activity, "every man desires to obtain additional wealth with as little sacrifice as possible."[10] The means to any one man's happiness may be private or public, economic or political. What matters is that both men and their means will be rational.

After assuming the existence of rational men, Liberals further assumed that such men are, or ought to be, the basic political components of the state.[11] This second tenet of Liberalism referred to an ideal state of affairs that may be known analytically as "atomism." Atomism may be said to exist when "every complex whole can be broken down or analyzed into its parts without remainder, the whole being no more than the sum of its parts."[12] Political atomism was implicit in the speculation of Jeremy Bentham when he argued, for example, that "the community is a fictitious body, composed of the individual persons who are considered as constituting as it were its *members*. The interest of the community then is, what?—the sum of the interests of the several members who compose it."[13]

The Liberal notion of atomism was especially significant because it disparaged and discounted the political role of groups. Liberals took it for granted that groups, or factions, are potentially dangerous entities because, as political actors, their particular interests conflict with the general welfare. This was the view of James Madison. In his classic Federalist Paper 10, he decried the existence of factions and explained how the American constitution would restrain them. He argued, indeed, that the chief virtue of the federal system, with its checks and balances and separation of powers, was its ability to curb the influence of factions.[14]

Madison's political theory was typically Liberal in that it assumed factions merely to be no more than groups of rational individuals united by a particular and often temporary self-interest; a man who today belongs to one group may then change his affiliation to another when his self-interest dictates it. This view emphasized individual interests as against the *gestalt* qualities of politically potent groups, qualities over and above the rational concerns separately animating a group's individual members, and in it, groups are simply less significant for political analysis than men. A similar notion permeated most Liberal writings. The epitome of Liberalism in this respect was the very popular nineteenth-century philosophy of Samuel Smiles, who expounded a sort of Horatio Alger thesis that "national progress is the sum of individual industry, energy, and uprightness, as national decay is of individual idleness, selfishness, and vice."[15] For such sentiments, Smiles' brand of Liberalism became known as "Individualism." It was perhaps unrealistic of Liberals to misjudge the significance of groups, but, as we shall see, they had good reason.

The final tenet of Liberalism was that only government based upon a democratic electoral system—one man, one vote—can truly represent the interests of all men in any given society. This grew out of the first two tenets. Liberals assumed that all men desire certain ends for themselves. Fortunately, however, because most men are rational their subjective perception of desires equates fully with their real, objective needs. That is to say, the interests such men do seek to satisfy are the ones that they *ought* to satisfy. Consequently, there is little danger in permitting most citizens to be represented in a community's government, because the real needs of the community must of necessity be the sum of the perceived desires of its members.

The people should govern themselves, then, but the form of self-government must serve several functional requirements. Because individual men are rational and know what they themselves want, when in power they may seek to secure only their own personal needs.[16] A democracy must therefore control the citizens it elevates to public office; in order to avoid tyranny, democratic government must place the governors under the continuous consent of the governed. This control may be achieved by the distinctively Liberal practice of frequent elections.[17] The justification for frequent elections is that they keep government officials constantly prepared to be judged by the voters. Under the circumstances, the best insurance of a vote of confidence is advocacy and execution of policies consonant with the interests of the electorate. The result of frequent elections will therefore be a balance of the self-interest of the governors and of the governed. Voters will express their perceived interests with their ballots, and government officials who wish to retain their offices and attendant privileges will serve the public desire expressed by their constituents. In the long run, both the elected and the electors should be satisfied.

But even within this system there persists a possible danger that the majority of voters might elect a majority of legislators who, with impunity, might pursue a policy oppressive to a minority of citizens. This undesirable end can be avoided by instituting checks and balances within government, by separating powers and distributing authority to different government agencies, and by granting inviolable civil rights, such as free speech and freedom of religion.[18] Liberals believed that such devices would make it difficult for a majority to accumulate enough power to act uncompromisingly toward a minority. Therefore these, and like political safeguards, were adopted by Liberal societies throughout the nineteenth century.

CONSERVATISM

An historical logic linked together the tenets of Liberalism and even explained the absence of certain beliefs among them. This logic cannot be demonstrated by perfectly unambiguous manifestations of cause and effect, yet we can say that in general the Liberal tenets were inversely related to those of the political culture Liberals sought to replace. In other words, one must seek the logic of Liberalism in Conservatism, in the ideas and practices of the old aristocratic society that Liberalism opposed.

Unfortunately, Conservatism is an amorphous political entity, and it is therefore just as difficult to define as Liberalism. Both dispassionate scholars and dedicated disciples of Conservatism agree, however, that the most typical and outspoken of its proponents was the eighteenth-century Englishman, Edmund Burke.[19] When Burke's writings are analyzed and their substance isolated from oratorical and polemical overtones, three basic political tenets emerge. These are: (1) most men are *not* rational; (2) groups in society are *more* important than individuals; and (3) governmental representation of political interests should *not* be based on direct suffrage. Significantly, these typical Conservative tenets are precisely the reverse of those of Liberalism.[20]

As a member of Parliament who identified himself closely with its aristocratic leaders, Burke could hardly assert that all men are equally reasonable; such an acknowledgement would have challenged the moral legitimacy of rule by a privileged nobility based on birth rather than merit. He argued, instead, that most men have only small capacity for reasoning and that they do well, therefore, to place little confidence in their own speculations on politics. In Burke's estimation, what we require are not personal political opinions but firm political convictions drawn from the experience of mankind over the centuries.

Burke expounded the Conservative tenet on incompetent men boldly: "We know that *we* have made no discoveries, and we think that no discoveries are to be made, in morality, nor many in the great principles of government, nor in the ideas of liberty, which were understood long before we were born."[21] Certain moral and political truths, then, which instruct us in the proper manner of forming governments and securing liberty, have been revealed over generations to the *collective wisdom* of men, and there is no more to be learned on these subjects. Such truths are woven into our culture, where they foster habits, or, in Burke's term, "prejudices." "Instead of casting away all our old prejudices," he argued, we should "cherish them to a very considerable degree . . . because they are prejudices; and the longer they have lasted and the more generally they have prevailed, the more we [should] cherish them. We are afraid to put men to live and trade each on his own private stock of reason, because we suspect that this stock in each man is small."[22] "The science of government," accordingly, is "a matter which requires experience, and even more experience than any person can gain in his whole life."[23] Men must defer to "precedent, authority, and example,"[24] or they must rely upon "instinct to fortify the fallible and feeble contrivances of our reason."[25] Clearly, Burke was saying it is a mistake for people to count on their own capacity to discover new political truths or to insist that the leaders of society yield to new ideas urged upon them. For this reason, the Conservatives saw no justification for democracy or widespread suffrage.

While Burke denied the competence of individual men, he did have faith in, and therefore emphasized, the political importance of groups. As a practical matter, he sought to preserve the remnants of a feudal society still controlled largely by the aristocracy, a society whose shape was determined by the pattern of its social and economic elements. Guilds, ancient corporations, chartered companies, noble orders, churches, commoners, and more—all these groups were linked by a complex configuration of privileges and duties. Burke, who insisted on retaining most of this configuration intact, was implying that a rightly ordered society must be composed of enduring groups whose positions vis-à-vis each other change slowly if at all.

A steady Conservative opposition to rapid social change was a constant theme in Burke's writings. "I may assume," he wrote, "that the awful Author of our being is the Author of our place in the order of existence—and that, having disposed and marshalled us by a divine tactic, not according to our will, but according to His, He has in and by that disposition virtually subjected us to act the part which belongs to the place assigned us."[26] All men are involuntarily situated in society, and they must remain in their places loyally, for "our country is not a thing of mere physical locality. It consists, in a great measure, in the ancient order into which we are born."[27]

It was within this "ancient order" that Burke saw established groups as serving the greater whole, and while he did not explore the role played by all existing groups, he took pains to defend

the aristocracy, in which he deemed himself an active partici-
pant. "A true natural aristocracy," he claimed, "is not a separate
interest in the state, or separable from it. It is an essential in-
tegrant part of any large body rightly constituted."[28] It is "the
leading, guiding, and governing part. It is the soul to the body,
without which the man does not exist."[29] From the Conservative
point of view, men's social stations are fixed, the social groups
they belong to are naturally endowed with purposes within the
state, and the aristocratic social group is peculiarly competent to
govern.

From these Conservative views of individual men and of
groups, it followed, as a third tenet, that the interests of men
should not be democratically represented in government through
widespread suffrage. Concerning the nature of a proper relationship between citizens and their government, Burke raised three
related points. To begin with, citizens should not enjoy the
power to change the form of government, since they are not wise
enough to improve the governmental institutions they inherit,
nor do they have the right to alter the fundamental structure of
society. "Society is . . . a contract," Burke argued. "It is a
partnership in all science; a partnership in all art; a partnership
in every virtue and in all perfection. As the ends of such a partnership cannot be obtained in many generations, it becomes a
partnership not only between those who are living, but between
those who are living, those who are dead, and those who are to be
born. Each contract of each particular state is but a clause in the
great primeval contract of eternal society [ordained by God]."[30]
The form of any government should therefore be beyond the
will of its populace at any given time in its history.

Moreover, no citizen should presume to instruct his elected
representatives as to what policies to support in the legislature.
In the last analysis, government and politics are matters of experience, a special expertise that the legislator is more likely to
have than the citizen. "Your representative," Burke told his own
constituents, "owes you, not his industry only, but his judgment;
and he betrays, instead of serving you, if he sacrifices it to your
opinion."[31]

Finally, not many citizens should demand that their government permit them to vote and thus participate directly in the

making of political decisions. According to Burke, it is sufficient if only a few men vote and the rest be "virtually represented." As he defined it, "virtual representation is that in which there is a combination of interests and a sympathy of feelings and desires between those who act in the name of any description of people and the people in whose name they act, though the trustees are not actually chosen by them."[32] Burke preferred this mode of representation to any other, because it frees government officials to deliberate and to formulate policy unhampered by the hue and cry of volatile public opinion.

This concept of "virtual representation"—as distinguished from direct and widespread suffrage—dovetailed neatly with the Conservative view of groups. Once it is assumed every man is a member of some order, part, or segment of society, a plausible argument can be made that he is represented, albeit indirectly, if the legislature seems to take into account the concerns of his peers. The right to vote, in that case, ceases to be a measure of adequate representation and responsible government. And Burke, at least, believed that England's eighteenth-century system of representation, based on a severely limited franchise, "has been found perfectly adequate to all the purposes for which a representation of the people can be desired or devised."[33]

THE LOGIC OF CONFRONTATION

Comparison of Liberal and Conservative political tenets reveals a consistent duality. In each of the major concerns the two ideologies opposed each other. There was a pervasive logical and historical appropriateness to their confrontation. The Liberal tenets marked a middle-class resolve to question the legitimacy of a society controlled by hereditary aristocrats; the Conservative tenets reflected an aristocratic need to justify a dominant role in that society. It was only natural, therefore, that Liberals should believe individual men to be reasonable and certain truths to be self-evident to those men; and it was as predictable that Conservatives would brand men as unreasonable and look to history and experience for political truths. The old order was entrenched in factions and other established interests, and so to the

Liberals all groups appeared pernicious; to the Conservatives, who dominated society in the existing structures, the status quo became divine. And so it went, always consistent, with Liberals wanting the people to speak directly to the government and Conservatives always defending quasifeudal representation. The logic of such a duality has been summed up by Louis Hartz, in a twentieth-century context, when he observed that "the inevitable perspectives of political controversy . . . compel a system to define itself in terms of the one it seeks to undermine. Its image of itself is a negation of what it seeks to destroy."[34]

The works of Herbert Spencer, a Liberal sociologist, offer proof of Hartz's thesis and a summary of the logically contradictory positions taken by Liberals and Conservatives. Writing in the late nineteenth century, Spencer reviewed modern English history and saw in it the two great political movements of Toryism and Liberalism, or, roughly speaking, Conservatism and Liberalism in the largest sense. Toryism and Liberalism, he observed, "at first stood respectively for two opposed types of social organization, broadly distinguishable as the militant and the industrial—types which are characterized, the one by the *regime* of status, almost universal in ancient days, and the other by the *regime* of contract, which has become general in modern days, chiefly among the Western nations, and especially among ourselves and the Americans."[35]

By "a regime of status," Spencer meant a society wherein a man's role is fixed by the social order into which he is born. Under a regime of contract, in contrast, a man's role can change in keeping with his productive efforts; he can thereby become a doctor, an artist, a businessman, or a banker if he works accordingly. In general, the regime of status was the hallmark of feudalism, in which men inherited their social position, and the regime of contract was the basis for capitalism, in which men advance on the basis of effort rather than birth. Under the old regime there was little social, economic, and political mobility; the new allowed a considerable amount of all three. The aristocrats were intent on preserving their rule, of course, and so took the Conservative view. Precisely *in order to overthrow* the established authorities, a Liberal view of men, groups, and representation was expounded by an ambitious middle class. This group aimed at reconstructing what remained of feudal society so that power, prestige, and ease would flow from a man's accomplishments rather than from his antecedents.

AMERICAN LIBERALISM

To understand the logic of the confrontation of Conservatism and Liberalism is to understand a vital aspect of American political thought, which, with few exceptions, has been so distinctively Liberal. During the nineteenth century, the three tenets of Liberalism coalesced and created an ideological vision of American society—how it was functioning, or how it would function in the future when all its members constantly improve their intellect and social condition by steady work and its remuneration. An hereditary aristocracy was not permitted, upward mobility was encouraged, and, especially on the frontier, men were esteemed in proportion to their contribution to the community. All the visible marks of a Liberal society were present and lauded: government by consent, separation of power, checks and balances, fundamental political rights, economic opportunity, and freedom of contract.

The faith that most Americans have always extended to this ideological vision has been demonstrated in both word and deed. Its general influence in the nineteenth century was apparent, for example, to astute foreign observers like Alexis de Tocqueville and James Bryce,[36] both of whom remarked on the democratic bias of American society. It frequently served as the rallying cry to all Americans in times of great stress. Thus Abraham Lincoln's poetic expression of Liberalism that "government of the people, by the people, and for the people, shall not perish from the Earth"; thus Woodrow Wilson's plea that Americans go to war in order "to save the world for democracy"; and, thus Franklin Roosevelt's announcement that America would become "the arsenal of democracy." In equally ceremonious language, the vision has been evoked again and again—in Flag Day speeches, at convocations, at cornerstone laying ceremonies, and at other public functions. Today, when Americans see themselves in ideological confrontation on a world-wide scale, belief in the tenets of

Liberalism is commonly equated with our national character. We define treason and our enemies as "un-American," which means, of course, that both are defined in terms of disdain for our political ideals.

SOCIALISM

Ideological orthodoxy, unfortunately, is not necessarily rooted in a sure grasp of the facts, and the great flaw in our Liberal ideology, a flaw that has a direct bearing on recent efforts to understand power in our communities, has been and still is its failure to describe adequately the political systems established or reformed in the name of Liberalism. Like Conservatives and Liberals, of course, Socialists differ among themselves, and to speak of Socialism as a single entity is as risky as speaking generally of Conservatism or Liberalism. Indeed, to the extent that some Socialists are quite democratic and advocate elections, civil rights, and competitive political parties (like the former British Prime Minister Harold Wilson or the late Norman Thomas), they are so similar to Liberals that they are not our concern here. Such men may be classified comfortably with the Hubert Humphreys and Barry Goldwaters of the Liberal political world. What should concern us here is the most radical expression of Socialism, that ideology most thoroughly hostile to Liberalism and everything that Liberalism endorses. This kind of Socialism assumed the shape of Marxism, and, if we figuratively place it on the Left, and Burkean Conservatism on the Right, we have the symmetry of Left, Right, and the Liberal Center.

MARXISM

The fact that Liberalism, and American Liberalism in particular, feels itself threatened by Marxist Socialism does not require emphasis here. If space were available, Marxism and its hostility to Liberalism might be traced to the beginning of the nineteenth century, to certain failures of revolution in Europe, to industrial unrest, to the writings of Karl Marx, Friedrich Engels, V. I.

Lenin, and others, to the Russian Revolution of 1917, and to the Marxian conversion of many Western intellectuals in the ideologically confused decade of the 1930s.[37] In America, Marxism was firmly opposed by the ideological mainstream, consisting of the mass media (excluding some avant-garde intellectuals but including *The New York Times, The Literary Digest, Time, Business Week,* and so forth), professional associations, religious groups, business organizations, veterans, and politicians. Spurred by ideological passion and by various political and economic interests, the middle class and those who thought of themselves as middle class[38] eventually joined ranks against Marxism in the great ideological struggle that developed into the Cold War.

Even without a cataloguing of details, the massive confrontation between American Liberalism and Marxism should be fairly clear to most readers. The question is: How may this conflict between Marxists and Liberals be defined in terms of their basic political tenets? What was the logical nature of the left-wing challenge to Liberalism? What did Marxists preach to undermine confidence in Liberalism, and what was the necessary response?

The principles of Marxism have been expounded, analyzed, acclaimed, and attacked by many scholars. Not all students of Marxism agree upon any one explanation of the relevant material, but it seems reasonable to relate certain basic axioms and beliefs of Marxists to parallel notions of Liberals and Conservatives, in particular, to notions already analyzed above. The picture that emerges does not explain the consequences of Marxism in China, the Soviet Union, Cuba, and elsewhere, but it can lead to an appreciation of the significance of community power studies. In very broad terms, Marxist theory can be portrayed as a conglomeration of Liberal expectations, Conservative observations, and revolutionary recommendations.

To begin with, Marx himself laid down a model of the nature of man. According to his early writings, and implicit in his later works, man "is a being for himself, and, therefore, a *species-being.*"[39] The essence of a distinctively *human species-being,* however, must be described in terms of the typically Liberal quality of rationality. As Marx put it, "free, conscious activity, is the species-character of human beings."[40] It is thus the rationality of man which sets him apart from other living creatures.

Marx expected that an ideal society would permit men to develop to the fullest their natural capacity for reason, but he argued that such growth was nowhere the case in Liberal societies. Under Liberalism, the capitalist economic system looks upon the average man as merely one among many instruments of production and, therefore, manipulates him as it does any inanimate object.[41] Working by the hour as wage laborers rather than as independent, creative artisans, most employees are spiritually stunted and effectively isolated from the very products they create. Operating around a cash nexus, most employers are similarly affected, for they relate to their business more in monetary terms than in terms of nonproperty, humane values.

The wage system, the cash nexus, the market economy, assembly lines of mass production, concentration of capital, absentee control of industry, and the general, ever-increasing complexity of modern economic life, all cause men in Liberal states to be psychologically *alienated*.[42] They work at repetitive and uninspiring jobs; they become greedy and acquisitive; their personalities are warped and perverted. In short, their common humanity is diminished and they cannot achieve their potentiality as *species-beings*.

Actually, what Marx envisaged was something Liberal—a society of rational, mature men. What he saw around him instead was a reality composed largely of irrational men, a reality that might just as well have been discovered by Conservatives. It can be said, therefore, that Conservatives and Marxists agreed that an ideal society cannot be built upon men as they are.

Marx's disciples were even more pessimistic than Marx himself. Lenin, for one, formulated a powerful theory of why most men in Liberal states, and the working class in particular, are unable to think clearly about their own affairs or even to understand their ultimate personal interests.[43] According to Lenin's concept of "spontaneity," workers in industrial societies blindly and impulsively seek shortsighted goals consonant only with immediate economic objectives. Through trade unions, and by voting in democratic parliamentary elections, they pursue a policy of "economism"; they demand more pay, more leisure, and better working conditions. In the long run, however, such demands neither make for change nor question the fundamental validity of the capitalist economic system. The normal, spontaneous activity of workers will therefore never destroy capitalism and replace it with an ideal society free from alienation and capable of permitting men to fulfill their proper ends as *species-beings*.

This debilitating process, whereby the existing environment entices men to complacent adaptation rather than toward any desire for change, depends upon a state of mind that may be labeled "false consciousness."[44] That is to say, most men are aware only of interests that are not in accord with their true needs. The Marxian recognition of this false consciousness was not unrelated to the Conservative notion of unthinking masses, although the terminology was, of course, quite different. There was a striking similarity between the two, however, because both agreed that the greatest number of men are unable to discover what is good for themselves. From both these points of view, and contrary to Liberal belief, the desires men feel subjectively are not usually informed by objective reason.

In the matter of political groups, Marxists shared a large area of agreement with Liberals. Marxists envisioned a utopia in which groups would be unimportant, where there would be only workers and thus, in effect, a classless society. Under such circumstances, all the inequalities and inequities flowing from status in modern society would cease. All men would be skilled and industrious; all men would be decent and humane; all men would be guided by reason and logic.[45] As Friedrich Engels put it, when this classless utopia is finally attained, man will become "the lord over nature, his own master—free."[46] It was a vision that appealed to a great many men of good will.

On the question of classes, Marxists shared a fundamental conviction that social conditions in capitalist societies are rotten to the core. This highly undesirable reality found its Marxian explanation in the theory of economic determinism, that "the history of all . . . society is the history of class struggles."[47] According to the theory, available techniques of production shape the institutions within which men must live. As a result, every social system is inevitably divided into economic classes, those that own the means of production and those that do not. Between the two, there is perpetual conflict to gain more of the benefits produced by the economy. In the capitalist social system, Marxists argued, the bourgeois middle class owns the factories, or the means of industrial production, and members of the working class have no choice but to labor for minimal wages. The result of Liberal freedom, then, is *not* a society in which groups count for little, but rather a society in which certain groups—in this case, economic classes—are penultimately important. As a member of the bourgeoisie, you may enjoy the comforts made possible by modern technology. If you belong to the proletariat, you will probably suffer the indignities and hardships of poverty.

Again it is clear that Marxists entertained Liberal expectations, since they looked forward to a society composed of independent men, men unrestrained by ties to permanent and entrenched social orders. However, it is also clear that they viewed the world with a Conservative eye, since they firmly believed that the natural configuration of power in every society correlates with great social groups and, short of radical changes, is likely to remain so.

Finally, Marxists, like Liberals, hoped eventually to enjoy a completely democratic society. They called their vision of the future "Communism," but Marx's writings reveal that in its mature form, Communism is to be a representative form of government, with public officials responding to the will of the people and with universal suffrage exercised by politically competent and reasonable men.[48] Unlike Liberals, however, Marxists assumed that before such a democracy could be established, there would have to be a transition period during which would be established a "dictatorship of the proletariat."[49] The precise meaning of this phrase, and the government it depicts, has never been clear, not even to Marxists themselves. But it surely cannot be equated with Liberal practices—with elections, separation of political powers, and due process of law. Evidently, Liberals expected their democracy to be established quickly, whereas Marxists insisted that true democracy can only come in an indefinite future.

The conflict between Marxists and Liberals on the issue of

democracy flowed from their contrasting perceptions of men and groups. Lenin, for example, explained that since most men *cannot* ascertain their own objective interests, they are incapable of exercising their democratic rights in a Liberal society except blindly, erroneously, and to the ultimate benefit of the rulers of that society. In the light of this presumed incompetence, he posited the need for a revolutionary party[50]—a secret, tightly knit organization that could act as a vanguard for the proletariat, serve the interests that the masses cannot perceive, erect a dictatorship on their behalf, liquidate all other classes, establish a classless society, educate men to their fullest capacity as rational *species-beings,* and then, upon all this, build a true democracy.

This was the famous Marxist doctrine of an elite, dogmatic Communist party, based on a rather Liberal vision of the future and a somewhat Conservative view of the political and economic situation existing in Liberal societies. With a confidence born of metaphysical certainty, the theory rejected Liberal democracy as a sham and labeled it harmful to Marxist ends. It was by such logic that the specter of violent revolution was raised. And in fact, the end result of Marxist theorizing was a broad and persistent recommendation for upheaval, to be led by a Communist party implacably hostile to the practices of Liberalism. According to the Marxian assessment of political reality, bourgeois rulers of Liberal states simply will not yield their power democratically and peacefully, and revolution is therefore absolutely necessary. Thus Marxists around the world, drawing from Liberal optimism and Conservative pessimism, planned violent and total destruction of Liberal political systems.

AGAIN, THE LOGIC OF CONFRONTATION

We have already seen how ideologies tend to define themselves in terms of their opposites, how Liberalism was formulated as a rejection of certain principles of Conservatism. In like fashion, Marxism was formulated as a rejection of Liberalism. Marxism is an extraordinarily complex philosophical construct, with an ingenious combination of explanatory theories and moral principles that can be almost theologically compelling. In its essence, nevertheless, it was designed to propel the lower class to power, to oust the middle class in industrial societies. Quite apart from how, and for what purposes, it has been used by assorted political movements from Russia to China to Cuba, in the abstract Marxism remains an ideology defined in terms of its perceived opposite, Liberalism. In the logic of political disputation, it was virtually predictable that Marxists, *in order to overthrow Liberalism,* would deny the validity of Liberal tenets and rationalize a position exactly opposite them.

This rationale for the Marxist position leads to a vitally significant fact, the intellectual commonality of Marxism and Conservatism. While both the Left and the Right have historically disagreed with the Center, ironically they have stood on common ground in ascribing fundamental faults to Liberalism. There are, after all, only a limited number of clearly distinguishable polemical positions in political debate and, therefore, as they had to do, both Conservatives and Marxists claimed—contrary to Liberal beliefs—that most men are not rational, that many groups are both vitally significant and persistent, and that democracy cannot work. The perspective differed, but in these conclusions they agreed.

In the last analysis, then, even though the two viewpoints critical of Liberalism were inspired by different aims, they both sought to disestablish its institutions and brought similar charges against those institutions. This mutual reinforcement of converging accusations from both ends of the political spectrum was cumulatively dangerous to Liberalism. At the same time, however, such limited focusing of many arguments exposed an intellectual Achilles heel in both kinds of critics who found fault with Liberalism. If Liberals could prove that men are in fact rational, that groups are at least flexible and responsive, or that democracy can work, Conservatives and Marxists would simultaneously and decisively be refuted. In other words, if Liberals could point to Liberal communities and show that power was distributed fairly and exercised reasonably in them, the polemical case in favor of Liberalism would be won.

Here was a promising opportunity, inherent in the very nature of the positions that logic dictated to the Right, Left, and Center. It arrived, unfortunately, precisely when developments in the various fields of social science brought to light certain very disturbing evidence contradicting all the tenets of Liberalism. Little by little, political reality in Liberal societies became almost an embarrassment to Liberal democratic theory.

NOTES

1/ (New York: Norton, 1969) .
2/ (New York: Random House, 1964) .
3/ (New York: Dell, 1966) .
4/ (New York: Random House, 1966) .
5/ The leading exponent of this point of view is Louis Hartz, *The Liberal Tradition in America* (New York: Harcourt, Brace, 1955) .
6/ The origins of the distinctively American use of the terms "liberal" and "conservative" are discussed in Samuel Beer, "Liberalism and the National Idea," in Robert A. Goldwin (ed.) , *Left, Right, and Center: Essays on Liberalism and Conservatism in the United States* (Chicago: Rand McNally, 1965) , pp. 143–150.
7/ Harold Laski, *The Rise of European Liberalism* (London: Allen and Unwin, 1962) , pp. 11–13.
8/ Harry Girvetz, *The Evolution of Liberalism* (New York: Collier, 1966) , p. 47.
9/ For the rationale of the Declaration, see Carl Becker, *The Declaration of Independence* (New York: Knopf, 1942) .
10/ The quotation is from Nassau Senior, the leading Utilitarian economist. See his *Outline of the Science of Political Economy* (orig., 1840; New York: Ferrar and Rinehart, 1939) , p. 26.
11/ Earl Latham, "The Group Basis of Politics: Notes for a Theory," *American Political Science Review* (June 1952) , p. 378.
12/ Girvetz, *The Evolution of Liberalism*, p. 41.
13/ Jeremy Bentham, *The Principles of Morals and Legislation* (orig., 1789; New York: Hafner, 1948) , p. 1.
14/ In Alexander Hamilton, John Jay, and James Madison, *The*

Federalist (orig., 1788; New York: Modern Library, 1937), pp. 53–62.

15/ Samuel Smiles, *Self-Help* (orig., 1860; London: John Murray, 1958), p. 36.

16/ James Mill, *Essay on Government* (orig., 1820; New York: Library of Liberal Arts, 1955), pp. 47–54.

17/ *Ibid.*, pp. 67–72.

18/ Some of these devices are discussed in Madison *et al.*, *The Federalist*, Essay 10, pp. 53–62. The rights are found in the Bill of Rights.

19/ For example, see Samuel Huntington, "Conservatism as an Ideology," *American Political Science Review* (June 1957), pp. 454–473; and Russell Kirk, *The Conservative Mind* (Chicago: Regnery, 1953).

20/ Like the very terms "Liberal" and "Conservative," the juxtaposition of Liberal and Conservative tenets above is merely a useful generalization. Scholars disagree on the characteristic tenets they attribute to both schools of thought; indeed, an intense academic controversy currently rages over the *true* nature of Liberalism. For example, interpretations of Liberalism that do not entirely agree with the analysis outlined in the text above are advanced in Sheldon Wolin, *Politics and Vision* (Boston: Little, Brown, 1960), pp. 286–434, and in C. B. MacPherson, *The Political Theory of Possessive Individualism* (New York: Oxford University Press, 1964). The opposition of Liberal and Conservative tenets outlined above is especially useful for our purposes, though, and exclusive of minor adjustments is consistent with the analysis set forth in Girvetz, *The Evolution of Liberalism*, pp. 23–149; and Huntington, "Conservatism as an Ideology," p. 456.

21/ Edmund Burke, *Reflections on the Revolution in France* (orig., 1790; New York: Library of Liberal Arts, 1955), p. 97.

22/ *Ibid.*, pp. 98–99.

23/ *Ibid.*, pp. 69–70.

24/ *Ibid.*, p. 36.

25/ *Ibid.*, p. 39.

26/ Edmund Burke, *An Appeal from the New to the Old Whigs* (orig., 1791; New York: Library of Liberal Arts, 1962) , p. 96.

27/ *Ibid.,* p. 97.

28/ *Ibid.,* p. 104.

29/ *Ibid.,* p. 105.

30/ Burke, *Reflections,* p. 110.

31/ Edmund Burke, "Speech of November 3, 1774," in Ross J. S. Hoffman and Paul Levack (eds.) , *Burke's Politics* (New York: Knopf, 1959) , p. 115.

32/ Edmund Burke, "Letter to Sir Hercules Langrishe, Bart., M.P., on the subject of the Roman Catholics of Ireland and the propriety of admitting them to the elective franchise, consistently with the principles of the Constitution, as established at the Revolution," in *ibid.,* p. 494.

33/ Burke, *Reflections,* p. 64.

34/ Louis Hartz, "Democracy: Image and Reality," in William Chambers and Robert Salisbury (eds.) , *Democracy in the Mid-Twentieth Century* (St. Louis: Washington University Press, 1960) , p. 14.

35/ Herbert Spencer, "The New Toryism," in Truxton Beale (ed.) , *The Man Versus the State* (New York: Mitchell Kennerley, 1916) , p. 7.

36/ Alexis de Tocqueville, *Democracy in America,* eds. J. P. Mayer and Max Lerner, trans. George Lawrence (orig., 1840; New York: Harper & Row, 1966) ; James Bryce, *The American Commonwealth,* ed., abr., and introd. by Louis M. Hacker (orig., 1885; New York: Putnam, 1959) .

37/ There are many comprehensive general works on the history and theory of Marxism. For example, see George Lichtheim, *Marxism* (New York: Praeger, 1961) , and *The Origins of Socialism* (New York: Praeger, 1969) ; Adam Ulam, *The Unfinished Revolution* (New York: Vintage, 1960) ; Bertram D. Wolfe, *Marxism* (New York: Delta, 1965) ; G. D. H. Cole, *The Meaning of Marxism* (Ann Arbor: University of Michigan Press, 1964) ; and Alfred G. Meyer, *Leninism* (New York: Praeger, 1962) .

38/ One of America's sources of strength in the battle of ideologies is that most of its people, regardless of their income or position in American society, *think* of themselves as middle class. The result of this widespread outlook is that Marxist theory, which emphasizes proletarian misery, is viewed by most Americans as irrelevant at best and pernicious at worst. On the prevalence of middle-class expectations and values, see Elmo Roper, "Fortune Survey: A Self Portrait of the American People," *Fortune Magazine* (January 1947), pp. 5–16.

39/ Karl Marx, "Critique of Hegel's Dialectic and General Philosophy" (1844), in T. B. Bottomore (ed.), *Karl Marx: Early Writings* (New York: McGraw-Hill, 1964), p. 208.

40/ Karl Marx, "Alienated Labor" (1844), in *ibid.,* p. 127.

41/ This contention, so basic to Marxism, pervades Karl Marx, *Capital* (orig., 1867; New York: Modern Library, 1906), Vol. I, and also Marx, *Early Writings.*

42/ See Marx, "Alienated Labor" in *Early Writings.*

43/ V. I. Lenin, *What Is To Be Done?* (orig., 1902; New York: International Publishers, 1929), *passim.*

44/ C. Wright Mills, in "The Middle Classes in Middle-Sized Cities," in Irving Horowitz (ed.), *Power, Politics and People: The Collected Essays of C. Wright Mills* (New York: Oxford University Press, 1963), p. 276, defines false consciousness as "the lack of awareness of and identification with one's objective interests."

45/ Some of the most optimistic passages about the ideal society yet to come are in V. I. Lenin, *State and Revolution* (orig., 1918; New York: International Publishers, 1932), pp. 73–74, 83–85.

46/ Friedrich Engels, *Socialism: Utopian and Scientific* (orig., 1880; New York: International Publishers, 1935), p. 75.

47/ Karl Marx and Friedrich Engels, "The Manifesto of the Communist Party" (1848), in Harold Laski, *Harold Laski on the Communist Manifesto* (New York: Vintage, 1967), p. 131. The best summary of the theory of economic determinism may be found in Engels, *Socialism,* pp. 54–75.

48/ Marx's democratic goal is one of the central themes of Shlomo Avineri, *The Social and Political Thought of Karl Marx* (Cambridge, Eng.: Cambridge University Press, 1968), *passim,* but esp. pp. 31–40.

49/ This regime is mentioned briefly by Marx in "Critique of
the Gotha Program" (1875), in Lewis S. Feuer (ed.), *Marx
and Engels: Basic Writings on Politics and Philosophy*
(Garden City, N.Y.: Doubleday, 1959), p. 127. Later, it became an important theoretical concept among those Marxists
who actively sought to produce revolutionary change. See
Lenin, *State and Revolution*, pp. 71–75.

50/ Lenin, *What Is To Be Done?, passim,* but esp. pp. 112 ff.

⭐ 2 ⭐

The Challenge to Liberalism:
Social Science and the Study
of Political Power

In general, Anglo-American Liberalism suffered a serious decline in faith during the first several decades of the twentieth century. Much of the disillusionment was due to events in the political world of that period; in particular, it was heightened by the inauspicious conduct of elected governments during World War I, by their inability to create an equitable peace and stable prosperity after that war, and by the rise of right-wing and left-wing dictatorships in Europe. It was difficult to remain optimistic about any political system, Liberal or otherwise, during such an era. At the same time, the spirit of Liberalism was additionally weakened by the research of social scientists. These men did not always intend to challenge Liberalism, but their findings were clothed with the apparent objectivity of science itself and therefore could not be ignored. The result was an intellectual crisis, a far-ranging confrontation between Liberal beliefs and the seemingly obdurate facts of power in Liberal communities.

Is democracy really possible? That became the crucial question. The moral raison d'être of Liberal societies depended on a favorable answer, since a negative one would have strongly implied that the great eighteenth-century revolutions, the hard won electoral reforms, the highly valued civil rights, as indeed all other fundamental elements of Liberalism, had been in vain. A negative answer would implicitly and convincingly demonstrate the validity of Conservative and Marxian political notions, and thereby add to the doubts which already plagued many twentieth-century Liberals.

Is democracy really possible? In the realm of social science, so far as democracy was defined by Liberals, the answer was "No." Beginning with a trickle of social research in the late nineteenth century and continuing with a massive outpouring of findings and hypotheses in the twentieth century, students in the fields of psychology, sociology, economics, and political science emphasized aspects of man and his behavior that thoroughly undermined the three basic tenets of Liberalism. Unwelcome facts of all kinds appeared in writings by the most influential scholars and social investigators, contradicted every Liberal hope and expectation, and, at the same time, seemed to support their Conservative and Marxian alternatives.

IRRATIONAL MEN

It will be recalled that the first Liberal tenet viewed men as naturally rational beings. Late in the nineteenth century, however, the developing science of psychology flatly denied that such people exist at all. Supported by the seminal theories of Sigmund Freud, psychologists insisted on the enormously significant distinction between mental processes that are conscious and those that are unconscious.[1] The very idea that there is a difference between the two was necessarily disturbing to Liberals because their common, everyday understanding of rationality, formalized in the utility calculus of Jeremy Bentham, presumed that reason is the mark of a deliberate intellect; rationality, to them, was the path followed by a conscious, thinking mind.

Freudian terms are so widely understood today that they may be used to demonstrate how severely Liberalism was challenged. Briefly, they describe the human personality as a composite of *id, ego,* and *superego.* The id is the "unknown and unconscious,"[2] rooted in men's basic and primordial instincts. Upon this id rests the ego, which Freud described as a "coherent organization of mental processes" including consciousness.[3] And above the ego stands the superego which, roughly speaking, is the awareness of moral imperatives constituting the conscience that seeks to guide the ego to patterns of behavior acceptable to society. In the most general sense, the id represents man's animal qualities, the ego represents his individual human nature, and the superego represents the social, communal aspects of his personality.[4]

The question is: Where does rationality reside, and in what measure? Freud himself concluded that "the ego represents what we call reason and sanity, in contrast to the id which contains the passions."[5] The id, then, is unreasonable. However, even if the ego is credited with reason, it enjoys that quality only to a limited extent. Powerful, irrational impulses in each man's id constantly surge forth, checked only weakly by his ego. Likewise, other irrational forces may be directed at one's ego by his superego, whose moral commands, unfortunately, may arise from the superstitious myths of religion, nationality, or class. And finally, the consciousness of the ego is itself weak, since any number of psychological processes, such as rationalization, may cause it to succumb to the strength of either id or superego and permit man to act without reason even while he is convinced that his behavior is thoroughly logical and objectively appropriate to his circumstances.

From a Liberal point of view, the personalities Freud discovered among his psychiatric patients in Vienna were imperfectly balanced. To those who assessed the component parts of men's minds, it was clear that the rationality required for democratic politics was in short supply. This fact was emphasized, to the embarrassment of Liberal theorists, by Graham Wallas, a professor of politics at the London School of Economics.

"We are apt to assume," Wallas observed, "that every human action is the result of an intellectual process, by which a man first thinks of some end which he desires, and then calculates the means by which that end can be attained."[6] Wallas labeled this assumption "the intellectualist fallacy," and charged that it was common among the theorists of democracy. "Intellectual political thinkers often assume," he remarked, "not only that political action is necessarily the result of inferences as to means and ends, but that all inferences are of the same 'rational' type."[7] In fact, however, politics "consists largely in the creation of opinion by the deliberate exploitation of subconscious non-rational inference."[8]

In technical terms, Wallas argued that politics is not based on reason but rather is a reflection of men's instincts—for example, the instincts he saw associated with fear, affection, property, family, hunger, fighting, curiosity, sex, and anger.[9] Motivated by the drives that reside in the Freudian id, political behavior is much more a matter of impulsive action than thoughtful premeditation. Indeed, the superstructure of politics—that is, the vocabulary of political discourse by which we conduct public affairs—is shaped by the totality of passionate forces that animate all men. Political discourse at home, in the streets, in election campaigns, and in official government policy statements, is definitely *not* designed to encourage men to think clearly and calmly. On the contrary, it is composed mainly of what Wallas called "entities," or collections of emotionally weighted symbols, which distort our thinking about political parties, states, and ideals.[10] Men talk to one another, and leaders speak to the electorate, largely in terms of crude stereotypes; and there is some doubt that political communication leaves any room at all for reasonable, dispassionate, detached thought. Consider, for example, modern terms like "fascist pig," "Red China," "clean bomb," "Chicago 1968," "law and order," "dove," or "hawk." Such terms are actually entities, so weighted by prejudice, passion, and preconception that they impede reason rather than permit it to function.

The observations made by Wallas served Liberalism in the same way as the small boy who pointed out the emperor's lack of clothing. The facts were plain to see, and practical politicians recognized them or were quickly driven into private occupations.[11] But Liberals were ideologically inhibited from admitting the highly visible facts of irrationality. Any admission that human desires that arise subjectively are not informed by objective reason would compel the further admission that the interests men seek to serve politically may be unwise. Moreover, if the desires men attempt to satisfy are only subjectively valid, perhaps Liberal societies would be better off *not* practicing democracy; perhaps they should, instead, search their ranks for those few men who are peculiarly competent to make political judgments. This reasoning was logically consistent, but it was either too inherently Conservative or too inherently Marxian to satisfy Liberals. Liberals were unable to ignore totally the existence of irrationality, but they could not comfortably accept it either.

UNIQUE GROUPS

The second Liberal tenet presumed the unremarkable nature of political groups, and held that they are no more than aggregates of rational men bent on a collective, premeditated purpose. This tenet also was denied by social scientists. Gustave Le Bon, a French student of collective behavior at the turn of the century, focused attention on the metamorphosis of men's personalities when groups form. "Under certain given circumstances," he asserted, "an agglomeration of men presents new characteristics very different from those of the individuals composing it. The sentiments and ideas of all the persons in the gathering take one and the same direction, and their conscious personality vanishes. A collective mind is formed . . . and is subjected to the *law of the mental unity of crowds.*"[12]

For Liberals and for democracy, the significance of the mental unity of crowds lay in the fact that, as Le Bon put it, "in the aggregate which constitutes a crowd there is no sort of summing-up of or an average struck between its elements. What really takes place is a combination followed by the creation of new characteristics."[13] Unfortunately, these new characteristics are generally undesirable, since they are dominated by men's unreasoning instincts.[14] Crowds may generate godliness and self-lessness; but more often, crowds will foster barbarity, bigotry, vengeance, and jingoism. In all their acts, group minds lack forethought and are susceptible to the exciting appeals of demagogy.

A similar view of groups was advanced by Freud, who provided conceptual categories to describe group personalities much as he described the minds of individuals. In psychological terms, Freud explained that when men associate, they "put one and the same object in place of their ego-ideal [i.e., superego]."[15] On the spur of the moment, the objectives of the group replace the consciences that society has implanted in each man for the benefit of all. Then, under the influence of the new collective superego and with its active approval, members of the group may be impelled to socially irresponsible behavior directed to the group's own narrow ends. In an extreme case, which Freud thought quite possible, a very large group may form around a narcissistic, maladjusted leader and, if it adopts his goals as the group's own, the result could be a totalitarian political party, unrestrained by the discipline of conscience.[16]

The description of groups offered by social science was a direct threat to Liberalism. It was seen that groups can be as unreasonable as individual men and this was distressing to Liberals who maintained, as their heir, former President Lyndon Johnson, did recently, that we can all "reason together." The indication that men may *not* be so capable brought into question the moral foundations of Liberal institutions. After all, group activity commands every level of democratic political life, from committees and juries to parties, electorates, nations, and races.[17] What if the rationality, and thus the wisdom, of all these is suspect?

Then too, social scientists in effect argued that groups are unique and cannot be ignored, as Liberal theorists were accustomed to doing. It might be possible to fashion a mechanical and automatic process for limiting the effects of faction, as America has done with its constitutional form of government. But the efficacy of such devices is not absolute; the peculiar qualities of groups can neither be channeled nor checked with assurance. By tapping the most primitive and passionate of men's impulses, groups might grow powerful enough to overcome constitutional restraints (for example, the Southern whites who have succeeded in tyrannizing Southern blacks and denying them effective citizenship for generations). They might be tenacious enough to outlive their original members (for example, the Democratic party, which originated in the political organization founded by Thomas Jefferson). They might not disband after their original cause is achieved or abandoned, but they might, instead, adopt successive new issues for the sake of perpetuating their organization (for example, the March of Dimes, Inc., which began by seeking a cure for infantile paralysis and now collects money to combat other diseases) . In several respects, groups have a vitality and a life of their own. They constitute something of a permanent element in society, a factor that must be reckoned with on its own account rather than in the simple, classic Liberal terms of the individual people who separately compose it.

But here was a cause for persistent concern. If groups possess peculiar qualities that Liberals had earlier denied, perhaps Conservatives were right when they claimed that society is composed of various kinds of associations, each with a separate and meaningful role, and each serving men in its own way. Or, perhaps Marxists were justified in their insistence that the shape of economic classes determines the distribution of property and the apportionment of justice in every society. It was not necessary for social scientists to join with particular Conservatives or Marxists in commending the virtue embodied in any established social group, be it the aristocracy or the proletariat. The very revelation of collective aspects of behavior struck a powerful, if unintentional, blow at the spiritual heart of Liberalism. In the last analysis, the clear implication was that groups are politically more important than individuals.

THE UBIQUITY OF OLIGARCHY

The final Liberal tenet was that government can be made democratic and responsive to the desires and needs of the governed. This tenet, too, was challenged by social science research. Social scientists claimed that the organizations that men form to restrain government officials—groups such as parties, lobbies, and ad hoc committees—themselves tend to get out of hand, to pass beyond the control of their members. This cast a serious reflection on Liberal institutions, since it meant that perhaps they do not give an effective voice to the ordinary men who constitute the great majority of citizens.

The undemocratic characteristics of organizations were highlighted by Robert Michels, a Swiss sociologist who postulated what he called the "Iron Law of Oligarchy."[18] According to this law, there is a propensity for all organizations to be at least partially unresponsive to the wishes of their members in two ways. First, it is inevitable that organizations will acquire a hierarchical structure of internal power. All the group members cannot exercise power directly, if only for technical and administrative reasons.[19] It must be expected, in any collection of men, that only a few possess the skills and expertise that the organization requires, and that those few will move into positions of leadership. Eventually, every organization is marked by a vertical alignment of authority, with the result that only a limited number of men make decisions and the rest, the rank and file, are content mainly to acquiesce.

If the leaders of any organization win their position and remain in it due to efforts on behalf of the men below them, the organization might be deemed democratically responsive, despite its hierarchical characteristics. The trouble is, observed Michels, that a second aspect of the "Iron Law of Oligarchy" may diminish the identity of interest between leaders and their followers. Leaders of various organizations may draw upon a source of power from beyond their own group in order to stay at the top. They may, in other words, maintain their positions without satisfying the group's membership. We see this when the leaders of diverse organizations band together, covertly or overtly, for mutual support.[20] In so doing, they escape the restraints nominally laid upon them by their original supporters.

Michels himself argued that the process of collusion between men at the top is inevitable; he cited, as an example, the cooperation between Socialist leaders and the leaders of non-Socialist parties in Germany to support World War I, in the face of a stated policy of the German Social Democratic party to oppose the war.[21] Had Michels crossed the Atlantic Ocean, he would have discovered American political practices that encouraged similar collusion. Unresponsive organizational behavior was present even then in the American Congress, where representatives elected in the name of ostensibly competitive parties befriended each other through the seniority system, often at the expense of rendering the Congress insensitive to public opinion. The conclusion to be drawn here is that the Liberal practice of frequent elections has never enjoyed more than imperfect control over the tacit conspiracies of leaders intent upon avoiding responsibility.

From the Liberal point of view, the tendency toward oligarchy is particularly dangerous because the great organizations that reveal it are characteristic of the twentieth century. They represent a necessary and irreversible principle of modern life. The great German sociologist Max Weber explained this phenomenon by observing that, as civilization grows more complex, it requires more and more specialization of labor.[22] Great organizations, which Weber called bureaucracies, therefore come into being to supply this necessary factor of production in the form of minutely refined skills, for both public and private realms of endeavor. Accordingly, hierarchies are inevitable in government, in commerce, and in manufacturing; indeed, they will be established in every field of activity where men congregate to pursue the vital business of a complex society. It is ironic, of course, that as the Liberal vision of prosperous, democratic polities was fulfilled, their very size and success generated the organizational structures that significantly lessened the opportunities for democratic participation in community affairs.

Implicit in their growing anxiety over the nature and the role of organizations was a characteristic Liberal concern with elites. If modern life is so complicated as to require oligarchical hierarchy and specialized expertise, men can hardly be viewed as substantially equal, interchangeable parts in an open, Liberal society. Instead, they are significantly unequal and necessarily differentiated from one another. As Conservatives and Marxists had long argued—albeit to press conflicting recommendations for political improvement—some must lead and others must follow. In fact, elite leaders seemed inevitable and necessary, both of which evoked approval from the Right and from the Left, and caused considerable Liberal anguish. The optimistic, nineteenth-century Liberal vision of an ideal man—for example, Andrew Jackson's egalitarian common man[23] or Mark Twain's omnicompetent Connecticut Yankee[24]—faded and gave way to the pessimistic, twentieth-century portrait of "mass" man. As José Ortega y Gasset, a Spanish Conservative, described him, the typical member of the masses in an industrial society is a creature of limited competence, whose culture must be created and preserved by his superiors.[25]

THE STUDY OF COMMUNITY POWER

The totality of early social science findings concerning reason, groups, and organizational structure contributed to the general loss of faith suffered by the advocates of Liberalism. It appeared that democracy was a glorious but unattainable ideal, and the joint contentions of Conservatives and Marxists seemed irrefutable. At the same time, however, there appeared within social science a small area of inquiry that promised a potential for eventually restoring men's confidence in Liberal politics; this was the study of community power. In America the study of community power expanded greatly after World War II in a series of scholarly works and commentaries. This literature is discussed fully in successive chapters below, and its enormous importance will then become clear. It may be helpful now, however, to analyze briefly some of the early efforts in this field, in order to lay the groundwork for an understanding of its later developments.

The theoretical relationship between community power studies and Liberalism may be demonstrated by the pre-World War I theory of an American political scientist, Arthur Bentley.[26] When we assume that men are rational, it is appropriate to study their utterances and avowed ideals, since these may then be taken as representative of what they will accomplish. From this point of view, Lincoln's Gettysburg Address proves that American government is "of the people, by the people, and for the people." On the other hand, if men are not rational, as social science has ascertained, and if their intentions and motivations are uncertain indicators of their eventual behavior, the study of politics is better served by observing only the relationships that actually exist among men. And as Bentley emphasized repeatedly, these relationships entail power.

Bentley himself was explicit on this point. He belittled all a priori axioms of politics, including Liberal notions, as unreliable guides to an understanding of politics. "Soul stuff," he derisively labeled such axioms.[27] They refer to mental attitudes, which cannot be grasped or examined and therefore are irrelevant to political analysis. What can be grasped, according to Bentley, are the *results* of our states of mind, outward behavior in itself only imperfectly understood. What can be examined are the vectors of political force created by human efforts. What can be analyzed are associations and institutions, the configurations of power that men create and manipulate in order to advance their subjectively determined interests. What ought to be studied, in short, is the distribution and exercise of power in our communities.

STUDIES OF GROUPS AND ELITES

While thinkers like Bentley provided theories to link the beleaguered tenets of Liberalism with the need for power studies, developing events suggested the practical need for such studies. On both sides of the Atlantic, democratic practices and policies were constantly being challenged. The realities of agrarian and industrial unrest, financial panics, governmental corruption, World War I, the Russian Revolution, the Great Depression, and the ascendance of Fascism, gave rise to new political movements. These movements, including American Populism and Progressivism, and English Guild Socialism, agitated and focused attention on existing conditions such as widespread poverty and business concentration in Liberal states. In popular writings called muckraking and in more technical works by distinguished scholars,[28] attempts were made to pierce the rhetoric of Liberalism and to uncover the actual facts of power. With or without knowledge of Bentley's formulation, many American and English students of politics became impatient with what they regarded as sterile democratic shibboleths and began to concentrate on reality. Their findings, at least until after World War II, did not encourage adherents of Liberalism, and in fact, suggested that notwithstanding all their democratic political practices, Liberal societies had fallen into an indefensible rut where most citizens were politically insignificant and only a few wielded decisive power.

Early studies in the field of community power fit in two categories: those that explained politics largely in terms of groups, and those that drew attention to elites. The group studies may themselves be divided into two classes: one distinguished by philosophical pluralism and the other by analytical pluralism.[29]

Philosophical pluralists, for the most part in England, criticized the wisdom of the Liberal electoral notion of one man, one vote. They argued that all men possess complex personalities which generate more than one interest, each requiring separate representation. It was observed that in life, unlike in theory, the same men join different groups in order to fully promote their diverse interests. Thus, a single man may be a member of an Anglican parish, a hunters' lodge, a country club, a professional society, a temperance league, and a neighborhood improvement association. In reality, then, politics consists of the clash between such groups rather than the registering of single votes on election day. And in evaluating electoral returns, politicians are interpreting them in terms of the group interests they reflect.

The philosophical aspect of this point of view, expounded by scholars like Harold Laski, G. D. H. Cole, and R. H. Tawney,[30] lay in the dissatisfaction these pluralists found in the existing array of groups. They claimed that groups protecting property, for example, were too powerful and far outweighed those groups concerned with the poor, with clean air and clean water, and with other amenities of life. Here was a problem for Liberalism, for if in reality certain groups are overly powerful, their narrow interests will be served at the expense of those of society as a whole. To remedy this imbalance, philosophical pluralists prescribed radical constitutional changes in Liberal societies, changes designed to establish and protect new groups as counterbalances to those already active in politics.[31]

Unlike philosophical pluralists, analytical pluralists were mainly American and more concerned with describing group behavior than with recommending reforms. Bentley himself, the forerunner of this school, argued that groups were preeminent in politics, but he did not go much beyond theoretical presumptions that this was true. This is the general substance and significance of his *Process of Government*. Later scholars engaged themselves deeply in research, though, and wherever they looked, they found groups to be the determinants of public policy. Pendleton Herring analyzed the whole range of lobby groups in

Congress; E. E. Schattschneider concentrated his attention on groups especially interested in the tariff, a single national issue; and Oliver Garceau carefully examined the political practices of just one powerful group, the American Medical Association.[32]

The challenge of such studies to Liberalism was summarized in the theories of group behavior offered by two other analytical pluralists, John Dewey and Walter Lippmann.[33] According to both, the public that Liberals had envisioned and relied upon takes little interest in the broad spectrum of political issues. Rather, each particular issue attracts relatively few partisans, who are usually divided along group lines for or against any proposal. Some unattached or unorganized citizens may inject themselves into a particular issue, but their power is only occasionally decisive. What became of the public of Liberals, the final arbiter of all political disputes, the guarantor of society's general interest? Lippmann went straight to the point: the public, he declared, is no more than a "phantom."[34] Groups are the only important structures of power.

While both the philosophical and analytical pluralists focused their attention on groups, other students of politics concentrated on the activities of the elite. Society's elite is composed of those few men and women who, by virtue of birth, superior intelligence, enterprise, luck, hard work, trickery, violence, or any other means, attain leading positions and exercise decisive power over social, economic, and political affairs. The phenomenon of elites stimulated commentary by many European and American social scientists now well known in the history of sociology—for example, Gaetano Mosca, Max Weber, M. Ostrogorski, Vilfredo Pareto, Pitirim Sorokin, Harold Lasswell, and Robert and Helen Lynd.[35] An American political scientist, Lasswell, argued that all political activity depends on "influence and the influential"— in a word, the elite.[36] Inevitably, members of the elite gain the lion's share of society's valued objects—deference, safety, income, and leisure. The Lynds, both sociologists, discovered a typical powerful elite in Muncie, Indiana, composed of the "X family," its relatives, and its friends. Describing the varied powers of this elite—powers extending to control over banking, jobs, the mass media, and local government—they claimed that the one family enjoyed the dominant influence over the entire town.[37]

The implications of elite power were similar to those of group power. Scholars might disagree as to whether the elite is more powerful than groups or vice versa, whether the elite is a group unto itself, or whether the elite works through groups. But regardless of the exact relationship between the two, according to Liberal ideology neither was a legitimate permanent force in society. In reality, however, both persevered and seemed capable of manipulating, or at least circumventing, the representative and legislative procedures that had been established in nominally democratic countries to place decision-making power in the hands of the entire citizenry. Indeed, entrenched groups and the elite enjoyed some of the unchecked powers of a privileged aristocracy, much to the dismay of Liberals.

THE PROBLEM OF METHOD

Despite the fact that most studies of community power seemed to validate Conservative and Marxian pessimism about man and democracy, Liberals made an effort to confound their critics. Some Liberal scholars, especially in America, made their own studies of community power in an effort to demonstrate that it was exercised democratically. One such scholar, typical and influential among political scientists of the interwar period, was Charles Merriam at the University of Chicago. Merriam contended that regardless of any limitation on man's rational behavior, and regardless of his propensity for establishing hierarchies, the common people of democratic societies maintain a considerable measure of control over their leaders. By means of active or passive resistance, through civil disobedience or general strikes, they can compel the removal and replacement of those in authority. In other words, the citizenry retain some kind of ultimate reserve power which they can exercise in time of need.[38] This line of argument was not entirely satisfactory, given original Liberal hopes and expectations. It was capable, nonetheless, of conveying some comfort in a century marked by authoritarianism, expanding bureaucracy, totalitarianism, and even bizarre forms of government.

Unfortunately, Merriam's analysis of power was flawed by

severe methodological deficiencies. As was true of many pre-World War II studies of community power, its conceptual scheme was extremely inexact. For this reason, Merriam and other scholars of the period could not measure precisely the influence wielded by groups or elites and, therefore, could not know how unreasonable and/or undemocratic the politics of any particular community were. The techniques available for analyzing power were largely unrefined, and the men who studied communities were quite confused about the subject. The problem was that there were simply too many revealed facts about power, all seemingly pertinent. But no one could say with certainty which ones were relevant to a true understanding of the configuration of power and its effect on democracy. Merriam himself, for example, while arguing that citizens collectively retain ultimate power over their government, noted that elements of power exist in wealth, patronage, prestige, administration, punishments, honors, force, tradition, and routine,[39] as well as in the special skills needed for administering bureaucracies and for controlling people through social work, medicine, and education.[40] Lasswell, a one-time student of Merriam, maintained that in order to study elites one must be aware of the power inherent in violence, goods, symbols, practices, skills, classes, personality, and attitudes.[41] And Bertrand Russell, in a general book on the subject of power, suggested that power be viewed as a social force analogous to the physical world's energy.[42] The analogy was valid, but it merely indicated the ubiquity of power and did nothing to help scholars measure its magnitude.

In retrospect, it is easy to see what happened. Studies of power became fashionable in academic circles, but even where those studies were optimistic about democracy, they were unable to define power in terms so simple that a convincing evaluation could be made of the actual or imagined threat to democracy. The scholarly achievements of men such as Bentley, Lasswell, Merriam, and Russell were unquestionably valuable, but their usefulness vis-à-vis the issue of democracy was at best limited. Prewar comments on community power were far from reassuring, given the serious challenges from Right and Left against Liberal faith in democracy. Further comments on community power might yet restore Liberal confidence, but a great deal of work remained to be done.

NOTES

1/ Sigmund Freud, *The Ego and the Id* (orig., 1927; London: Hogarth Press, 1935) , p. 9.

2/ *Ibid.,* p. 28.

3/ *Ibid.,* p. 15.

4/ *Ibid., passim.*

5/ *Ibid.,* p. 30.

6/ Graham Wallas, *Human Nature in Politics* (orig., 1908; Lincoln: University of Nebraska Press, 1962) , p. 45.

7/ *Ibid.,* p. 18.

8/ *Ibid.*

9/ *Ibid.,* pp. 53–75, *et passim.*

10/ *Ibid.,* pp. 81–117.

11/ For example, see British Prime Minister Benjamin Disraeli's novel *Coningsby* (orig., 1844; New York: Signet, 1962) , p. 111: " '. . . you must have a good cry,' remarked Taper. 'All depends upon a good cry.' 'So much for the science of politics,' concluded the Duke."

12/ Gustave Le Bon, *The Crowd* (orig., 1895; New York: Viking, 1960) , pp. 23–24.

13/ *Ibid.,* p. 27.

14/ *Ibid.,* p. 32.

15/ Sigmund Freud, *Group Psychology and the Ego* (orig., 1932; New York: Bantam, 1960) , p. 61.

16/ *Ibid.,* pp. 62–77.

17/ Le Bon, *The Crowd,* pp. 155, 207.

18/ Robert Michels, *Political Parties* (orig., 1915; New York: Free Press, 1966) , pp. 342–356.

19/ *Ibid.,* pp. 61–114.

20/ *Ibid.,* p. 343 ff.

21/ Seymour Martin Lipset, Editor's "Introduction" to *ibid.,* pp. 19–20.

22/ See the section entitled "Bureaucracy," in Max Weber, *From*

Max Weber, eds. Hans Gerth and C. Wright Mills (New York: Galaxy, 1958) , pp. 196–244.

23/ Andrew Jackson, "First Annual Message to Congress, 8 December, 1829," in Alpheus T. Mason (ed.) , *Free Government in the Making: Readings in American Political Thought,* 3rd ed. (New York: Oxford University Press, 1965) , p. 447: "The duties of all public officers are, or at least admit of being made, so plain and simple that men of intelligence may readily qualify themselves for their performance. . . . In a country where offices are created solely for the benefit of the people no one man has any more intrinsic right to official station than another."

24/ Mark Twain, *A Connecticut Yankee in King Arthur's Court* (orig., 1889; New York: Signet, 1963) .

25/ José Ortega y Gasset, *The Revolt of the Masses* (orig., 1930; New York: Norton, 1957) .

26/ Arthur Bentley, *The Process of Government* (orig., 1908; Cambridge, Mass.: Harvard University Press, 1967) .

27/ *Ibid.,* p. 19 ff, *et passim.*

28/ The former writings include Lincoln Steffens, *The Shame of the Cities* (New York: McClure, Phillips, 1904) ; Henry D. Lloyd, *Wealth Against Commonwealth* (New York: Harper & Row, 1894) ; and Ida Tarbell, *The History of the Standard Oil Company* (New York: McClure, Phillips, 1904) . The latter works include Charles Beard, *An Economic Interpretation of the Constitution of the United States* (New York: Macmillan, 1913) ; J. Allen Smith, *The Spirit of American Government* (New York: Macmillan, 1907) ; and John Dewey, *The Public and Its Problems* (New York: H. Holt, 1927) .

29/ The terms "philosophical pluralism" and "analytical pluralism" are suggested by Earl Latham, "The Group Basis of Politics: Notes for a Theory," *American Political Science Review* (June 1952) , pp. 380–381. One of the most thorough and clearest expositions of the philosophical pluralist view may be found in G. D. H. Cole, *Social Theory* (New York: Frederick Stokes, 1920) .

30/ Harold Laski, *Authority in the Modern State* (New Haven: Yale University Press, 1919) , and *The Foundations of*

Sovereignty and Other Essays (New York: Harcourt, Brace, 1921) ; G. D. H. Cole, *Social Theory, and Guild Socialism Restated* (London: L. Parsons, 1920) ; and R. H. Tawney, *The Acquisitive Society* (New York: Harcourt, Brace, 1920) .

31/ For example, see Sidney and Beatrice Webb, *A Constitution for the Socialist Commonwealth of Great Britain* (London: Longmans, Green, 1920) .

32/ Pendleton Herring, *Group Representation Before Congress* (Baltimore: Johns Hopkins University Press, 1929) ; E. E. Schattschneider, *Politics, Pressures and the Tariff* (New York: Prentice-Hall, 1935) ; Oliver Garceau, *The Political Life of the American Medical Association* (Cambridge: Harvard University Press, 1941) .

33/ John Dewey, *The Public and Its Problems;* and Walter Lippmann, *The Phantom Public* (New York: Macmillan, 1925) .

34/ Lippmann, *ibid.*

35/ Gaetano Mosca, *The Ruling Class* (orig., 1896; New York: McGraw-Hill, 1939) ; Max Weber, *From Max Weber;* M. Ostrogorski, *Democracy and The Origins of Political Parties,* 2 vols. (orig., 1902; New York: Anchor, 1964) ; Vilfredo Pareto, *The Mind and Society* (orig., 1916; New York: Dover, 1935) ; Pitirim Sorokin, *Social Mobility* (New York: Harper and Brothers, 1927) ; Harold Lasswell, *Politics: Who Gets What, When, How* (orig., 1936; New York: Meridian, 1958) ; Robert and Helen Lynd, *Middletown* (New York: Macmillan, 1929) , and *Middletown in Transition* (New York: Harcourt, Brace, 1937) .

36/ Lasswell, *Politics,* p. 13.

37/ The Lynds, *Middletown in Transition,* pp. 74–101.

38/ Charles Merriam, *Political Power* (orig., 1934; New York: Collier, 1964) , pp. 157–181.

39/ *Ibid.,* p. 287.

40/ *Ibid.,* p. 286.

41/ Lasswell, *Politics, passim.*

42/ Bertrand Russell, *Power: A New Social Analysis* (New York: Norton, 1938) , pp. 12–15.

∘ **3** ∘

The Process Theory of Democracy: Joseph Schumpeter

The central issue for over a century in the confrontation of Liberalism by both Conservatism and Marxism has been democracy: Is it immediately possible and desirable? Marxists and Conservatives alike have taken a negative position on this question, and the fact that both oppose the Liberal faith in democracy has created a peculiar but logically preordained situation: evidence supporting the principles of Marxism and/or Conservatism automatically weakens the case for Liberalism, and vice versa.

In recent generations, such evidence has accumulated and the intellectual tide has run strongly against Liberals. Research by respected social scientists has reinforced repeated suggestions that all the traditional tenets of Liberalism are false and misleading, that the many rational individuals posited by Liberals do not in fact exist, and that, therefore, the nominally democratic structure of Liberal societies cannot work as expected and is either a fraud or a sham.

In addition to the dialectic of intellectual disputation and confrontation, various political events of the nineteenth and twentieth centuries have stimulated doubts in Liberalism and have made men receptive to the aspersions that social science cast upon Liberal beliefs. Those events, continued into the 1930s, and during that time, in combination with social science findings, they encouraged widespread anxiety among middle-class

Liberal thinkers. Many lost faith in their own political institutions and embraced what was, for them, a new "ism," be it Fascism, Marxism, or Conservatism. Political conversions abounded in the West, and even in America, the citadel of pure Liberalism, confidence did not remain entirely unshaken.[1]

Yet in America, on the whole, Liberals remained more optimistic than their counterparts in England or on the Continent, with some American scholars using their studies of community power as the foundation for reassuring comments on the condition of Liberal democracy. These studies were often haphazardly organized, however, because their theoretical framework lacked precision. In order for Liberals to tread the narrow path between Right and Left confidently, their studies of community power needed a new theory of democracy that could deal successfully with the discouraging realities affirmed by social science. The theory would have to assimilate certain disturbing facts and satisfactorily explain them as desirable or, at least, inoffensive. Thus the intellectual stage was set for new speculations on power and democracy in the 1940s.

The new theory that finally emerged to fill the need, the "process theory of democracy," sought to redefine the fundamental functional nature of democracy. Its origins are obscure but it appears that during the decade of the 1940s the process theory arose somewhat spontaneously in response to the need for a defense of Liberal societies, and there came into being a tacit, widespread understanding that this was the most appropriate argument in support of Liberalism. Uninspired by any brilliant seminal statement, it simply developed into the conventional academic wisdom.

The process theory runs through many of the community power studies undertaken by American scholars in the 1950s, and by the late 1950s it had become the ruling theory in the writings of most scholarly advocates of American democracy. It did not penetrate to the folk level of society, but the academic shift to the process theory was so marked, and the change in academic approach was so significant, that it requires some explanation here. The matter must be analyzed logically, of course, because the theory does not seem to have had an original, outstanding author, and any theory that has no identifiable founder must have impersonal, historical reasons for its success. What, then, was the background to the process theory? How can we explain, or at least understand, its widespread adoption in American community power studies?

JOSEPH SCHUMPETER

Curiously, the most complete understanding of the background of the process theory may be obtained by analyzing the writings of a man who was *not* a native American, Joseph Schumpeter. Schumpeter was a Liberal economist, a native of Austria, and a World War II refugee who joined the faculty of Harvard University. His book, *Capitalism, Socialism and Democracy*, published in America in 1942,[2] which consisted mainly of a sophisticated historical and philosophical analysis of economics and politics, concluded with a process theory of democracy and, overall, told a revealing story about the alternatives that preceded that theory and that were rejected by Schumpeter as untenable. One must bear in mind that there is no evidence demonstrating Schumpeter's influence on scholars who used the process theory in their own work. But the book does provide an insight into the logic of the theory. That it was written by a European is perhaps only a reflection of the American propensity for leaving to foreigners the traditional realm of great social theory.

SCHUMPETER'S EXPOSITION OF THE PROCESS THEORY OF DEMOCRACY

The very title *Capitalism, Socialism and Democracy* indicates the great issues Schumpeter was willing to engage. Starting with an analysis of the economic ideas of Karl Marx, he went on to discuss the practice of capitalism in Liberal societies and to relate that practice to Marx's criticism of capitalism as a unique system of ownership and economic activity.[3] Schumpeter argued that Marx had been correct, that capitalism is destined to collapse and that its characteristically private ownership of the means of production will be replaced by arrangements whereby the greater part of every state's industrial capacity will be owned and operated under collectivist, and therefore Socialist, forms of control. In disagreement with some of Marx's predictions, however, Schumpeter maintained that Socialism will arrive without the midwifery of violent revolution.[4] The middle class in Liberal societies will eventually tire of the frugality and sacrifice necessary for privately accumulating capital, and its members will become less and less willing to endure the insecurity of doing business in an uncertain, competitive marketplace. Moreover, large quantities of capital will be accumulated by joint-stock corporations, and the entrepreneurial skills by which bourgeois capitalists traditionally ran their enterprises will more and more be provided by the bureaucracies of great corporations, such as General Motors. In the end, economic collectivism will be embraced, almost by default, in return for its stability and its capacity to apportion economic rewards and risks more evenly than capitalism.

An urgent political question emerged from this Schumpeterian view of economic history: What political procedures and institutions will be adopted by the Socialist society of the future? Schumpeter was somewhat ambiguous on this point, but he did seem to assert that Socialism may enjoy democratic practices or it may suffer from authoritarian politics.[5] And because both of these two political ends are possible, Schumpeter argued that it is our responsibility at least to understand fully the alternative political principles that various Socialists expound. Only so forewarned and forearmed can we choose the principles most instrumental to a free society.

Marxism, of course, expounds the most radical form of Socialist theory and the disciples of Marx, both within and without the Soviet Union, have created totalitarian political movements. Herein lies the gravest danger to Liberalism—that the economically collectivist society yet to come will be controlled by such extremists and not by democratic Socialists such as are found in England or Scandinavia. Schumpeter's explanation of all this was that some Socialists, and especially Marxists, cling to a common, yet outdated and impractical view of the nature of democracy. Tracing this view back to certain origins in the eighteenth-century Enlightenment, Schumpeter summarized its significant elements in a brief passage: "The democratic method is that institutional arrangement for arriving at political decisions which realizes the common good by making the people itself decide issues through the election of individuals who are to assemble in order to carry out its will."[6] Over many generations, of course, this definition of what democracy actually is has inspired some great efforts, some decent policies, and some worthy accomplishments; even in the twentieth century it enjoys widespread and continuing popularity. Nevertheless, regardless of its commendable principles and inspirational value, Schumpeter argued that it is mistaken in its presumptions and, in the modern world, even dangerous.

This understanding of democracy is invalid, according to Schumpeter, mainly because it presumes the existence of rational citizens, men who join together in order to decide issues. Speaking with the confidence of a social scientist, Schumpeter claimed that such men are quite rare, and he pointed to the studies of researchers like Le Bon, Freud, and Wallas, who demonstrated that for the most part people behave irrationally.[7] Speaking as an economist, Schumpeter also remarked on the nature of marketing techniques—advertising and the calculated manipulation of consumer tastes—which convinced him that most men are incapable of responding deliberately and reasonably when subjected to similar flimflam devices in political campaigns.[8] The net effect of aggregated irrational behavior, he concluded, is that "the people" are unable to recognize the "common good" and therefore can hardly be relied upon to transmit an electoral mandate framing its essence to "the individuals who are to assemble in order to carry out its [the people's] will." Under the circumstances, those who believe in the people's rational ability are likely to be misled by their own convictions, and there is a real danger that totalitarian leaders and parties will arise, as in the Soviet Union, speaking in the name of the people but in reality acting in consonance with predetermined principles that the people can neither choose nor reject.

But if men are unable to think calmly and clearly on important matters, one must conclude that true democracy in terms of the eighteenth-century ideal is impossible. The apparently desirable political institutions which now function in Liberal states —parties, elections, and juries—must therefore be explained in other terms. Using the United States and Great Britain as examples, Schumpeter insisted that if we are to describe the reality of their political practices and accomplishments, we must formulate a new definition of what democracy actually is. He provided that definition in these words: "The democratic method is that institutional arrangement for arriving at political decisions in which individuals acquire the power to decide by means of a competitive struggle for the people's vote."[9]

Here, finally, was the new and much needed process theory of democracy, the one which became the subject—implicit or explicit —of influential works by David Truman, Floyd Hunter, C. Wright Mills, and Robert Dahl (see Chapters 4 through 8 below). Today, Schumpeter's version is only one among many, but in his phrasing there appeared clearly the crucially characteristic element of process, the focus on practices, the emphasis on a freely functioning political operation. As for any particular substantive result which may flow from the ever-continuing process—hopefully a common good—that matter stands apart from any description of the process itself. The logical appeal of this new theory will best be seen if the meaning of Schumpeter's succinct phrases is considered.

THE REJECTION OF CLASSICAL LIBERALISM

It must first be noted, as a very general observation, that while the process theory ostensibly contradicted extreme Socialism, and thereby also opposed dogmatic Marxism, it ultimately denied the moral foundations of Liberal ideology. The eighteenth-century view of democracy, which Schumpeter denounced in the hands of Marxists, equated perfectly with Liberal beliefs in rational men and responsive governments directed by mandates from below. There is a similarity of Liberal and Marxist expectations, and Schumpeter himself described Marxism as an offshoot of nineteenth-century Liberalism.[10] While he was certainly aware of the linkage between the two, there is no way of knowing whether he consciously intended to derogate the beliefs of Liberals along with Marxists. Still, he did contend that regardless of who held the eighteenth-century theory of democracy, it was dangerous and should be discarded.

What Schumpeter argued, in effect, was that the process theory should replace the more naive theory of democracy in the calculations of Liberals who seek to preserve their political way of life. The vision of an ideal society might thus be attenuated, but the theory did legitimize all those representative institutions that Liberals had already established, institutions that provide stability and a considerable measure of political choice. In Schumpeter's opinion, these were two valuable political conditions that may be retained even when the capitalist economy of Liberalism is changed to collectivism. In the last analysis, it is not that Socialism is *necessarily* incompatible with democracy; it is only that Socialism *might be* undemocratic.[11] As Schumpeter saw it, there is no reason why a Liberal society may not choose a collectivist economy together with a noncollectivist political superstructure. All that is required is an understanding of, a willingness to believe in, and a resolve to fight for democracy as defined and described in the process theory.

THE ASSERTION OF A NEW LIBERALISM

The process theory fully deserved to be called a new Liberal theory of democracy because it endorsed many political practices in existing Liberal states, and because it did this so ingeniously that the findings of social scientists were affirmed and deemed acceptable. Indeed, if the process theory is taken as correct, Liberal states will be found to possess electoral practices consonant with it. Moreover, the existence of irrational men, irrational groups, and powerful elites will not be cause to call those states undemocratic. This conclusion enjoys great potential for restoring the self-confidence of Liberals; its reassuring rationale via the new theory is important enough, consequently, to merit our closest attention.

To begin with, social scientists had overwhelmingly denied the rationality of individual men, thereby causing Liberalism considerable embarrassment. In the new Liberal theory, however, rational behavior by citizens was not a requisite for a properly functioning democracy. The subjective desires of men need not equate with any standards of objective reason, for there is no "common good" that men are to determine electorally. In fact, it is taken for granted that in a real democracy men choose their rulers like they choose soap or automobiles, on the strength of whim, fancy, or fleeting desire. The polity is actually a sort of political free-enterprise system, with each man acting the role of political consumer. Each man receives, then, what he electorally chooses to purchase.

Just as the lack of reason in individual men did not strain the process theory, so the irrationality of groups also created no problems. It is true that groups are driven by unpredictable and unreasonable impulses, and of course their ends may lead to socially irresponsible behavior. But these facts are simply extensions of individual irrational activity. Groups are no more than collections of individuals, after all, and if the subjective nature of one man's behavior fits comfortably into the process theory, so does the subjective nature of his group.

Was there not some cause for concern, though, in the fact, confirmed by social scientists, that group power far outweighs the political influence of the individuals who, in the abstract and the concrete, inspired early Liberals to cherish the theory and practice of democracy? No, the new understanding of democracy coexisted easily with the daily political impotence of most men. The process theory did not at all preclude a key political role for groups, and Schumpeter himself pointed out that groups will undoubtedly participate in the struggle for the people's vote.[12] Parties, corporations, ad hoc associations, pressure groups of all kinds, and lobbies may operate as powerful influences without contradicting the process definition of democracy.

The last realm of power to be explored by social scientists was the activity of elites, the rich, the prestigious, the clever, the unscrupulous, the lucky, and the enterprising, among others. The concentrated power wielded by such people had deeply disturbed Liberals, for its very existence seemed to foreclose ordinary citizens from participation in political decision-making. The role assigned to elites in the process theory was therefore exceedingly important. By accepting the reality that elections are usually contested by only a few, the process theory conceded what every social scientist had already confirmed—that in all of men's associated efforts, there comes into play a natural principle of hierarchy whereby the course of events is shaped by a few men at the top while most other men remain in subordinate positions with only limited influence.[13] If Liberals espouse the process theory, then, they need not be discouraged by the mere presence of elites.

There was even more to the new theory that gave Liberals comfort. While admitting that only a few men are politically important, the process theory demanded that in a democracy those few must compete for the support of the men below them. From this it followed that even though most men in a democracy cannot, and do not, participate continually in political affairs, they may periodically be offered choices of policy by their leaders. By exercising the franchise, subsequently, the great majority of citizens may elect to office those few of the elite who uphold the electorate's interests. With this safeguard, government may be responsive and the political system may justifiably be called democratic.[14]

In respect to individual unreason, group irrationality, group power, and elite dominance, the process theory was eminently agreeable to Liberals because it could embrace various seemingly undesirable phenomena and call them democratic. Here was no small accomplishment. The new theory enjoyed an additional, enormously appealing virtue. Not only did it legitimize the real behavior of men in Liberal states, it also sanctioned the outcome of that behavior. This last aspect of the theory was subtle but far-reaching in its consequences.

It will be recalled that early Liberals were quite optimistic, since they believed that men's objective reason leads them to make political demands on their government which, when aggregated, are equivalent to the needs of the entire community. Schumpeter noted this point in the eighteenth-century outlook on democracy, wherein "the people" seek a "common good." He observed, however, that in reality men are too unreasonable to agree on the substance of such an excellent end. What should be done if this is the case even in Liberal states? Schumpeter's answer made no attempt to reconcile convictions and reality. He simply urged that we relinquish our ideological expectations in this area.

If we give up our hopes for attaining some sort of common good, we ought nevertheless to maintain and support Liberal polities as the best possible kinds of government. After all, if everyone is inherently unreasonable, no man is more qualified than another to identify the common good or to judge a society's actions by his own standards. In that case, one can argue that every man is the best judge of his *own* interests, and a political system is desirable to the extent it permits each man to pursue his own, subjectively defined needs. If a political system is kept open, if citizens are provided with inviolable civil rights, if the electoral system compels elites to compete in order to retain leadership, if, that is to say, citizens are assured the power thereby to choose policies consonant with their individual sense of need, little *more* can justifiably be expected of any real political system composed of real men.[15]

Such a polity, characterized by freedom of choice, may be viewed as the political equivalent of a capitalist economy. In the political realm, men struggle for the power to make great decisions; in the economic realm, they compete in order to gain profits.[16] In both realms, it can be said that citizens receive precisely what they deserve—what they vote for and what they choose to buy. So long as they are free to select from among politicians and among pills, the only standard of judgment that need be applied is an ancient one: *caveat emptor.*

OVERCOMING THE PROBLEM OF METHOD IN COMMUNITY POWER STUDIES

From the foregoing, it is clear that the process theory of democracy fit the requirements for a more realistic Liberal view of politics. Once adopted, it would permit Liberals to stand their ground with solid confidence between the Left and the Right, to gird up their intellectual loins, so to speak, by affirming the findings of social scientists while still maintaining non-Conservative and non-Marxian conclusions about the worth of existing Liberal institutions. In the writings of scholars after Schumpeter, the process theory was elaborated, refined, qualified, and otherwise modified as befits a newly espoused conventional wisdom.[17] We shall analyze some of the applications of the theory in later chapters, but before leaving Schumpeter's bare-bones version of the new view, one final aspect should be noted, a point that probably contributed greatly to the eventual adoption of the process theory by so many American scholars.

During the 1930s community power studies in the United States were methodologically confused, unable to isolate one locus of power from another, and therefore, unable to argue persuasively just what degree of democracy in fact existed in American politics. Here is where the process theory matched its ideological fitness with a methodological appropriateness. By stressing the importance of the "competitive struggle for the people's vote," what it said, in effect, was that a very narrow realm of power—electoral politics—constitutes the critical field of human behavior that can prove whether or not we practice democracy. Are there several candidates in every election? Do they espouse alternative political principles? Do their proposals differ? Do citizens feel they are offered a choice on election day? These are some of the key questions for the process theory. They may be difficult to answer, but they are simplicity itself when compared with the extremely broad questions about power raised earlier by men such as Charles Merriam, Harold Lasswell, and Bertrand Russell.

There was an additional but complementary reason for narrowing the field of inquiry into power in Liberal societies. Quite apart from any concern for developing the process theory of democracy, during the 1940s political activity related to elections was becoming more and more attractive as the substance of American scholarly research. Primarily, this was because such activity could be treated empirically, and empiricism was coming into academic vogue. Facts related to the electoral process were often quantifiable and could therefore be weighed and assessed by careful analysis of voting returns, legislative roll calls, and well-constructed survey questionnaires; extensive, hard information could be converted to data easily manipulated by the statistical formulas and electronic computers that were rapidly proliferating. By happy coincidence, at that point the process theory appeared and suggested that community power studies pay special attention to precisely those realms of politics that American scholars were increasingly disposed to study for professional reasons. Although such matters do not lend themselves with certainty to cause and effect analysis we may conclude that while American Liberals were driven by the harsh realities of a developing Cold War to assume a positive ideological stance, and while students of politics were zeroing in on phenomena related to the electoral process, it was almost inevitable that process notions of democracy would become a central concern of American community power studies.

THE WEAKNESS OF THE PROCESS THEORY

As a brief introduction to the community power studies of David Truman, Floyd Hunter, C. Wright Mills, and Robert Dahl, which constitute the hallmarks of American community power research in the 1950s, it is worth noting certain failings of the process theory. The strengths of the theory did lead to its broad acceptance. Its weakness was in its applicability to politics in the United States. Indeed, every recent American community power investigator has either modified the theory so that it might more faithfully reflect the facts of our political life or has recommended reforms such as to alter existing political conditions to fit the theory.

The weaknesses of the theory were of two kinds, methodological and ideological. At the outset there was the extremely difficult problem of measuring the precise degree of political power exercised by various factions in the political process. By narrowing the field of power inquiry to the electoral process, the new theory undoubtedly represented an advance over democratic theory in the 1930s when so many elements of power were listed that no one could say which in the mélange was greatest. But it is not enough to say *electoral* power is *significant* power, for such a conclusion does not of itself answer the nagging questions of who has such power, how much of it they have, what resources produce it, how it is exercised, and what its results are. There is unquestionably some measure of pluralism in American life, and on the surface many Americans do seem to enjoy a range of alternatives among candidates, policies, parties, television programs, automobiles, cigarettes, recreation, and so forth. But how meaningful are our political choices? Are the alternatives offered to us significantly different? This was a central issue in the studies of Truman, Hunter, Mills, and Dahl, and what was in question was the degree of power in fact exercised by all the actors on the political scene. If, by their votes, citizens do wield a determinative measure of ultimate power, then the choices our society affords us do reflect the desires of the citizenry, choices that groups and elites are compelled to offer to the electorate. If, on the other hand, citizens wield little real power, but are manipulated or deceived by political campaign tactics, then the choices which American pluralism offers are not free at all, but are the limited alternatives which powerful groups and elites choose to present. Reliable measurements of power in the electoral arena are a minimum requirement, then, if we are to know when our political process is working sufficiently well to deserve the title of democracy.

The second weakness of the process theory had to do with moral questions that flowed from the fact that the theory was no more than a jargonized description of certain actual political practices in the United States and Great Britain. In his version of the theory, Schumpeter admitted this to be so; indeed, he explicitly defined democracy in terms of what Liberal states had managed to create, rather than what they aspired to create. Labeling the procedures of the United States and Great Britain democratic, however, has not convinced all men that such is the case. Indeed, it can be argued that the process theory begged the very question it presumed to answer—that is, what is democracy?—by calling what is, democracy.

A propos this question-begging, a number of studies of community power in the United States have revealed that there are many undesirable aspects of American politics—some of them very obvious, like the political insignificance of the poor, the tragic order of priorities concerning urban problems, the sacrosanct goals of certain small but influential groups such as farmers, veterans, and doctors, the increasing sense of alienation and isolation felt by black Americans, and the general sense of futility experienced by individual citizens. Insofar as we all assume that democracy is per se a desirable state of affairs, can these facts of community power, and other facts like them, be contained comfortably within our ideal of democracy? Or are they instead contemporary reflections of the irrationality and unresponsiveness which social scientists have long observed in men and their governments? In other words, can we be satisfied with the political system merely because the process theory says it deserves to be called democratic? In accepting the theory and thereby renouncing Marxist objectives, must we also be tolerant of conditions that mock our historic Liberal vision of a good society and a decent life? Together with methodological difficulties, this difficult moral issue has been a continual theme in community power studies.

NOTES

1/ A frequently cited volume dealing with political conversions during this period is R. H. Crossman (ed.), *The God That Failed* (orig., 1950; New York: Bantam, 1959). In it, six Western intellectuals—Andre Gide, Richard Wright, Ignazio Silone, Stephen Spencer, Arthur Koestler, and Louis Fischer —recount the personal experiences that led them to Marxism. The editor, himself a British democratic Socialist, concludes that "the only link, indeed, between these six very different personalities is that all of them—after tortured struggles of conscience—chose Communism because *they had lost faith in democracy* and were willing to sacrifice 'bourgeois liberties' in order to defeat Fascism" (p. 4, italics added).

2/ Joseph Schumpeter, *Capitalism, Socialism and Democracy*, 3rd ed. (orig., 1942; New York: Harper & Row, 1962).

3/ *Ibid.*, pp. 5–58.

4/ *Ibid.*, pp. 61–163.

5/ *Ibid.*, pp. 235–240, 296–302.

6/ *Ibid.*, p. 250.

7/ *Ibid.*, pp. 256–263.

8/ *Ibid.*, pp. 263–264.

9/ *Ibid.*, p. 269.

10/ *Ibid.*, pp. 298–299.

11/ See "Preface to the 3rd English Edition," *ibid.*, p. 411.

12/ *Ibid.*, pp. 270–271. Here Schumpeter observes that the theory encompasses "group-wise volitions" and "sectional interests."

13/ *Ibid.*, p. 270–272.

14/ This point was argued by Seymour Martin Lipset in his "Introduction" to Robert Michels, *Political Parties* (orig., 1915; New York: Free Press, 1962), pp. 15–39. Lipset strongly objected to the inferences Michels drew from the fact of hierarchy within organizations.

15/ Schumpeter did contend, however, that an adequate choice of policies requires the existence of certain conditions. These include the presence of a dedicated upper-class elite who will provide capable leaders if elected, the steady work of an efficient bureaucracy, and the healthy political balance which ensues when leaders are trusted and permitted fairly free rein by the electorate. See Schumpeter, *Capitalism, Socialism and Democracy*, pp. 290–296.

16/ *Ibid.*, p. 282.

17/ One of the most comprehensive analyses of democracy in terms of the process theory is expounded by political scientist Henry B. Mayo. See his *Introduction to Democratic Theory* (New York: Oxford University Press, 1960).

The Group Theory of Democracy:
David B. Truman

Between the end of World War II and the very early 1960s, hundreds of community power studies were conducted,[1] a number so large as to clearly indicate great concern for the condition of democracy. One can best comprehend this outpouring of research by concentrating on the major analytical devices that scholars developed for discovering, marshalling, and interpreting the revealed facts of power. In general, there were four such devices: the group theory of democracy, the reputational theory of elitism, the positional theory of elitism, and the pluralist theory of democracy.

Of course, the men who employed these various theories were often concerned with narrow, detailed questions of fact and procedure whose importance was by and large shortlived. It is therefore not necessary to explore all the issues they raised or even to examine a substantial portion of the numerous studies they conducted. We can confine ourselves instead to matters bearing on the great overriding issue of democracy. And on that issue each of the four theories was conveniently exemplified by the work of a single researcher, usually in one of his major writings. As so often happens in the course of intellectual history, a controversial point of view was expressed by one scholar; others attacked his work; an opposing point of view was formulated by a second scholar; criticism of his opinion then accumulated; and so on. Consequently, it is possible in retrospect to analyze certain key points in the field of community power studies through examples drawn from the writings of outstanding and representative scholars. Such examples are provided by David Truman for the group theory, Floyd Hunter for the reputational theory, C. Wright Mills for the positional theory, and Robert Dahl for the pluralist theory.

Before proceeding to an analysis of Truman's group theory, a word of qualification is required. Scholars usually draw a distinction between community power studies at the national and the local levels. This leads to the notion that one cannot legitimately compare the methods and findings of a man like Mills, whose book *The Power Elite* analyzes power in America's national community, with the approach and conclusions of Dahl, whose book *Who Governs?* examines power only in New Haven, Connecticut. In regard to democracy, however, there is very little difference between most national and local studies; what mainly interests us are not the particular facts any study reveals but, rather, the analytical logic that is employed in all of them. What concerns us is the way facts are assessed, circumstances weighed, appearances judged—in short, how scholars draw significance from the subject matter they study. This process of reasoning is the same regardless of whether national or local political affairs are being analyzed.

THE GROUP THEORY AS A PROCESS THEORY OF DEMOCRACY

In 1951 Truman's *The Governmental Process*[2] was published, a book whose very title revealed its intellectual debt to Bentley's earlier theory of groups in *The Process of Government* (1908). More than forty years after Bentley's pioneering efforts, Truman found it worthwhile to gather some of the available empirical data about political groups and use that information to bring Bentley's theory up to date—that is, to demonstrate that the political process in America is dominated by the behavior and attitudes of groups. In the post-World War II era, many political scientists were already convinced that groups are the most important forces in democratic politics. What Truman provided, then, was a framework of analysis to explain the origins and functions of groups, a framework that quickly became common currency in textbooks and scholarly articles about American government.

No framework of analysis, of course, can be entirely impartial, and Truman openly asserted the values that underlay his. He said these were "first, a preference for the essential features of representative democracy and, second, a belief in the virtues of peaceful change."[3] In light of these values, it followed that "what we seek are correctives, protections, or controls that will strengthen the practices essential in what we call democracy and that will weaken or eliminate those that really threaten that system."[4] What appeared, in short, was a process theory of democracy in the Schumpeterian sense. Truman presumed that what existed in the United States was actually democratic, and that it only remained to explain how the system operated and, if possible, how it might be strengthened and preserved.

THE FOCUS ON GROUPS

According to *The Governmental Process,* the American political system depends on group political pressures and can be understood almost entirely in terms of group behavior. Using technical terms of social science, Truman defined the group as a collection of people interacting "with some frequency on the basis of their shared characteristics."[5] As far as he was concerned, all left-handed people did not constitute a group unless they organized themselves for activity predicated on their mutual left-handedness, for example, to play left-handed softball games or to manufacture left-handed fountain pens. As Truman defined groups, "it is the interaction that is crucial . . . not the shared characteristic."[6]

Among groups, Truman paid special attention to what he called the "interest group." This entity he defined as "any group that, on the basis of one or more shared attitudes, makes certain claims on other groups in the society for the establishment, maintenance, or enhancement of forms of behavior that are implied by the shared attitudes."[7] In other words, an interest group is one that acts within the political process, and it is for that reason of particular concern to political scientists. The study of other groups may be left to other academic disciplines such as economics, sociology, or anthropology.

From these other disciplines, however, political scientist Truman borrowed a general theory of the origins of all groups, including interest groups. He claimed that the wide range of existing groups represented a modern specialization of labor, that in the course of history groups have appeared in order to provide the skills and information that progressively more complex societies require.[8] Thus men have formed economic groups, religious groups, social groups, or political groups in order to supply their needs when they could not be met by hunting, harvesting, praying, and otherwise acting alone. In short, the more complex a society, the more interacting groups of all kinds it is likely to embrace.

Using this theory of groups as the foundation for his understanding of men's collective activity in general, Truman asserted that "the dynamics of groups are not essentially different because the groups are labeled 'political.' Basically they show the same regularities as do other continuing social patterns."[9] This notion was pivotally important to Truman's view of the political process. It had the weakness, however, of being extrapolated from research focused mainly on the behavior of small and private groups, whereas Truman, for the most part, sought to explain the workings of a political process dominated by large and public groups. Here the logic of Truman's theory suffered a serious shortcoming.

THE CHARACTERISTICS OF GROUPS

Truman's elaboration of the group theory did not unfold via consecutive analytical concepts, but an overall view should take into account at least six of the points he discussed: potential groups, multiple group memberships, access, rules of the game, equilibrium, and the public interest. If these are examined separately, their necessary relationship to one another will become apparent.

The notion of "potential group" flowed logically from Truman's definition of a group as a collectivity of men interacting on the basis of shared characteristics. If interaction is the distinguishing sign of groupness, Truman argued, then some groups will be marked by a great deal of interaction; such groups are therefore likely to be formally organized with titles, headquarters, officers, dues, newsletters, and frequent meetings. Other groups, however, may not interact intensively and therefore they probably will not be formally organized. Indeed, a political analyst might overlook the pressure of unorganized groups on the political scene and be tempted to attribute predominant political power to visible groups with imposing reputations and unquestionably great resources—for example, the National Association of Manufacturers, the American Medical Association, the American Federation of Labor–Congress of Industrial Organizations (AFL–CIO), or various chambers of commerce.

According to Truman, the significance of groups with low interaction is that they have a potential for high interaction; such groups are, in fact, always present and often influential. Their interests are usually weak and dispersed—for example, many of us are occasionally but not collectively concerned about consumer protection, conservation of natural resources, and air and water pollution control. Nonetheless, in the last analysis "if these wide, weak interests [potential groups] are too flagrantly ignored, they may be stimulated to organize for aggressive counteraction."[10]

Potential groups, then, act as an important restraint on the very real and substantial power enjoyed by formally organized men. A second restraint exercised on the formally organized is what Truman called "multiple group memberships" or "overlapping memberships." As he put it, "no individual is wholly absorbed in any group to which he belongs"; and furthermore, "this characteristic is true . . . of all groups in . . . society."[11]

A dentist may thus simultaneously be a town councilman, a Democrat, a Lutheran, a stamp collector, a vegetarian, a Mason, and a skier. Consequently, he may belong to a variety of separately concerned groups: a church, a fraternal lodge, a philatelic society, and more. His associates in those several groups, however, will also maintain multiple group memberships, to the point where any single American group is composed of men whose allegiance to the interests of that entity is offset by their concerns in other groups.

Overlapping membership forces moderation on all groups, for none can be assured of perfect and unswerving loyalty from its members. Indeed, if any group advances its interest against all other men too vigorously and without qualification, its own members may defect and refuse to support its extreme demands.[12] A group theorist might therefore contend that a manufacturers' association will hesitate to demand the right to build factories in wilderness areas if some of its board members are conservationists. More pessimistically, on the other hand, the group theorist might observe that the same principle explains why neither great American political party has been able to implement a satisfactory program of equal racial opportunity. Evidently both parties attract at least some men whose personal interests and views strongly oppose such a policy, and the effect of overlapping memberships may thus not be an unqualified benefit to society. In the long run, however, Truman claimed that the fact that "memberships in organized and potential groups overlap . . . imposes restraints and conformities upon interest groups on pain of dissolution or of failure."[13]

The main objective of any group's activity is presumably to gain recognition and satisfaction for the desires of its members. This requires what Truman referred to as "access" to the decision-making process whereby government decides which of society's interests shall be served. According to the group theory, groups seek to maintain channels of access and to guarantee a sympathetic response to their needs at every level of government. They therefore publicize their views, support candidates, lobby to have sympathetic officials appointed to government agencies, seek appropriate gerrymandering of constituencies, and act in many other ways to implement their programs. Political parties, of course, often serve group interests, but parties are only the most obvious and commonly recognized conduits for such interests. In fact, many government agencies, many legislators, the President, and even the courts serve the expressed needs of particular groups in American society.[14] For example, certain congressmen are notably solicitous of agricultural interests while others look after the welfare of the military; rural areas and small towns are favored by many state legislators; veterans are the special province of the Veterans Administration; the railroads are influential within the Interstate Commerce Commission; and the nation's banks have the friendly and attentive ear of the Federal Reserve Board.

But because American groups do seek and require access to government in order to advance their interests, and because some groups patently enjoy such access, a democratic commentator must explain how access is in fact assured to all our groups. After all, only if every group may gain access can those who do be said to represent collectively the manifold interests present in American society. Truman explained that access is guaranteed by what he called the "rules of the game" or the "democratic mold."[15] This aggregation of procedures—for example, fair play, free speech, free assembly, the right to petition, and the right to vote—permits new groups to form, allows them to publicize their cause, and encourages the public and the government to listen to them. The rules of the game, at least in Truman's theory, make it virtually impossible for established groups to entrench themselves in government, hold their privileged positions indefinitely, and pursue their separate interests unrestrained.

The open framework of American politics is surely the key to the degree of democracy we enjoy; on this point, Truman reiterated the obvious. But how is the vital framework maintained? Here was a crucial point in Truman's analysis of group activity. The rules of the game, he argued, are enforced because they are constantly supported by "unorganized or potential groups; [and] the generality of their [the rules'] acceptance is such that their claims do not require organized expression except when their notions are flagrantly violated or when they are in the process of alteration."[16] In other words, except for public spirited groups such as the American Civil Liberties Union, the necessary support for the rules of the game come from all Americans, and any groups or individuals who attempt continually and flagrantly to violate the rules will sooner or later be thwarted by an adverse reaction from the electorate, other groups, or government officials. Indeed, in the day-to-day operation of government, certain officials believe themselves to be invested with a special responsibility to guard democracy's rules. Truman noted this in the cases of judges, leaders in Congress, and the President.[17] Because of the peculiar nature of their constituencies or the terms of their offices, such men serve what Truman called "majority interests."[18] These interests, including the rules of the game, are ideologically instilled by our American education and are therefore deep-rooted and powerful.[19] They overlap all other group affiliations and direct us collectively to broad, common goals as a society.

With the American polity composed of groups and potential groups, with all interests seeking access to government when they deem it necessary, and with that access accorded them by virtue of the rules of the game, Truman contended that the political system could reach an equilibrium.[20] Every society requires such an equilibrium "if it is to survive."[21] Of course, there will be occasions when the balance will be upset—for example, by great ethnic injustices, by demographic shifts, or by rapid technological changes. In such cases, new groups will probably struggle to form, to express new demands like those for civil rights in the 1950s and 1960s. If the new groups can be accommodated successfully a new equilibrium will emerge, with a new political configuration of power, privileges, and responsibility. If they cannot be accommodated, misery, alienation, oppression, and even civil war may ensue. In *The Governmental Process,* written in 1951, Truman expressed the belief that the fundamental health of American democracy is demonstrated by the fact that its political system did, on the whole, permit the formation and activity of new groups in ways that were generally conducive to restoring equilibrium peacefully in a changing society.[22]

"Peaceful change," which Truman advocated as one of the virtues of democracy, would seem to be a matter of successive equilibria. Are these equilibria at any moment equivalent to a "public interest"? Do they serve a common, public good? On this point, there was considerable ambiguity in the group theory, for Truman explicitly rejected the traditional concept of public interest familiar to political philosophers. "In developing a group interpretation of politics . . . we do not need to account for a totally inclusive interest, because one does not exist."[23] What Truman seems to have meant is that the nation is not an organized group but only a potential group, and therefore one cannot state its interests definitively until the potential group mobilizes and thereby indicates its desires and its needs.[24] What we can infer from this analysis, however, is that the public interest in Truman's group theory is a combination of organized and unorganized interests, an entity whose contours cannot be ascertained precisely because it is not manifest in coherent form. This inference warrants another, that the public interest, which cannot be ascertained even by the observant political scientist, can best be fostered by permitting the interaction between organized and potential groups to proceed at its own pace. This may be accomplished by guaranteeing access and stability.

It may be argued from all this, even if Truman eschewed traditional terminology, that equilibrium—itself a sign of stability and workable access—may be taken as an index of the public interest, of what the sum total of American groups wants and needs. In this sense, Truman's group theory of democracy can instructively be compared to that of Schumpeter. In both, the emphasis was on leaving the democratic political system open to let citizens decide, in moderate and civil ways, what they need. Once the democratic process was seen to be operating smoothly, the commentator generally refrained from a detailed analysis of its results.[25] Such was the process theory of democracy.

THE STRENGTH OF TRUMAN'S THEORY

On the whole, *The Governmental Process* was well received by fellow political scientists who have reported on the activities of political groups and made them a central factor in the study of politics since World War II. The theory was popular for two reasons. First, it was realistic in its emphasis on the importance of group behavior in American society. Research data confirmed the common sense view that the facts of group influence at every level of government require our attention and understanding. Organized groups such as labor unions, business groups, and professional associations are certainly a key element in politics. Potential groups also exist—witness the rise of collective opposition to the Vietnam war. And the rules of the game are undoubtedly present and powerful, as the forced resignation of Supreme Court Justice Abe Fortas demonstrated in 1969. What Truman provided, then, was a broad theoretical framework for placing some of the obvious phenomena of American politics in manageable perspective. Second, this same theory could easily be viewed as an attractive alternative to the Marxist theory of how Liberal political systems function. As Truman himself put it, "The evidence regarding individual differences stemming from multiple group memberships is of . . . importance. . . . It challenges the Marxist assumption that class interests are primary."[26] Highlighting the fact that Americans have many partial interests and can join many narrowly concerned groups, the group theory concluded that as Americans we are not motivated by any allegiance to the very large collectivities which Marxists call classes. The theory was thus ideologically reassuring, for it explained how our Liberal "representative democracy" provides us with a variety of social and political choices, thereby avoiding class conflict and conditions requiring revolutionary change according to the Marxian tenets.

SOME CRITICISMS OF GROUP THEORY

Although Truman's group theory was realistic and persuasive to many, some felt instead that it was misleading and overly optimistic. The criticisms advanced by such men were valid enough so that, with time, Truman's group theory was gradually abandoned by political scientists in favor of the more complex understanding of groups offered by the pluralist theory of Robert Dahl in the late 1950s and early 1960s. If we are to appreciate the ingenuity and serviceability of Dahl's theory (discussed in Chapters 7 and 8), we must here examine the charges against Truman's.

The many scholars who rejected the group theory cited different reasons applying to various points of its analysis of American politics; their objections, therefore, were not centered on any single theme or argument. However, many of the objections can be related to a fundamental element in Truman's understanding of the nature of groups. As noted above, Truman first posited a general theory of group formation—that groups arise to serve the specialized needs of a complex society—and then went on to presume that political groups resemble all others. In effect, however, when stating the general theory of groups in support of a framework of political analysis, Truman simply extrapolated from observations of small groups by sociologists, anthropologists, and others, to an implicit presumption that the *large* political groups of our society behave in much the same way. It was a quantum leap with serious consequences, and it drew many critics.

As economist Mancur Olson observed, the presumption of Truman's group theory was that small and large groups differ only in *degree* (size), but actually they may differ in *kind* (structure and cohesiveness) as well. Olson argued that most political groups provide what economists call collective or "public goods" for their members. As he put it, "A common, collective, or public good is . . . any good such that, if person x_i in a group x_1, . . ., x_i, . . ., x_n consumes it, it cannot feasibly be withheld from the others in that group."[27] Examples of such goods are common in political affairs. Thus, if you are a black man, and the National Association for the Advancement of Colored People (NAACP) lobbies successfully for certain civil rights, those rights cannot be withheld from you or any other black man. Or, if you live in New York City and air pollution laws are strictly enforced by community authorities, the clean air that results cannot be denied you or any other person in the city. Or, if consumer advocate Ralph Nader succeeds in convincing the Congress to compel automobile manufacturers to incorporate safety devices into the design of automobiles, all drivers, not just some of them, will acquire safer cars.

The difficulty with public goods, as economists have long recognized, is that people are reluctant to pay for them. We may, after all, receive such goods even if we do not pay. So even when the expected benefits of a collective action are clear to all men, they may separately decline to supply a portion of the cost and effort that action requires.[28] As Olson remarked by way of illustration, we are all members of the same nation, and we all enjoy the stability, peace, order, and prosperity that our government promotes; yet that government can hardly rely on voluntary taxation to acquire the money to provide us with those benefits.[29] What is in effect here, and what is always related to public goods, is a peculiar but significant propensity in social affairs, namely, that individuals may refuse to support collective efforts they know to be beneficial to their own interests.

Small groups have no great problem in organizing and obtaining support, because they enjoy close personal contacts which encourage members to cooperate,[30] and because they enjoy a favorable, visible ratio between each man's contribution and the benefit he will receive *only* if the group receives enough of such contributions.[31] In contrast, large groups find it much more difficult to gain support, get organized, and provide collective benefits. Their members can easily hold back as individuals, make no contribution of money or effort, and wait for others to provide these and thereby the collective good. The NAACP is a case in point. For years it has suffered from lack of funds and members, despite the fact that all black men in America are potential beneficiaries of the service it could provide were it adequately supported by them.

When large groups do gain support, it is usually because they have found a way of enforcing a "selective incentive" as well as providing a public good.[32] We see this when citizens who pay taxes receive public goods in return, but go to jail if they *stop* paying. The threat of jail constitutes a selective incentive aimed at individual members of the polity and is designed to encourage their support when the public good fails to do so. Such selective incentives probably are found wherever a politically potent, large group functions successfully. Thus the American Legion stimulates veterans to enlist in its ranks by offering valuable assistance to any member who seeks to gain benefits from the Veterans Administration.[33] And thus labor unions improve working conditions generally but compel workers to join union shops or possibly suffer the hardship of unemployment.[34] And thus the American Medical Association (AMA) motivates doctors to join its ranks by offering them prestige, various certification credentials, and the privilege of working in most hospitals.[35]

In the last analysis, the concept of public goods offers a technical explanation of what many students of politics observe in a general way—that large, potential groups in American society find it enormously more difficult to get together, and work effectively, than do small groups. But if there is a valid distinction to be drawn between large and small groups, Truman must have erred when he argued that the difference between organized and potential groups is *merely* a matter of degree of interaction.[36] In reality, that degree is the most important factor in the group political process, and it merits the closest possible scrutiny. Indeed, it marks the difference between the National Rifle Association and individual citizens who favor gun control legislation, between the Detroit automobile moguls and many irate car owners, between a disciplined army and an anarchic mob.

In this matter of degree, it is instructive to observe the kinds of groups that actually organize within what is commonly known as free and open conditions in the American polity. E. E. Schattschneider, who analyzed a representative sample of thousands of American interest groups, argued that they constituted a "pressure system"—a small, politically effective sector of the larger polity that embraces all Americans—and observed that most of them were composed mainly of businessmen and upper-class joiners.[37] Referring to great and small economic interest groups, and to the prevalence of upper-class membership in such entities, Schattschneider claimed that "the flaw in the pluralist [group theory] heaven is that the heavenly chorus sings with a strong upper-class accent. Probably about 90 per cent of the people cannot get into the pressure system."[38] In reality, then, the group process of politics is not representative of all the interests of the community.

Group theorists would reply that even if existing groups seem for the most part to be business, upper class, and/or narrow in scope of concern, they have no choice but to serve public needs; otherwise potential groups will form to oppose them. In practice, the critics respond, this assertion simply cannot be proved. As Theodore Lowi has observed, formulations such as "potential interest group" are exasperatingly imprecise.[39] After all, how can the power of a potential group be measured if it does not reveal itself in any perceptible way? How can we gauge the intensity of an apprehension? Does the American Mining Congress, a mining lobby group, refrain from acting to increase the depletion allowance on copper, zinc, and lead because of an apprehension that *if* discontent were to ensue, and *if* leaders were to arise, and *if* time were to permit, and *if* funds were to become available, *then, perhaps,* a potential group *might* coalesce, *might* oppose the increase in the depletion allowance, and *might* even seek to reduce such tax benefits for mining in the United States? Some apprehension there may be, but how much? Enough to say that potential group power was exercised?

The difficulty in measuring potential group power is neither more nor less than calculating the significance of a *nonevent,* something that does *not* happen—for example, the American Mining Congress is *not* lobbying to increase the depletion allowance. Such a circumstance lends itself to speculation but not measurement. It entails mental processes and states of mind, two political factors that Bentley and Truman had sought to remove from their group theories, precisely because such factors are exceedingly difficult to weigh and assess. In fact, potential group influence may be as ephemeral as the feelings that Bentley referred to as "soul stuff," and no easier to deal with in research.

Doubts that the concept of potential group was useful were related to the fact that critics were dissatisfied with Truman's theory because it failed to rank groups, because it failed to assess differentially the resources and attributes of those that dominate our polity and those that do not. The extraordinary variety of American associations is often taken as evidence of a considerable and satisfactory measure of political pluralism, but "the uncomfortable question of the practical effects of serious power disequilibrium among them [groups] is often avoided."[40] It is not that scholars who employ the group theory cannot rank groups; it is just that they usually do not and there is little in the theory that can help them do so. Indeed, the concept of potential groups militates against ranking, for it suggests that if not now then surely when necessary, existing groups will be opposed by new groups. What seems clear, however, from long-standing and recent evidence, is that certain important interests are persistently weak, continually ineffective, and repeatedly disregarded in the process of political bargaining. Consumers are in this category, since they lack powerful organizations, as do migrant farm laborers, white-collar workers, the poor, and "multitudes with an interest in peace."[41]

If some groups are perennial losers, perhaps it is because they are unable to gain access to the political system, that access which Truman emphasized as the key to interest group satisfaction. On this point, a powerful critique of group theory has been advanced by several men, including Theodore Lowi, Grant McConnell, and Henry Kariel. Their common complaint is that during the last few decades a new kind of political arrangement has evolved in American government. Lowi calls it "interest group liberalism," by which he means the theory and practice of officially linking private group interests to government activity.[42] At both the state and the national level a great many government agencies delegate power, formally or informally, to concerned private groups. The United States Department of Agriculture, for example, permits the American Farm Bureau Federation, a farmer group, to appoint county officials in the government's agricultural extension program;[43] the Alabama Medical Association is authorized by the Alabama legislature to certify doctors for the practice of medicine in Alabama;[44] and Congress grants the National Rivers and Harbors Congress, a wide-ranging lobby organization embracing private interests and local officials in every state of the nation, de facto control over Congressional "pork barrel" legislation affecting dams, dikes, harbors, pollution control, and the like.[45]

The danger in such relationships, which become symbiotic between private interest groups and public agencies, is that established groups acquire some of the power of the state and can use it to discipline their own members and prevent the rise of groups with opposing interests and alternative policies. Radical doctors who favor socialized medicine, for example, will not greatly influence the practice of medicine in Alabama so long as the Alabama Medical Association, a branch of the AMA, is already legally empowered to issue credentials for physicians there.

The marriages of convenience between existing groups and the governmental power structure are an indication of what Kariel called "the decline of American pluralism,"[46] since, to the extent they continue, choices are limited for a great many Americans. Existing entrenched groups simply do not serve all interests. *The Governmental Process* argued, at one point, that the powerful white Delta planters in Mississippi had to speak on behalf of "their Negroes in such programs as health and education."[47] This may have been true; but they could hardly have done so with great conviction or adequate results. In the case of farm interests, McConnell accused the dominant private farm groups of drawing their constituencies "so as not to include the rural poor, among whom the major problems of the farm population are concentrated."[48] And, surely, in the case of restricted labor unions, which share government power through influencing the appointment of officials to the National Labor Relations Board, black workers in the building trades have been ill served.

Where "interest group liberalism" is widespread, it may be dangerous for still another reason; it may, in effect, negate the restraining influence of what Truman called overlapping membership. One might argue that many interest groups engage in "logrolling" rather than "compromise,"[49] that they selfishly serve each other's narrow interests without regard to any need for attending to widespread, general, public interests. This may occur because, while interest group liberalism makes it difficult to establish new groups, those that exist can afford to be persistent and even extreme in their demands. For example, minority views cannot be fostered in the Alabama branch of the AMA if its members are effectively prevented from organizing other medical groups in Alabama.

THE PROBLEM OF EQUILIBRIUM

An analogy may be drawn between the various criticisms of Truman's group theory and a line from George Orwell's allegorical satire *Animal Farm*. The pigs, who lead the other barnyard animals in the nominally egalitarian Animal Farm, become more and more powerful until, finally, they justify their rule by the comprehensive social and political principle that "all animals are equal, but some animals are more equal than others."[50] If we substitute "groups" for "animals," the statement would seem applicable to American politics. To comment meaningfully on the democratic quality of American society, it is necessary first to know what kinds of inequalities exist and who benefits from them. The group theory did not tell us this, and therefore it was never entirely persuasive in its explanation of how well Liberal democracy in America functions.

It is worth noting that the issue of precisely who receives the fruits of the American political system was thoroughly blurred by Truman's concept of equilibrium, his term for describing the condition under which various groups are balanced and various interests are served. An effective political system such as ours, he claimed, would permit new groups to form, to present their demands, and to shift the equilibrium to a new level peacefully. Conversely, a stable and peaceful equilibrium may be taken as an indication that demands are being met and a considerable measure of justice attained.

The shortcoming of this concept of equilibrium is that an equilibrium may exist without providing for all substantial interests. Economists are very much aware, for example, that the economy may be well balanced with a fairly high rate of unemployment, as was the case during the Great Depression and subsequent recessions.[51] Are such equilibria desirable simply because they manage to maintain various forces in balanced juxtaposition? Are the relative positions of all affected groups—consumers, labor, management, or the elderly—justifiable? An equilibrium in the American polity existed for more than a hundred years while black citizens were excluded from its benefits. Was that equilibrium desirable?

Questions about the business cycle and segregation indicate that equilibrium must remain a central concept in commentary about American politics. But it should constitute the foundation of analysis—the point of departure—rather than the goal at which point analysis rests, fulfilled. What is the meaning of any particular equilibrium at any specific time? But this, after all, is merely a restatement of the question of groups in general: Who are they, and whom do they benefit?

THE OVEREMPHASIS ON GROUPS

Most of the shortcomings of Truman's group theory vis-à-vis questions of democracy can be traced to his attempt to explain everything in politics by reference to groups and their activity. The key points of the theory—potential groups, multiple group memberships, rules of the game, and the others—together constitute a presumption that, barring genetic factors of causation, everything in political affairs has its origins in group behavior. Truman's consistency may be viewed as a manifestation of the recent quest by some political scientists for "scientific" rigor in their discipline. Thus, in search of objectivity and reputation as unbiased observers of social affairs, political scientists since World War II have often sought a single fundamental and measurable force, a basic factor in political matters similar, perhaps, to energy in the physical world or money in economic affairs. As a theory that analyzed the entire political process in terms of one variable, however, Truman's group theory sought to explain everything and found itself at times explaining nothing. It failed to provide distinctions between the various group interests that succeed in gaining representation, and it therefore failed to identify the people who consistently manage to acquire benefits from the political system. Yet these are precisely the matters such a theory must deal with if it is to comment satisfactorily on the quality of democracy in America.

THE NEED TO STUDY ELITES

The long and the short of Truman's analysis and that of his critics is this: the group theory was a process theory of democracy, which stood revealed as insufficiently refined to locate significant power and overly optimistic about the general excellence of political results flowing from that power, wherever it may be. The theory presumed that our Liberal political institutions are democratic and that they assure us choices of social policy, the same choices Schumpeter had deemed vital to a free society. But this view of America was too abstract, too often unconcerned with specific facts. It did not assess and compare the roles of particular political actors, such as the NAACP, the Kennedy family, Richard Nixon, the AMA, the Department of Agriculture, and the National Rivers and Harbors Congress. Indeed, the fact that some Americans are always actors on the political stage, and others always onlookers, was not adequately discussed, explained, or justified.

The clue to the group theory's fundamental failure lay in its single-minded devotion to groups alone. Social scientists in the first few decades of the twentieth century had noted the importance of the influence of elites as well as the importance of group power. But Truman argued at some length that the leaders of groups—elites according to Robert Michels' Law of Oligarchy—are by and large controlled by the groups they represent;[52] he was in this way able to discount and disregard elites as if they were ultimately powerless. It is possible, nonetheless, that elites are considerably more independent than Truman believed, and that they play significant and even pivotal roles in the political process. If so, studies of the behavior of elites might explain a great deal that group theory did not explain; in particular, the rank of powerful leaders in American politics and the distribution of benefits from political activity. Truman himself seems to have become aware of the need for a more thorough understanding of elites after publishing *The Governmental Process*. In 1959 he contended that, in light of occasionally widespread and undesirable behavior such as McCarthyism, perhaps the rules of the game in American democracy would best be upheld by knowledgeable and moderate elites rather than a nationwide potential group composed largely of the masses.[53]

A more adequate understanding of elites was the missing element in academic appreciation of community power. It is not surprising, then, that the two influential theories of community power to appear directly after Truman's were the reputational theory of elitism and the positional theory of elitism. As we shall see, the prominence these two theories attained was at least partly due to their logical relationship to the group theory, constituting, as it were, the second side of power which had been passed over lightly. The intense debate over their validity, by supposedly dispassionate scholars, was impressive evidence that their various conclusions about community power severely threatened the ideological assurance provided by the group theory.

NOTES

1/ For bibliographies of this literature, see Charles Press, *Main Street Politics: Policy Making at the Local Level* (East Lansing: Institute for Community Development and Services, Michigan State University, 1962) ; Roland Pellegrin, "Selected Bibliography on Community Power Structure," *Southwest Social Science Quarterly* (December 1967) , pp. 451–465; Willis D. Hawley and Frederick M. Wirt (eds.) , *The Search for Community Power* (Englewood Cliffs, N.J.: Prentice-Hall, 1968) , pp. 367–379; and Edward Keynes and David M. Ricci (eds.) , *Political Power, Community, and Democracy* (Chicago: Rand McNally, 1970) , pp. 255–277.

2/ David B. Truman, *The Governmental Process: Political Interests and Public Opinion* (New York: Knopf, 1951) .

3/ *Ibid.,* p. xi.

4/ *Ibid.,* p. 12.

5/ *Ibid.,* p. 24.

6/ *Ibid.*

7/ *Ibid.,* p. 33.

8/ *Ibid.,* pp. 24–26, 52–57.

9/ *Ibid.,* p. 15.

10/ *Ibid.,* p. 114.

11/ *Ibid.,* p. 157.

12/ *Ibid.,* pp. 157–167.

13/ *Ibid.,* p. 168.

14/ *Ibid.,* pp. 264–270.

15/ *Ibid.,* pp. 129–139, 159, 348–350, 448–449, 486–487.

16/ *Ibid.,* p. 448.

17/ *Ibid.,* pp. 449, 486.

18/ *Ibid.,* p. 512.

19/ *Ibid.,* p. 514.

20/ On equilibrium, see *ibid.,* pp. 26–33.

21/ *Ibid.,* p. 27.

22/ This was the general, implicit position taken in *ibid.*, Chapter 16, "Group Politics and Representative Democracy," pp. 501–535. See pp. 516–524, however, where Truman discussed the possibilities, "not necessarily imminent," for conditions which could upset the "present effectiveness" of our open political system.

23/ *Ibid.*, p. 51.

24/ *Ibid.*, pp. 50–52.

25/ Notice how Truman refrained in *ibid.*, p. 38: "[I]s an interest group inherently 'selfish'? . . . [S]uch judgments have no value for a scientific understanding of government or the operation of society. . . . Judgments of this kind are and must be made by all citizens in their everyday life, but they are not properly a part of the systematic analysis of the social process."

26/ *Ibid.*, p. 165.

27/ Mancur Olson, *The Logic of Collective Action: Public Goods and the Theory of Groups* (Cambridge, Mass.: Harvard University Press, 1965), p. 14.

28/ *Ibid.*, pp. 9–16.

29/ *Ibid.*, pp. 13–16.

30/ *Ibid.*, p. 50.

31/ *Ibid.*, pp. 22–36.

32/ *Ibid.*, p. 51.

33/ This assistance offered by the Legion was noted by Truman, *The Governmental Process*, p. 203.

34/ See Olson, *The Logic of Collective Action*, pp. 66–73, on selective incentives in unions.

35/ The powers of the AMA were noted by Henry S. Kariel, *The Decline of American Pluralism* (Stanford: Stanford University Press, 1961), pp. 108–111.

36/ Truman, *The Governmental Process*, p. 36: "Organization is merely a state or degree of interaction."

37/ E. E. Schattschneider, *The Semi-Sovereign People: A Realist's View of Democracy in America* (New York: Holt, Rinehart and Winston, 1960), pp. 20–43.

38/ *Ibid.*, p. 35. Schattschneider did not use the term "pluralist" with the same connotations it possesses generally in this and other chapters of the text.

39/ Theodore J. Lowi, *The End of Liberalism: Ideology, Policy, and the Crisis of Public Authority* (New York: Norton, 1969), p. 49.

40/ Robert Presthus, *Men at the Top* (New York: Oxford, 1964), p. 16.

41/ The last phrase is from Olson, *The Logic of Collective Action,* p. 166. What he probably intended it to describe were those who are unorganized and ineffective against what has come to be called the "military-industrial complex."

42/ Theodore J. Lowi, "The Public Philosophy: Interest-Group Liberalism," *American Political Science Review* (March 1967), pp. 5–24, and *The End of Liberalism,* pp. 55–97.

43/ On entrenched groups in the Department of Agriculture, see Lowi, *The End of Liberalism,* pp. 102–115; Kariel, *The Decline of American Pluralism,* pp. 76–87; and Grant McConnell, *Private Power and American Democracy* (New York: Knopf, 1966), pp. 230–243.

44/ Kariel, *ibid.,* pp. 104–105.

45/ On the politics of inland waterways, see McConnell, *Private Power and American Democracy,* pp. 221–229.

46/ Kariel, *The Decline of American Pluralism, passim.*

47/ Truman, *The Governmental Process,* p. 512.

48/ McConnell, *Private Power and American Democracy,* p. 342.

49/ The use of these two phrases in opposition to each other was suggested by McConnell, *ibid.,* pp. 110–112.

50/ George Orwell, *Animal Farm* (New York: Harcourt, Brace, 1946), p. 112.

51/ Lowi, *The End of Liberalism,* pp. 50–51, suggests comparing economic and political equilibria, both suffering shortcomings.

52/ Truman, *The Governmental Process,* pp. 188–193, esp. p. 191: "the group . . . exerts in the long run a control over the fortunes of aspiring leaders."

53/ David B. Truman, "The American System in Crisis," *Political Science Quarterly* (December 1959), pp. 481–497.

✪ **5** ✪

The Reputational Theory of Elitism: Floyd Hunter

In 1953 Floyd Hunter published *Community Power Structure: A Study of Decision Makers;* in 1956 C. Wright Mills released *The Power Elite.*[1] Both men elaborated a common theme, that American politics must be analyzed with reference to influential elites. The two books were distinguished by markedly different techniques for discovering exactly who is powerful, techniques which will be examined in this and the following chapter. Their methods apart, the authors agreed on certain presumptions about the basic configuration of power in our communities. If we are to appreciate their theories of elitism, we must begin by understanding those presumptions.

TWO ACADEMIC PERSPECTIVES ON POWER

The fact that both Hunter and Mills wrote as sociologists is of considerable importance. Although it is not entirely fair to characterize academic disciplines in sweepingly general terms, there are many persuasive indications that sociologists and political scientists entertain significantly different presumptions about power.[2] Sociologists tend to look on any community as an enduring thing, an aggregation of human institutions that is greater and more permanent than the sum of its parts. They make much of the fact that each man's life is relatively short, while his community outlives him. One may therefore presume that the community possesses some structure of power, some network of stable relationships which permits it to endure largely unchanged. The community's lasting organized parts *must* collectively have this power, else they could not last. As Robert Lynd, one sociologist, put it: "Organized power exists—always and everywhere, in societies large or small, primitive or modern—because it performs the necessary function of establishing and maintaining the version of order by which a given society in a given time and place lives."[3] We may expect, then, that particular men at specific times will wield great power, but only insofar as they are in control of the community's enduring constituent parts. As Hunter wrote: "Power of the individual must be structured into associational, clique, or institutional patterns to be effective."[4]

Political scientists, on the other hand, are inclined to think of power more as a personal possession. As a group, their view of American society seems to be that of a fluid, ever-changing interplay of influence relationships between men who seek and wield a somewhat free-floating substance of power. David Truman, for example, described the national political system as a hodgepodge of groups, some rising and some falling, some entering and some leaving, some old and some new. He did not suggest, as a sociologist might, that certain groups continually remain strong, and that the men who lead those groups are therefore continually powerful solely by virtue of the permanence of their power base, the groups per se.

These two disparate views of power in our communities are worth noting, even though the preference of sociologists for the former and of political scientists for the latter are only imperfectly understood.[5] What should be remembered is simply this: there are apparently some differences in outlook, and yet, in their studies of community power, most scholars are firmly convinced that their respective conceptions of power are positively valid. To Hunter, the various postulates he expounded about structured power seemed to be "self-evident propositions,"[6] and to Mills, "the hierarchies of state and corporation and army constitute the means of power."[7] But to Nelson Polsby, a political scientist, the "basic presupposition of the pluralist approach is that nothing categorical can be assumed about power in any community."[8] The result of such conflicting presumptions is that some sociologists and some political scientists, at least, have emphasized contrasting manifestations of power. The ideological consequences of this duality are enormous, as we shall see, with nothing less than the issue of democracy at stake.

THE REPUTATIONAL METHOD OF STUDYING COMMUNITY POWER

In *Community Power Structure* Hunter set out to examine power in the city of Atlanta, Georgia. From the obvious fact that Atlanta was a community of intense business activity—with factories, railroads, highways, airports, and a constant stream of goods and people entering and departing—Hunter concluded that "a social order, or system, must be maintained there."[9] This was the sociological point of view, from which Hunter inferred that of necessity the maintenance and continued existence of such a system was effected by all its citizens collectively, while changes of importance were probably caused by only a few.

Here was an important distinction that guided Hunter in his research. *Maintenance* of a community is assured by the continuing activity of many men at work, at play, and in politics, although an investigator may expect to find some people enjoying more power and influence than others in daily affairs. *Changes* in the community, however—large-scale projects or innovative legislation—are distinctly the province of only a few citizens, men whom Hunter called leaders. He explained their positions sociologically: "The difference between the leaders and other men lies in the fact that social groupings have apparently given definite social functions over to certain persons and not to others."[10] To distinguish between the influence exercised by leaders and by lesser persons, Hunter used the term *policy* to describe political acts of change, whereas *power* was simply a common force that, when exercised to a greater or lesser degree, resulted in policy decisions or less important activity.[11]

A crucial question then presented itself. How can we identify the men and women who wield *great* power and therefore control policy in Atlanta? In order to answer this question, Hunter devised a simple method for locating power, a new research technique that might be used to study any community. He described it as follows:

> In [Atlanta] the men of power were located by finding persons in prominent positions in four groups that may be assumed to have power connections. These groups were identified with business, government, civic associations, and "society" activities. From the recognized, or nominal, leaders of the groups mentioned, lists of persons presumed to have power in community affairs were obtained. Through a process of selection, utilizing a cross section of "judges" in determining leadership rank, and finally a further process of self-selection, a rather long list of possible power leadership candidates was cut down to manageable size for the specific purpose of this study. Forty persons in the top levels of power in [Atlanta] were selected from more than 175 names. Many more persons were interviewed than the basic forty, but they were interviewed in relation to the forty.[12]

Expository precision was not Hunter's forte, but from this passage and others,[13] it appears that he drew up a list of persons who were reputed to hold commanding positions in the economic, political, and social life of the community. Then he invited fourteen judges—local people with great knowledge of Atlanta affairs—to pare down the list of one hundred seventy-five to the forty who, in the opinion of the judges, were the most powerful. Finally he interviewed twenty-seven of the forty finalists, plus an indeterminate number of other people with some knowledge of local policy-making. The interviews served two purposes. They tested, and consequently confirmed, the judges' choices, as all the people interviewed were asked if more names should be added to the list, yet they did not significantly agree that any leaders had been overlooked. The interviews also provided information about the manner in which the forty leaders actually exercised the power they possessed, how they initiated policy changes in Atlanta, and how they could effectively bar changes they disapproved.

Taken together, the techniques of first listing persons of repute and then interviewing to validate the list have become known as the reputational method, even though in a sense this title is a misnomer. It is true the lists were originally composed according to reputations for leadership; it is also clear, however, that the interviews refined the lists by introducing corroborative opinions and substantive information about policy-making by men directly familiar with such matters. Therefore the interviews, at least, constituted direct proof far closer to reality than the indirect evidence seen in simple reputation. Still, Hunter's research scheme is usually called the reputational method, and his critics have emphasized its reputational component and focused largely on the weaknesses appearing in that component.

THE POWER STRUCTURE OF ATLANTA

After his interviews had revealed a great deal about the most powerful forty leaders in Atlanta, Hunter was able to describe them and their activities in detail. The most noteworthy common characteristic of both men and activities was patently financial. Eleven of the leaders were from commercial enterprise, seven were from banking and investment, five were from industry, five were people of leisured wealth, six were professionals, four were with government, and two—the least powerful—were representatives of labor unions.[14] Among the most powerful forty, then, twenty-eight leaders were clearly identified with business resources or accumulated wealth, and the six professionals were doubtless financially secure. The power of money in the city was further highlighted when Hunter refined the list of forty by inquiring, in the course of the interviews, which men were the most influential of all. A group of about ten or fifteen top leaders emerged, and these were almost all associated with the community's business life.[15]

Hunter also discovered that the top leaders and the forty leaders in general were not uniformly interested in every matter affecting the community. Instead, some were interested in one issue and some in another. The result was a pattern of "cliques" and "crowds," each consisting of five or six leaders, and each dealing with matters of particular interest to its members.[16] One clique might form around men concerned with the affairs of banking; another might form around men associated with the chemical industry. The structure of power in Atlanta therefore resembled a collection of little pyramids of power, each clique standing somewhat by itself from day to day.[17] Even here, however, the financial factor was ubiquitous, for Hunter found that the dominant members of each clique invariably belonged to "a major business enterprise within the community."[18] The cliques stood separately, so there was no political boss who single-hand-edly controlled politics in the entire city.[19] But they also consulted each other frequently to gain approval of most of the leadership before embarking on a policy decided within any single clique.[20] In light of such interaction, one could argue that the city was controlled by one overriding interest—the acquisition and security of private property[21]—even though it lacked an ultimate ruler.

As Hunter put it, "men of independent decision"—the policy-makers—were not a large group.[22] Below them were a great many other men of considerable social stature and visible influence, political actors who formed what Hunter called the understructure of power. This understructure embraced all the varied associations constituting the celebrated pluralism of American life—churches, schools, the Chamber of Commerce, the Community Chest, the Rotary Club, the YMCA, the Bar Association, the Community Council, and many others.[23] On ordinary occasions, and in regular meetings, the understructure groups carried on their affairs from day to day, maintaining the community in its existing form. On extraordinary occasions, however, when more significant matters were at stake—policy questions—the understructure served merely as an instrument for implementing decisions of the leaders. Policy was formulated in the cliques, and then introduced to various associations throughout the city. Many leaders held important positions in those associations and could therefore easily place items on their agendas.

When the associations constituting the understructure were willing to support proposals from above, broadly based and enthusiastic coalitions of civic groups, politicians, and socialites could quickly be assembled. And when they were unwilling, the leaders could exercise several powers to encourage compliance.[24] Enjoying great private wealth, they could tighten the purse strings of organizations to which they usually contributed, such as the Community Chest or the YMCA. Or, with control over most of the city's sources of private credit, leaders could withhold normally required financing. Or, by virtue of their dominant positions in business, commerce, and industry, they could harass and even threaten to discharge their own employees, thus compelling those men, at least, to support their employers. In the long run, leaders could virtually dictate their preferences on policy matters; it was not difficult for them to gain the approval of organizations with widespread membership and considerable reputation for public-mindedness. And if, in any particular case, none of the existing associations seemed to fit a special need—as, for example, to persuade new industries to locate in the Atlanta area—the community's leaders could arrange the creation of an ad hoc committee whose members could be manipulated from behind the scenes.[25]

CONTINUITY IN ATLANTA

A leadership elite, several cliques, and an understructure consisting of associations with large memberships and small powers: such was the community power structure of Atlanta. What held it together and perpetuated it, if there were a half million people in the city and most of them were excluded from significant power? Hunter argued that the leaders did not conspire to carry out their effective rule in secrecy;[26] their power was usually acknowledged freely and openly, even if its involuntary and undemocratic aspects were not stressed. Presumably, therefore, the community knew of the existence of elite influence, yet that influence was never massively and radically challenged. Indeed, it must have been widely viewed as generally legitimate, for there was no outcry from the vast majority of local citizens who, as Hunter remarked without elaboration, were generally passive men even though they had "no voice in policy determination."[27]

One might conclude from all this that the leaders of Atlanta were doubly blessed by the economic system they dominated in the city: first because they enjoyed its direct benefits and could easily work together to secure perpetuation of the system, and second because the rest of Atlanta's citizens were sufficiently convinced of the excellence of capitalism and the "American way of life" to permit themselves to be ruled by the modern lords of a privately oriented economy. The elite was internally cohesive because it shared common interests, and it was externally protected in its exercise of power by the prevailing sentiment of the community. Hunter asserted the first point in so many words;[28] the second was implicit in the passivity of most Atlantans and the fact that Atlanta was an American city, not a Russian town.[29] (The Russians, we know, have their own ideologically sanctified elites.)

HUNTER'S CONCLUSIONS

After surveying Atlanta's power structure, Hunter assessed its worth to the community. The trouble with elite rule, he argued, was that it remained unresponsive to many interests other than those of the elite.[30] Fearful of losing their dominant power, the leaders tended to support the status quo, the arrangement which made their power possible. As a result, the needs of blue and white collar workers, professionals, and blacks were usually excluded from policy considerations, from decisions that might have altered the status quo in their favor. The political and economic system of Atlanta was thus perpetuated, but always for the disproportionate benefit of a few.

The solution to this unjust imbalance, according to Hunter, was to increase group activity.[31] Just as the power of leaders was structured into cliques and often exercised through associations in the understructure, in like manner individuals who were disadvantaged by the status quo would have to collect their separate powers and reinforce each other through group politicking. Some basic organizations and interest groups already existed and could be strengthened; others could be created and maintained. In this way the power structure would be enlarged, the leaders would have to take into their calculations interests other than their own, and government policies would necessarily constitute social planning for the entire community. We cannot expect to bar the elite from the halls of power, since they will always be capable of paying the price of admission; nevertheless, it may be possible to force entrance for a few more men, men more responsive to the needs of all.

THE DENIAL OF THE GROUP THEORY
OF DEMOCRACY

Community Power Structure and other reputational studies carried out later were scrutinized intensively by political scientists; in fact, much of the commentary on Hunter and his scheme of research was more than merely intense, it was decidedly hostile. One early scholarly review, for example, concluded that Hunter's "findings must . . . be regarded as intuitive—mature and rich in insight, but intuitive all the same—rather than scientific."[32] In the modern world of social research, of course, labeling a man's work unscientific is unmistakably a mark of intellectual disdain. Another critic advanced a similarly disparaging assessment: "The power data now being accumulated by Hunter's method ought [to] be viewed as a mound of smelter's ore, offering promise of further refinement and use."[33] This remark, directed at research publications that abounded in complicated charts and statistical tables and that clearly strove for the greatest possible precision and accuracy, was little more than a gratuitous insult.

The reason for such a reception may be surmised by comparing the fundamental approaches of Hunter's and Truman's respective theories of community power. What happened, and it was an event of distressing ideological significance, was that Hunter's theory of elitism in effect denied the major propositions of the group theory of democracy. It did so without explicit challenge—Truman and his work were never even mentioned—but to the extent that the group theory was then broadly acceptable to political scientists and Liberal sentiment, the reputational theory of elitism was emphatically unacceptable. Its ideologically suspect elements were obvious to its critics.

It will be recalled that Hunter presumed every community to be *maintained* by the many, and *changed* only by the few. In light of this presumption, the numerous and varied groups of the political *understructure* in Atlanta exercised day-to-day power in ordinary affairs, but only the *elite* exercised the degree of power necessary for deciding *policy* questions, matters of change. The pluralistic component of American political life—the arena of group activity which had engaged Truman's attention on the national level—was relegated therefore to relative unimportance in comparison with the activity of elites in our society. To argue this point, moreover, was tantamount to ranking political actors. It meant that there were some who were plainly and persistently more powerful than others, and this was a reality that was either deliberately or unconsciously avoided by both the author and advocates of the group theory.

Indeed, according to Hunter's findings the group theory was entirely misleading when it optimistically suggested or implied that potential groups exercise influence over those men currently in power, or that if necessary most citizens will form groups to advance their fundamental interests. Hunter discovered, instead, that Atlanta's elite took little account of the needs of potential groups such as blacks, white collar workers, professionals, and ordinary nonunion workers. Moreover, by strongly urging such people to organize, Hunter highlighted the fact that they had failed to do so despite their possession of all the varied political rights and privileges stressed by Truman. Why had the nonelite not banded together? Hunter answered this vital question little by little as he analyzed power in Atlanta.

The elite stayed in power and the nonelite were left out, and their respective positions—their ranking—remained roughly the same because the political system was much more closely inter-related with the economic system than Truman had admitted.[34] The elite of Atlanta threatened to withdraw contributions, credit, and jobs; it was thus private economic power they used to gain benefits through the political system.[35] Since their source of such power had long endured unimpaired, of necessity they were constantly more powerful than any of the nonelite. It could be argued, indeed, that regardless of the formal equalities guaranteed by the political system—voting rights, free speech, the right to a lawyer, and others—control of certain resources in the economy will always permit certain men to dominate the polity.

Here was an ideological nettle that the group theory had failed to grasp. There are a great many equalities and legal safeguards to guarantee them written into the political side of American life, and these the group theory had described more or less accurately. But in a society pervaded by the ethics of capitalism, which sees itself engaged in a world-wide struggle against the ethics of collectivism, no one expects economic hierarchy and inequality to vanish. Indeed, according to our commonly accepted principles of practical virtue—material incentives, business competition, entrepreneurial imagination, and hard work—enormous disparities of income and economic power are held to be legitimate, even necessary. The inevitable result, in Hunter's theory of elitism, is a polity dominated by economic elites, where "there appears to be a tenuous line of communication between the governors of our society and the governed . . . [and where] our concept of democracy is in danger of losing vitality."[36]

CRITICISMS OF HUNTER'S WORK

Hunter's findings and his conceptualization of power in Atlanta posed such a threat to the conventional wisdom of political science in the 1950s that opposition to both was inevitable. But it was difficult to criticize *Community Power Structure* and its author, since Hunter was the only social scientist at that time who possessed research data and concrete facts about political life in Atlanta. Opponents therefore could not attack him on substantive grounds; they could not justifiably complain that he had misjudged the role of any actual man or group in the city. Instead, they were limited to challenging the validity of the reputational method in general. On this score, they could charge that *regardless* of the actual configuration of power in Atlanta, Hunter's rationale for ascertaining the situation there was faulty. It turned out to be a clever strategy, for the embarrassing facts could thus be quarantined, so to speak. They could rhetorically be isolated in Atlanta while political scientists argued at length that Hunter's scheme of research was invalid and could not reliably be applied to any other American communities, there to discover similar facts.[37]

Of the great many criticisms advanced against the reputational method in the five or six years following 1953, some were directed at the rationale inherent in Hunter's research and others were aimed merely at inconsequential or obscure passages in *Community Power Structure*. In the course of this persistent fault-finding, it was rejection of the fundamental rationale that became the foundation for a rival theory of community power, the pluralist theory of democracy expounded by Robert Dahl. We shall extensively examine that theory's component parts in later chapters; therefore only a few of the major objections to Hunter's work need be described briefly here.

According to his critics, there were three outstanding weaknesses in Hunter's methodological approach to community power: the first, a matter of simple logic; the second, a difficulty in acquiring reliable data; and the third, a problem in assessing the facts once they are collected. The first was labeled the fallacy of infinite regress; the second cast doubt on judges and the practice of interviewing; and the third concerned Hunter's conclusion that the revealed facts proved the existence of a dominant elite.

The fallacy of infinite regress[38] was said to have occurred when Hunter argued that men in the political understructure, those who in fact handled the community's day-to-day affairs, were not the true decision-makers in Atlanta. To most observers, it appears that local officials in community-wide organizations are the real movers of their groups; to Hunter, on the other hand, such men were little more than willing or unwilling agents for a small coterie of leaders who made all important decisions behind the scenes. The flaw in this analysis, according to critics, was that it proceeded on an assumption that significant power was always to be found beyond the range of our direct perceptions—at least one step removed from our observations—in the hands of a few. It presumed that a great deal of power is exercised informally and privately, and therefore investigators cannot be present to record its immediate effect. Under such a presumption, however, the existence of an elite can never be *disproved*, because it can always be expected to lie just beyond the hard facts—beyond voting records, minutes of meetings, newspaper and radio stories, or eye-witness reports—available to everyone.

The fallacy of infinite regress resulted from a presupposition about elite power which was allegedly self-validating and impossible to prove. Although critics did not make the point, it would appear that this presupposition was related to the sociological view of power as something necessarily structured and persistent. If it is so persistent, it will not be found in the possession of men who come and go relatively rapidly in associational affairs. Rather, it will attach to individuals who have solid institutional power and who do not quickly pass from the scene.

The reliability of both the judges and the interviewing process was a second challengeable point in Hunter's research, occasioning several related charges. Raymond Wolfinger suggested that Hunter's judges identified supposedly powerful leaders merely on the basis of reputation, and that those who were reputed to be extraordinarily powerful in local affairs might actually exercise only slight influence.[39] This charge, that *status* is not necessarily the equivalent of *power,* that a *reputation* for power does not necessarily reflect the *reality* of distributed power, struck at the logic of Hunter's method rather than at his sociological bias. A similar charge, that all the local people interviewed ranked leaders on the basis of misinformation and misperceptions of one kind or another, completed the blanket criticism that both judges and respondents were not objectively qualified to supply the facts of power in Atlanta.[40] If this were so, Hunter's research scheme should not be applied again in community power studies. For, as Dahl remarked, "How does our investigator know that the panel consists of experts, unless he can test their expertness? Yet he cannot test their expertness unless he already knows the answer to the question he seeks. Here is a dreadful and baffling circularity."[41] And therefore, as Polsby concluded: "It can be cogently argued that the researcher should . . . make it his business to study the requisite behavior directly, and not depend on second-hand opinions."[42]

The charge that Hunter committed the logical fallacy of infinite regress and the complaint that his sources of information were unreliable both enjoy a measure of abstract plausibility.

And yet it should be remembered that in effect Hunter's critics accused important and successful people in Atlanta of collective ignorance of the political facts of life surrounding them. After all, Hunter and other reputational researchers who followed him sought out local respondents whose answers to questions about power were constantly double-checked, cross-analyzed, and ordered for consistency. In the last analysis, reputational researchers thereby do obtain a composite portrait of each community *as it sees itself.*[43] It is theoretically possible that some communities are unaware of their own power configurations but it is an unlikely event in reality, since most communities and their major institutions seem to function passably well on the basis of such perceptions. Moreover, if after years of constant self-scrutiny and conducting its own affairs successfully any community does *not* perceive its own power accurately, it is hardly likely that outside researchers such as Hunter's critics can arrive on the spot and improve the situation. This was, nevertheless, the claim of critics who later devised the pluralist theory of community power to perform just such a feat.

The final criticism of Hunter charged him with assessing his evidence, such as it was, incorrectly. It was said that *Community Power Structure* failed to prove cohesion among the various Atlanta leadership cliques, that it ignored the possibility of their separate concerns actually bringing them into conflict with each other. A clique devoted to real estate interests, for example, might well oppose the proposals of another clique seeking a freeway, which causes urban blight. If Atlanta's cliques were not cohesive, perhaps their members did not wield general, all-embracing power; perhaps they were influential only in limited areas.[44] But if different leaders were powerful in diverse areas of controversy, and if they could not rely on the cooperation of other leaders, it would follow that no *elite* existed in Atlanta, that in fact some men were powerful on some matters and others powerful on entirely different matters. If power were thus divided, the possibility always existed for enlisting some leaders in a political struggle against other leaders, and this competitive situation should be judged democratic and desirable rather than elitist and regrettable. In fact, the eventual picture would fit well with Joseph Schumpeter's definition of a democratic process.

The charge of noncohesion among elites was signally important because it suggested the existence of politics based on temporary and shifting factions rather than on more permanent upper-class/lower-class divisions of interest.[45] Such a system would resolve political issues by a clash of opposing forces cutting across class lines, with each side gaining the support of a few leaders, part of the understructure, and some of the masses. If it could be demonstrated that such a political system is in fact characteristic of our communities, it would provide comforting assurances of an anti-Marxian reality, and thus conform to American Liberal sentiments. The charge of noncohesion, then, automatically implied some version of the group theory of community power. Indeed, when the charge was incorporated into the pluralist theory of democracy, it became a necessary component of that theory's assessment of group politics in America.

THE CHALLENGE TO LIBERAL THINKING

If Hunter was right, the process theories of both Schumpeter and Truman were, at the very least, inapplicable to American democracy at the local level; the former because Hunter discovered noncompetitive local elites, and the latter because in Atlanta the plurality of groups was not a sign of widely shared community power. Of course, both Schumpeter and Truman had written mainly of democracy in very broad terms, with the national community in mind. But it would be difficult to maintain confidence in the theories of either man if local communities, of which the nation is composed, are obviously undemocratic by the very standards and logic that Schumpeter and Truman used to evaluate politics at the higher level. In the dialectic of intellectual disputation, therefore, steps had to be taken to establish, or reestablish, an assuring view of American politics. Before this was done, however, Mills introduced his theory of elites to the scholarly world. Where Hunter's study, with the reputational method, had found elites at the local level of politics,[46] Mills' research, based on a positional technique, discovered elites in national affairs. Here was a second challenge to Liberal thinking, reinforcing the first.

NOTES

1/ Floyd Hunter, *Community Power Structure* (orig., 1953; New York: Anchor, 1963) ; C. Wright Mills, *The Power Elite* (orig., 1956; New York: Galaxy, 1959).

2/ For a discussion of this difference, see Thomas J. Anton, "Power, Pluralism and Local Politics," *Administrative Science Quarterly* (March 1963), pp. 425–457.

3/ Robert Lynd, "Power in American Society as Resource and Problem," in Arthur Kornhauser (ed.), *Problems of Power in American Democracy* (Detroit: Wayne State University Press, 1957), pp. 3–4.

4/ Hunter, *Community Power Structure,* p. 6.

5/ See John Walton, "Discipline, Method and Community Power: A Note on the Sociology of Power," *American Sociological Review* (October 1966), pp. 684–689, and "Substance and Artifact: The Current Status of Research on Community Power Structure," *American Journal of Sociology* (June 1966), pp. 430–438. But for a different point of view, see also Terry Clark, *et al.,* "Discipline, Method, Community Structure, and Decision-Making: The Role and Limitation of the Sociology of Knowledge," *The American Sociologist* (August 1968), pp. 214–217. Even if sociologists do tend to perceive power differently from political scientists—and there are exceptions, of course, such as Seymour Martin Lipset, Daniel Bell, William Kornhauser, Talcott Parsons, and David Riesman—we still do not know why this is so. Do certain men become sociologists *because* they have a certain outlook? Or do they *acquire* that outlook as a result of professional pressures for conformity? And what of political scientists? How does one explain their largely similar outlooks? By the morally and analytically crude theory that many of them have such close and rewarding contacts with government officials that they tend to mirror the government's own view of itself?

6/ Hunter, *Community Power Structure,* p. 6.

7/ Mills, *The Power Elite,* p. 5.

8/ Nelson W. Polsby, "How to Study Community Power: The

Pluralist Alternative," *Journal of Politics* (August 1960), p. 476.

9/ Hunter, *Community Power Structure,* p. 10.

10/ *Ibid.,* p. 2.

11/ *Ibid.,* pp. 6–7.

12/ *Ibid.,* pp. 11–12. In the original of this passage, as throughout *Community Power Structure,* Hunter used the pseudonym "Regional City" to refer to Atlanta. For convenience, Atlanta is used in the text.

13/ See esp. *ibid.,* "Appendix: Methods of Study," pp. 255–263.

14/ *Ibid.,* p. 13.

15/ *Ibid.,* pp. 67–74.

16/ *Ibid.,* pp. 77–79.

17/ *Ibid.,* pp. 62–74.

18/ *Ibid.,* p. 78.

19/ *Ibid.,* p. 48.

20/ *Ibid.,* p. 79.

21/ *Ibid.,* p. 104.

22/ *Ibid.,* p. 66.

23/ *Ibid.,* pp. 65–66, 81–86.

24/ On the powers of leaders, see *ibid.,* pp. 169–202.

25/ *Ibid.,* pp. 87–93.

26/ *Ibid.,* pp. 177–178.

27/ *Ibid.,* p. 242.

28/ *Ibid.,* pp. 104, 223–228.

29/ Hunter noted the capitalistic frame of reference surrounding American community power, but he did not attempt to analyze it in detail, *ibid.,* p. 5.

30/ *Ibid.,* pp. 223–254.

31/ *Ibid.,* pp. 228–254.

32/ Herbert Kaufman and Victor Jones, "The Mystery of Power," *Public Administration Review* (Summer 1954), p. 208.

33/ Laurence J. R. Herson, "In the Footsteps of Community Power," *American Political Science Review* (December 1961), p. 825.

34/ Hunter specifically noted the ties between economy and polity, *Community Power Structure,* pp. 100–101.

35/ *Ibid.,* pp. 169–202. Here, Hunter examined the fact that public power and private power tended to merge in the hands of the leaders.

36/ *Ibid.,* p. 1.

37/ Kaufman and Jones, "The Mystery of Power," p. 207: "Hunter may . . . be right or wrong about the social structure of Regional City [Atlanta], but that is beside the point if his methods are faulty. Unfortunately, they are, and these shortcomings are probably more important than any chance accuracy in his conclusions."

38/ See Nelson W. Polsby, *Community Power and Political Theory* (New Haven: Yale University Press, 1963), pp. 34, 50–51, 59; and Robert A. Dahl, "A Critique of the Ruling Elite Model," *American Political Science Review* (June 1958), p. 463.

39/ Raymond E. Wolfinger, "Reputation and Reality in the Study of Community Power," *American Sociological Review* (October 1960), p. 640.

40/ *Ibid.,* pp. 638–644.

41/ Robert A. Dahl, "Hierarchy, Democracy, and Bargaining in Politics and Economics," in Heinz Eulau, Samuel J. Eldersveld, and Morris Janowitz (eds.), *Political Behavior* (Glencoe, Ill.: Free Press, 1956), p. 85.

42/ Nelson W. Polsby, "Three Problems in the Analysis of Community Power," *American Sociological Review* (December 1959), pp. 796–797.

43/ In another reputational study, several panels of judges were employed, their answers compared, and no significant differences between panels appeared. See Robert O. Schulze and Leonard V. Blumberg, "The Determination of Local Power Elites," *American Journal of Sociology* (November 1957), pp. 293–296. On the uniformity of judges' perceptions, see also Harry R. Dick, "A Method for Ranking Community Influentials," *American Sociological Review* (June 1960), pp. 395–399.

44/ Wolfinger, "Reputation and Reality," pp. 438–439; and Dahl, "Critique of the Ruling Elite Model," p. 118.

45/ Wolfinger, *ibid.,* p. 643; and Polsby, *Community Power and Political Theory,* p. 118.

46/ Hunter did use the reputational method in a study of national power, but the field of relationships was enormous and the study was not convincing. It left little mark on the scholarly field of community power studies, which was already devoted to heated discussion for and against Mills' *The Power Elite*. See Floyd Hunter, *Top Leadership, U.S.A.* (Chapel Hill: University of North Carolina Press, 1959) .

⚙ **6** ✪

The Positional Theory of Elitism:
C. Wright Mills

Whereas Hunter's work suggested that the reasoning employed by Schumpeter and Truman could not validly be extended to local political affairs, C. Wright Mills' controversial community power study, *The Power Elite* (1956),[1] posed an even greater threat to the uncertain confidence engendered by the process theory of American democracy. It focused attention directly on national power and national political actors, and could therefore be read as a deliberate contradiction of the facts that Truman claimed to have discovered. Hunter's findings might be belittled as pertaining only to Atlanta, and thereby irrelevant to an understanding of power in other local communities and/or the national political arena. But Mills analyzed exactly the same locus of men and events that Truman did, and consequently his adverse judgment of it was especially disturbing.

THE POSITIONAL METHOD OF STUDYING
COMMUNITY POWER

Like Hunter, Mills used a methodological technique rooted in a sociological view of community power. This view, as we have observed in Chapter 5, entails the presumption that every community is an enduring thing, with steady and persistent power entrenched in its continuing institutions. Mills himself argued that in regard to power the crucial institutions were those that comprised the state, the military establishment, and the corporate economy. In his words, they "offer us the sociological key to an understanding of the role of the higher circles in America."[2]

In Mills' opinion, if the most powerful, the most wealthy, and the most famous men in the United States were to be separated from their institutional positions, as, for example, Chairman of the Board of Alcoa, President of the Chase Manhattan Bank, Director of the United States Information Agency, Ambassador to the Soviet Union, Chief of Staff of the Army, Secretary of Defense, or Speaker of the House of Representatives, and if the same men were thereby deprived of the resources those positions dispose, they would become politically impotent, poor, and unknown.[3] "For power is not of a man. . . . To be celebrated, to be wealthy. to have power requires access to major institutions, for the institutional positions men occupy determine in large part their chances to have and to hold those valued experiences."[4] It is true that "not all power . . . is anchored in and exercised by means of such institutions, but only within and through them can power be more or less continuous and important."[5] Thus men of crucial influence, the men who shape the community's affairs, the men who make key decisions, the men who wield the ultimate instruments of change or delay—in short, the men who may be counted as truly and notably powerful— these men may be identified by a simple standard: the controlling position they acquire and retain in the hierarchies of society's great institutions.

In this understanding of community affairs lay the rationale for Mills' approach to national politics, an approach that has been labeled the positional method for studying community power. In *The Power Elite* he first discussed the few institutions that demonstrated to his satisfaction their enormous influence over national events and national policy. He then argued, on the basis of his sociological view, that the men who held dominant positions—"strategic command posts"[6]—in those few institutions constituted the "power elite" of American society. And finally, he intensively analyzed the characteristics and behavior of such men, for, as he put it, "the problem of the nature and the power of this elite is the only realistic and serious way to raise . . . the problem of responsible government."[7]

THE POWER ELITE

In Mills' terminology, the power elite was composed of "the war-lords, the corporation chieftains, [and] the political director-ate."[8] He did not dogmatically offer their smoothly operating partnership as proof of a general hypothesis that every society must have a similar elite; the convergence of events that produced our peculiarly American, tri-partite constellation of the most powerful was not at all inevitable. In fact, during most of our history men of the economic realm and men of the political realm have at times ruled alternately and at times shared dominance, and therefore the military have usually been controlled by civilians.[9] During the 1940s, however, the attention of the nation turned sharply to international affairs and to the Cold War. Accordingly, warfare came to be viewed as "the only reality,"[10] and "men in authority" began to speak about " 'emergency' without a foreseeable end."[11] Under these circumstances, the permanent military establishment was greatly enlarged, the counsel of its leaders was highly regarded, and the Pentagon became the seat of the third branch of the national power elite.

In what sense did Mills claim that this elite ruled America? He carefully noted that it was not omnipotent,[12] that it was not engaged in a "secret plot," and that there was no "co-ordinated conspiracy" among its members.[13] On the contrary, he asserted that the elite was "frequently in some tension," because it came together "only on certain coinciding points and only on certain occasions of 'crisis.' "[14] Policy decisions for most everyday affairs were in fact made and promulgated in middle and lower levels of power, in state legislatures, bureaucracies, and like places. The elements of the elite at the pinnacles of influence and authority ordinarily went their separate ways and attended to their diverse concerns.

The collective role of the power elite can only be understood, then, in relation to moments of "crisis." Day-to-day political activities, minor decisions, and short-term policies by and large suffice. But finally and inevitably, there comes a time in the life of every community when great decisions must be made, decisions upon which all else depends, decisions effecting "great changes."[15] As Mills described it, "in our time the pivotal moment . . . [arises], and at that moment, small circles . . . decide or fail to decide."[16] In his era these small circles—the power elite according to Mills—embraced those who decided to drop atomic bombs on Japan, to go to war in Korea, and to refrain from war in Indo-China in 1954.[17] A more recent positional theorist of elitism, G. William Domhoff, extended such analysis of top leadership to philanthropic foundations, law firms, the Central Intelligence Agency, the Federal Bureau of Investigation, universities, and more.[18] The point of seeking to identify crucial decision-makers is that we must live with the consequences of great decisions, and therefore we would be well advised to inform ourselves about the relatively few men who make them.

THE ELITE'S UNITY

If Mills had gone no further than to complain of a minority making the most important decisions in American life, his work would have faded quickly and deservedly into obscurity. After all, since Robert Michels' early study of oligarchy every student of community power has been aware of the fact that in one way or another only a few men actually participate in society's key decisions. The important question therefore is: Whom do the few represent? If they in fact represent the voices of various and competing interests, as Truman contended, then at least American democracy might be said to operate satisfactorily according to the process theory. But Mills flatly rejected this comforting contention, and argued at length that in many significant ways the elite are of one mind and a single interest. In his opinion, their unity results from three contributing factors, which we may call cooptation, circulation, and class identity.

The term "cooptation" describes the complicated way in which individuals advance from the lower to the higher ranks of organizational hierarchies. Within such hierarchies, aspiring candidates are usually selected for advancement by their already entrenched superiors, and therefore conformity to the prevailing institutional norms of conduct and conviction is constantly enforced. Under the circumstances, uniformity of outlook is doubly likely: first, because only men who at least seemingly conform will be advanced, and second, because outward behavior turns into inner belief under the relentless psychological pressure exerted by the organizational environment.

Cooptation, then, is an administrative and intellectual process that assures the continuity of large organizations. It dissolves many of the differences that may originally separate those men who seek to lead others. Potential leaders may come from vastly different backgrounds—from families of poverty and of great wealth, from families of genteel tradition and those obsessed with status insecurity, from black families and from white ones. Nonetheless, the ultimately successful organization leader will probably be cordial, expansive, and moderate; in a word, he will be interchangeable with his peers.[19]

Mills argued that the various phenomena of cooptation, which produce similar outlooks and therefore similar perceptions of interest, operated strongly within the military establishment, the corporate economy, and the political realm. The military devices for molding conformity—the service academies, the interservice rivalries, the pomp and ceremony, and the authoritarian chain of command—were quite obvious.[20] In corporate circles, the many management training programs for junior executives served the same function, and produced the "sound man with well-balanced judgment."[21] And in the highest realm of politics, in the executive branch of government, cooptation was the rule.[22] Carefully selected "political outsiders" abounded during the Eisenhower years. As Mills defined him, the political outsider was a high-ranking official with no independent political base, a man chosen deliberately from corporate and military ranks for the appropriateness and consistency of his views. In fact, only three of the top fifty political leaders of the Eisenhower Administration were *not* outsiders in this sense of the term.[23] The result was a striking similarity of personalities and convictions in that administration.

There might be some cause for democratic optimism if the various components of the power elite were distinctive in outlook, if the generals and admirals, the politicos, and the economic notables did represent diversified institutional viewpoints. But according to Mills' analysis this was not at all the case. In the national arena as he saw it, elites kept circulating from one realm of power to another, continually mingling with each other, and thereby substantially eliminating whatever significant differences might originally have marked them in background, interest, and temperament.

The proof of elite circulation was the movement of leaders from one power realm to another in the post-World War II era.[24] Military men like Generals Dwight Eisenhower and George Marshall turned into statesmen as President and Secretary of State. Corporation men became politicos, the archetypical example being Secretary of Defense Charles Wilson, former President of the General Motors Corporation. Moreover, politicians were awarded high-ranking reserve commissions in the armed forces; military men went to work for corporations heavily engaged in defense contracts; Wall Street lawyers entered the State Department; and the Central Intelligence Agency acquired its share of economic and military notables. Indeed, Mills perceived a very clear triangular pattern of personnel circulation among top military, economic, and political positions. The result was cooptation on a grand scale: a blurring of distinct interests, a merging of ostensibly separate viewpoints, and a growth of mutual confidence and trust among men who moved easily from one realm of power to another as if there were virtually no differences among the responsibilities in each of the separate realms.

Here was a key point in the study of community power. Mills claimed that members of the power elite circulated without changing their deepest convictions. He noted that a corporation man could and did equate the interest of his corporation with the interest of the United States, even after he had formally left the private economy to assume the public obligations of a Cabinet position.[25] There were therefore no strong competitors devoted to politics, to military affairs, or to economic matters; there were no staunch and persevering representatives of three separate realms of interest and outlook. There was only an all-embracing, single group of men—the power elite—who circulated from one position to another while apparently agreeing that the interests of General Motors and the United States, or Lockheed and the Pentagon, or Wall Street and the Treasury, were precisely the same.

Complementing the cooptation and the circulation of the power elite was a third sign indicating identity of interest among the most powerful men on the national scene. Although Mills extensively described the contours of this power factor, he did not analytically define it satisfactorily; rather, he referred to it broadly as consciousness of "class."[26] The word "class" is unfortunately elastic, for it has been widely used by scholars and ideologues with respect to more than one social phenomenon. Mills himself attached great significance to certain social realities: many members of the power elite sent their children to the same prep schools, enrolled them in the same Ivy League colleges, dined and danced in the same country clubs, worked in the same prestigious law firms, were listed in the same Social Register, and married people of similar occupations and social stature.[27] Such common experiences generated common privileges, preferences, and prejudices, and were undoubtedly linked to a tendency to belong to "overlapping 'crowds,' and intricately connected 'cliques.' "[28] Of course, there were factions among the elite, and therefore some led the Democratic party and others led the Republican party. But Mills was convinced that "more powerful than these divisions" were "the internal discipline and the community of interests" that bound the power elite together as a single entity.[29] He did not succinctly state the precise nature of this discipline and these interests. We may assume, however, that he had in mind the commitment to defend and profit from a private property society in a world increasingly devoted to the ethics of collectivism. On this score the corporate-politicos, the military-politicos, and the military-industrialists surely saw eye to eye.

THE MIDDLE LEVEL AND THE MASS

Although Mills was concerned mainly with the behavior of the power elite, his analysis of the national political system revealed additional noteworthy political actors. He classified all of these into two categories: those in the "middle level" of power and those among the "mass." Both of these lesser power centers played active, if ultimately insignificant, roles in community politics.

"Immediately below the elite are the professional politicians of the middle levels of power, in the Congress and in the pressure groups."[30] In fact, Mills argued, "what is usually taken to be the central content of politics, the pressures and the campaigns and the congressional maneuvering, has, in considerable part, now been relegated to the middle levels of power."[31] Here was a direct challenge to Liberal confidence. Mills intentionally lumped together professional politicians, Congress, pressure groups, and campaigns—all at the "middle level"—in order to derogate the ever-present signs of Liberalism in action.

The Power Elite advanced two reasons to justify the label of middle level for ordinary national politics—the kind reported nightly to millions of Americans by commentators like Harry Reasoner, David Brinkley, and Walter Cronkite—and both were drawn from the unique coincidence of multiple historical forces that had shaped conditions favorable for the rule of the power elite. On the one hand, modern exigencies requiring speedy national decision-making had naturally shifted "the center of initiative and decision" from a plural, and therefore slow moving, Legislature, to a unitary Executive.[32] Beginning in the Depression years of the 1930s, and continuing into the hot and cold war years of the 1940s and 1950s, the transfer of initiative was epitomized by the "executive agreements" which presidents made with foreign governments, agreements committing America to vital courses of action without prior consent of the Congress.[33] On the other hand, the Congress had failed to radically reorganize itself into a smoothly operating and effective force, and therefore had failed to devote itself to issues of great consequence. It was dominated by a great many state and local interests, by splintered parties, and by an outworn combination of committees and gerontocratic committee chairmen incapable of permitting thorough and reasoned debate on most matters of urgency.[34] Moreover, the scattered constituencies and crazy-quilt pattern of local electoral units made it impossible to elect a Congress on the basis of nation-wide political consciousness. Significant political issues were therefore, in the end, resolved by the White House with the advice and consent of the power elite. Congress labored and labored, but brought forth little that was in any sense decisive.

The mass of ordinary citizens constituted the lowest level of power. Undoubtedly this entity engaged in a variety of political activities. It voted; it attended meetings and hearings; it made campaign contributions; it wrote letters; it formed ad hoc committees for many purposes; and it occasionally agitated over particular issues. In substance, however, its efforts were for the most part inconclusive. Mills attributed this lack of significant effect to changes both in the mental makeup of the individuals who constitute the mass and in the nature of opportunities for political action available to them.

Originally, Liberals relied on the public as "the very balance wheel of democratic power."[35] It was presumed that the public exercised its electoral power as a court of last resort for aspirants to public office and therefore effectively instructed the government as to the nation's needs. According to Mills, however, in the modern age most people are less competent to express opinions than to receive them. This is at least partly true because the instruments of the mass media—radio, television, and the press—monopolize communications, in large measure impede intelligent discourse among ordinary men and women, and tend to frustrate efforts to organize a public awareness and a public will. Even if members of the modern mass could communicate with each other easily, however, it is by no means certain they can effectively express their own opinions. The mass media are so pervasively influential that most citizens think prepackaged thoughts rather than make personal observations and reflections. Under such circumstances, democratic public opinion—alert, spontaneous, independent public consciousness—cannot exist.[36]

Mills offered another reason why the great majority exercised little real authority in national political affairs, why it merely reflected forces more powerful than itself. If ordinary men are to express their own opinions honestly and persistently, they must be financially independent; so long as they are beholden to others they will usually seek safety in conformity of outlook. Yet

Mills argued that precisely such dependence and consequent conformity had appeared in America as a result of the decrease in size and influence of a formerly large class of small property owners. The gradual shrinkage of the farm population and the metamorphosis from an economy of small businesses to one of great corporations combined to produce a post-World War II mass composed mainly of white collar workers and wage employees at even lower ranks. According to *The Power Elite,* people in both of these groups are aware that their jobs, their incomes, and their extremely modest properties are dependent upon the continued good will of their superiors. Even labor leaders, who seem powerful because of their union support, are actually insecure because they and their men achieved positions of some influence because of government legislation establishing and protecting the right of workers to organize. Yet in the judgment of many capitalist-minded Americans, union activities are not entirely acceptable and unioneers realize that at any time they might again be weakened by antiunion laws such as the Taft-Hartley Act of 1947. The men of the mass are therefore not entirely free to have, to hold, or to vent their own opinions, and neither the conformity nor the obsequity they are sometimes required to adopt are signs of a healthy and vigorous political entity.[37]

MILLS VERSUS TRUMAN

Since *The Power Elite* presented more than 400 pages of strong polemical criticism of American society, we can discuss here no more than the key points in Mills' understanding of power as it related to the overriding issue of democracy. Some of these crucial concepts—the tri-partite power elite, the middle level of power, and the qualities of the mass—do manage, however, to reveal the basic format of a pervasive and consistent criticism of any Trumanesque optimism that could conceivably be grounded on a pluralistic array of American groups.

Primarily, of course, there was the power elite. Acting at moments of crisis, it allegedly stood *above* the political actors Truman examined and discussed. If Mills' contentions about the extent of its influence were valid, the complex maneuvering and political in-fighting among groups that Truman assiduously analyzed were simply irrelevant to the issue of democracy. If, to use a recent illustration, the nation can be propelled into a land war in Asia virtually by Executive fiat, the day-to-day deliberations of Congress and the various regulatory agencies are exposed as relatively unimportant. The commentator who exhaustively describes all this hustle and bustle is merely tracing the choreography of an elaborate but insignificant political minuet.

The Congressional minuet presumably took place at the middle level of power. Mills would have agreed with Truman that at this level there were some subtle and self-adjusting devices—for instance, overlapping memberships in interest groups —which served to promote moderation, balance, and compromise. He would have disagreed, however, that such devices were proof of a flourishing democracy. In the long run they merely perpetuate the stalemate of local interests and local forces which engage so large a portion of every Congressman's time and energy. They therefore fail to reverse the recent trend shifting decisive power from the Congress to the White House.

When Mills argued that a stalemate existed at the middle level of power, his analysis paralleled and contradicted Truman's notion of a balance of interests, an equilibrium of forces. The term " 'balance of power,' " Mills remarked, "implies equality of power, and equality of power seems wholly fair and even honorable, but in fact what is one man's honorable balance is often another's unfair imbalance."[38] Balance, equilibrium, and stability may in fact exist at the middle level, but, when placed in the perspective Mills suggested, they did not constitute compelling evidence of democracy and political satisfaction of the nation's needs. From the sociological point of view, the middle level— with its continuity and unchanging shape—represented the politics of the status quo, the configuration of forces that perpetuates any community from day to day. Whoever is dissatisfied with the fundamental outlines of the status quo must turn to those *above* the balance for relief, to those who have the power to effect changes. And it was at this point, for Mills, that real, significant, ultimate power asserts itself. Yet at this point relatively few men were in command.

Below the middle level of power Mills found the mass, and an instructive comparison may be drawn between his understanding of this political factor and Truman's parallel understanding of the public at large. Truman argued that the ordinary men who together are called the public constituted any number of potential groups, all of them capable in the normal course of events of coalescing and exercising formidable power in a democratic sense, and this despite the reality that most political events are in fact determined by the activities of organized pressure groups. It was by such reasoning that Truman emphasized the importance and the ultimate power of the franchise and the electoral system, whereby potential groups may eventually act. Mills, on the other hand, concluded that the mass was incompetent to recognize its own interests, much less express them. And if, in rare cases, men of the mass did discover their interests, they were not entirely free to express them openly and effectively. It followed—as Mills saw it—that the mass wielded no decisive power.

MILLS AND HUNTER VERSUS TRUMAN

The basic data that Mills examined were components of the national political system and therefore his power study stood directly and empirically opposed to that of Truman, who also appraised the national scene. In addition to disputed facts, the two studies were opposed ideologically, in a realm of logic where all community power studies are ultimately related. In this regard, there was a similarity between the logic of Mills' analysis and that of Hunter's; indeed, the two men pursued a common rationale which challenged the group theory point-blank. Several elements of this rationale are noteworthy because they clarify the paramount issue of democracy which pervades all community power studies, national and local.

Mills' emphasis on moments of crisis was a case in point, for he in effect reiterated Hunter's distinction between policy matters and ordinary politics. For Hunter, policy decisions can change the shape of a local community's affairs and, accordingly, were made only by the elite of Atlanta. For Mills, decisions during moments of crisis may change the shape of national affairs and, therefore, were made only by the power elite. Both men saw two distinct levels of decisions and politicking: a higher level of elites and a subordinate stratum comprised of pluralistic groups and associations. The logic of analysis was the same; the only differences between Mills and Hunter appeared in their respective and belittling labels for local and national pluralism. Hunter referred to Atlanta's groups as the political "understructure" and Mills assigned the nation's groups to the middle level of power.

The mere ranking of decisions automatically ranks political actors either into an elite class or a nonelite class and is therefore of itself a threat to the optimistic group theory of democracy. Mills and Hunter both went further, however, by suggesting that existing rankings were, by and large, very durable and therefore unrepresentative from one year, one decade, or even one generation to another. The general thrust of Mills' analysis of American national democracy coincided exactly with Hunter's findings in Atlanta: both men concluded that our economic and political systems were so closely intertwined that the nominal and cherished political equality of all citizens was overshadowed by the ever-present differential in their relative access to economic resources.

As we have already noted, herein lies the severest challenge to a reassuring view of politics as it is practiced in a capitalistic society. Mills stated the problem bluntly: "America is now in considerable part more a formal political democracy than a democratic [egalitarian] social [economic] structure."[39] But the inequality that exists is closely linked to capitalism itself, which characteristically offers equal opportunities for men to become unequal. Then too, the inequality that exists is defended as a *necessary* evil, an *inevitable* by-product of the pecuniary system accepted as the last hope of free men in a world threatened by Communism.[40] If this pecuniary system endures, though, along with its revered structure of incentives, students of American politics cannot avoid reckoning with Mills' basic contention: "We must . . . revise and relocate the received conception of an enormous scatter of varied interests," for those "that count in any balance are few in number and weighty beyond comparison with the dispersed groups on the middle and lower levels of the power structure."[41]

SOME CRITICISMS OF MILLS

Adverse responses to *The Power Elite* were immediate and emphatic. No doubt this was more than partly due to the tenor of Mills' remarks, which one critic compared to "an intellectual lynching bee."[42] But polemical or otherwise, Mills' charges against American politics required refutation if only because of their logical assault on the comforting categories of analysis contained in the process theory, the categories of balance, access, representativeness, and satisfaction of various political needs. Among the many counter-charges that were advanced against *The Power Elite*,[43] three emerged as fundamental and persistent. Like the criticisms of Hunter's work, these were to become part and parcel of Robert Dahl's pluralist theory of democracy, which we shall examine extensively in the next several chapters. It is therefore worthwhile to note them here only briefly and thereby indicate the general direction in which defenders of American democracy had to move.

One revealing complaint against *The Power Elite* was that Mills failed "to identify the major mechanisms" of collusion among the most powerful.[44] His positional theory presumed that power flows from commanding positions in great institutions and organizations, but what was it—his critics asked—that united the men at the top? As one critic observed, there cannot be a power elite "without a *community of interests*. Mills implies one: the interest of the elite is in the maintenance of the capitalist system as a *system*. But this is never really discussed or analyzed in detail."[45]

We have already noted that Mills only vaguely mentioned the subject of class interest. But without detailed and convincing evidence of the power elite's class interest, it could plausibly be argued that American leaders who make key decisions do so on behalf of their formal constituents rather than as a result of their common outlook or shared prejudice. It could then also be said that regardless of superficial similarities among decision-makers —similarities of temperament, status, occupation, and so forth— such men do in fact believe themselves obliged to discharge certain official roles according to the constitutional and electoral requirements of their offices.[46] The service of constituent interests may therefore be more important to office holders than the service of any abstract, poorly defined class interest. At any rate, lacking direct proof of collusion or class interest, it is possible to assert with confidence that decisions made at moments of obvious crisis—such as the decision to drop atomic bombs on Japan— were made by leaders who, to the best of their ability, did what they thought the nation would have wanted.[47]

Closely related to the questionable assertion of cohesion among the elite were various uncertainties about the nature of political resources available to concededly powerful men in American society. Again and again in *The Power Elite* Mills argued that all such resources—money, prestige, status, and others—are directly associated with one's position in great institutions.[48] Accordingly, the men who hold high positions possess all these resources in large amounts and thereby ultimately enjoy commanding power in our society. Could it not as well be true, instead, that different positions in society yield different kinds of resources, political or otherwise? The president of a corporation may wield only private economic power while the chairman of a board of education controls and directs a whole public education system. Perhaps in like fashion only prestige flows from the Social Register while bloc voting strength is reserved for men with special ethnic backgrounds or skin colors at appropriate times and places. And whereas men control the stock of a great corporation, real power over the institution may be exercised by its management hierarchy. In short, to what extent does real power depend on special skills, or unique talents, as distinguished from mere ownership of wealth? What if political power is in reality a multifaceted composite of many kinds of power, all flowing from diverse resources that are not dominated by a few key, strategic positions in society?[49]

To raise such questions about the sources and locations of political resources was to challenge the notion of a single, cohesive, cooperating power elite by conceptualizing power instead as an extremely complex phenomenon. If resources were in truth widely dispersed, it followed that there would always be need for negotiated compromises, for a balancing of conflicting interests among the many centers of partial power. How might such compromises be effected? This question implied the importance of what Mills chose to derogate as the middle level of power.

What Mills called the middle level consisted of party activity, group pressures, bureaucratic lobbying and inertia, and most other organized politicking. If power resources were not as concentrated as Mills suggested, all the actors at the middle level possessed part of the total power needed to get things done in our political system. Mills argued that the men of the middle level were actually stalemated, but it could be contended, instead, that men in society's highest positions were also stalemated, by lack of cohesion. Yet if our political system suffers a general, widespread standoff, the politician must be viewed as an important and pivotal figure. He must be the political actor responsible for achieving satisfactory compromises and bargains. He must therefore be the catalyst of democracy, cajoling, demanding, pleading, fighting, arguing, conniving, and otherwise avoiding political paralysis. But the politician is the very epitome of middle-level politics, and if he wields significant influence, then the appurtenances of his activity—the intricate movements of legislature, parties, and campaigns—are supremely important,[50] even decisive, elements of community power, notwithstanding Mills' contentions that they were merely a kind of distracting sideshow.

THE NEED FOR A NEW THEORY

Thus the three fundamental charges against *The Power Elite*— its failure to prove cohesion, its mistaken notion of concentrated resources, and its derogation of the middle level of power—raised serious doubts about the usefulness of Mills' conceptual categories, and about the validity of some of his conclusions. Nevertheless, there was apparently enough unshakeable truth in his work, and in Hunter's before him, to discredit the one-sided view of community power advanced in Truman's *Governmental Process,* with its concentration solely on groups. Continued confidence in American democracy required a new theory, a new and optimistic understanding of our politics that would account for both groups *and* elites. This was the function served by the pluralist theory of democracy.

122 · COMMUNITY POWER AND DEMOCRATIC THEORY

NOTES

1/ C. Wright Mills, *The Power Elite* (orig., 1956; New York: Galaxy, 1959) .

2/ *Ibid.*, p. 5.

3/ *Ibid.*, p. 10.

4/ *Ibid.*, pp. 10–11.

5/ *Ibid.*, p. 9.

6/ *Ibid.*, p. 4.

7/ *Ibid.*, p. 25.

8/ *Ibid.*, p. 9.

9/ *Ibid.*, pp. 171–183.

10/ *Ibid.*, p. 202.

11/ *Ibid.*, p. 184.

12/ *Ibid.*, p. 26.

13/ *Ibid.*, p. 292.

14/ *Ibid.*, p. 276.

15/ *Ibid.*, p. 1.

16/ *Ibid.*, p. 22.

17/ *Ibid.*

18/ G. William Domhoff, *Who Rules America?* (Englewood Cliffs, N.J.: Prentice-Hall, 1967) .

19/ The leader of a revolutionary band of self-styled "freedom fighters" may be abrasive, narrow-minded, and volatile. But even he will resemble his peers, and if his group becomes a lasting institution, that is, a governmental party, he will probably change his idiosyncratic ways or be replaced by a bureaucrat or *apparachik*.

20/ Mills, *The Power Elite*, pp. 193–197.

21/ *Ibid.*, pp. 141–146.

22/ *Ibid.*, p. 235.

23/ *Ibid.*, pp. 228–235.

24/ *Ibid.*, pp. 287–292, *et passim*.

25/ *Ibid.*, pp. 284–285.

26/ *Ibid.*, p. 283.

27/ *Ibid.*, pp. 47–70.

28/ *Ibid.*, p. 11.

29/ *Ibid.*, p. 283.

30/   *Ibid.*, p. 4.

31/   *Ibid.*, p. 28.

32/   *Ibid.*, p. 229.

33/   *Ibid.*, p. 255.

34/   *Ibid.*, pp. 251–257 ff.

35/   *Ibid.*, p. 298.

36/   The foregoing analysis of the "mass" appears in *ibid.*, pp. 302–304 ff.

37/   Mills' discussion of white collar and unionized workers appears in *ibid.*, pp. 261–263 ff.

38/   *Ibid.*, p. 246.

39/   *Ibid.*, p. 274.

40/   That economic inequality in the United States is persistent may be seen in Gabriel Kolko, *Wealth and Power in America* (New York: Praeger, 1962) ; and Herman Miller, *Rich Man, Poor Man* (New York: Signet, 1964). That inequality is deemed inevitable may be deduced from President Nixon's 1969 recipe for halting inflation: money became more expensive to borrow, thereby increasing the profits of banks and wealthy lenders; and unemployment became more prevalent, thus reducing the income of unskilled workers and blacks. The fact that the general public tolerated this program for fiscal "soundness" indicates that inequality is widely considered to be a necessary part of the capitalist way of doing business.

41/   Mills, *The Power Elite*, p. 266.

42/   Richard Rovere, "The Interlocking Overlappers," in G. William Domhoff and Hoyt B. Ballard (eds.) , *C. Wright Mills and The Power Elite* (Boston: Beacon, 1968) , p. 183.

43/   Some of the notable critical discussions of *The Power Elite,* Mills himself, or his research technique are: Daniel Bell, "The Power Elite—Reconsidered," *American Journal of Sociology* (November 1958) , pp. 238–250; Robert A. Dahl, "A Critique of the Ruling Elite Model," *American Political Science Review* (June 1958) , pp. 463–469, and "The Concept of Power," *Behavioral Science* (July 1957) , pp. 201–215; William Kornhauser, " 'Power Elite' or 'Veto Groups'?" in S. M. Lipset and L. Lowenthal (eds.) , *Culture and Social Character* (New York: Free Press, 1961) , pp. 252–267; Talcott Parsons, "The Distribution of Power in American Society," *World Politics* (October 1957), pp. 123–143; and Nelson W. Polsby, *Community Power and Political Theory* (New Haven: Yale University Press, 1963).

44/ Kornhauser, *ibid.,* p. 265.

45/ Bell, "The Power Elite—Reconsidered," p. 242.

46/ On the question of role behavior, see Peter Rossi, "Community Decision-Making," *Administrative Science Quarterly* (March 1957), p. 423 ff.

47/ Rovere, "The Interlocking Overlappers," pp. 177–189.

48/ For example, see Mills, *The Power Elite,* pp. 84, 110, *et passim.*

49/ This question is more fully examined, with appropriate citations, in connection with the concept of "noncumulative resources" in Chapters 7, 8, and 9.

50/ Parsons, "The Distribution of Power," pp. 134–135; Kornhauser, " 'Power Elite' or 'Veto Groups'?" p. 264; and Arnold Rose, *The Power Structure* (New York: Galaxy, 1967), pp. 29–39, *et passim.*

✪ 7 ✪

The Pluralist Theory of Democracy: Robert A. Dahl

Between the years 1957 and 1959, Robert Dahl and two of his associates at Yale University—Nelson Polsby and Raymond Wolfinger—conducted an extensive community power study; as a result, two books were published. Dahl himself wrote *Who Governs? Democracy and Power in an American City* (1961), and Polsby wrote *Community Power and Political Theory* (1963).[1] In these works, and in a number of scholarly articles related to the same study, all three men analyzed and evaluated political conditions and events in the city of New Haven, Connecticut.[2] From their writings, there emerged in comprehensive outline what has since been called the pluralist theory of democracy, a complex explanation of how and why political power is in fact widely and democratically dispersed in our communities.

Although the pluralist theory flowed from the combined efforts of all three men, Dahl may be singled out as the dominant scholar among them. Moreover, the fullest account of politics in the city is to be found in his book. In this chapter we shall examine the pluralist theory by explicating *Who Governs?* as its basic text, with other works by Dahl, Polsby, and Wolfinger serving to clarify or amplify assertions made there.

The view of politics expressed in *Who Governs?* flatly contradicted virtually every significant notion advanced in Hunter's *Community Power Structure* and Mills' *The Power Elite*. What

125

amounted to a complete rejection of the reputational and positional theories of elitism was not always directly and explicitly argued, however, and some vitally important points of scholarly controversy were obscured by the easy-going, matter-of-fact style of Dahl's description of political life in New Haven. If his pluralist contribution to the continuing debate over community power is to be placed in usable perspective, it will be necessary to select a number of points that provided an analytical framework for his evaluation of what he observed in the city. On the basis of this abstraction, it is apparent that regardless of the way Dahl chose to tell the story of New Haven's political drama in *Who Governs?*, his understanding of power denied the validity of the work done by Hunter and Mills.

THE DECISION-MAKING METHOD OF STUDYING COMMUNITY POWER

Underlying the pluralist theory was a set of interrelated presumptions about the nature of power and how it is exercised in our communities. Just as the sociological view of power pervaded the works of Hunter and Mills, so also *Who Governs?* embraced a series of presumably self-evident truths about power, as seen by political scientists. The first of such truths was that there is a substantial distinction between power that is actual and power that is merely potential.[3]

The difficulty with most commonly accepted indices of power —standards based on wealth or position—is that if we measure power in terms of any particular resource, we have no assurance that men well-supplied with that item will actually attempt to use it to exert influence in the affairs of their communities. The Army, for example, is inseparably linked to enormous military resources—guns, tanks, planes, supplies, disciplined cadres, and more—but it does not employ them to impose a military dictatorship on the United States.[4] Likewise, a rich man in New Haven may be assured access to great personal wealth, and yet he may choose to use it to subsidize the ballet rather than dabble in community politics.[5] From such realities, the pluralist theory of democracy was constructed, presuming that the potential power a man enjoys bears no necessary relationship to the actual power he wields. For community power studies, this simple proposition bore far-reaching implications.

By distinguishing between potential and actual power, Dahl and his colleagues rebuked both reputational and positional researchers for asserting that persons who control great economic resources and positions also exercise great community power.[6] From this rebuke it followed that the sociological perspective should be rejected. We may not presume that certain people always make policy, although they obviously control resources of great potential power. We may not presume that certain individuals are continually powerful, although they are widely reputed to possess resources sufficient to dominate future events. We may not presume, finally, that certain positions within particular institutions actually afford their occupants dominant power, although such positions seem to dispose of overwhelming potential power resources. In sum, we may not justifiably entertain any presumptions whatsoever about the distribution—temporary or enduring—of power in any community: this was the methodological commandment Polsby laid down as the cardinal, negative rule of pluralist theory.[7]

If one cannot infer from sociological indices of potential power that people actually hold power, how should researchers proceed to identify the most influential members of a community? Once one rejects the sociological view of the community as a continuing web of relationships between men and institutions whose power is more or less permanent, what method should students of community power employ? The answer in *Who Governs?* was clear: one must study events, situations in which power is being exercised. In a word, one must study *decisions*.

As Polsby explained the pluralist method which was applied in the New Haven study, the pluralist investigator makes "an attempt . . . to study specific outcomes, in order to determine who actually prevails in community decision-making."[8] This approach was no more than the logical outcome of pluralist criticisms against the reputational and positional methods. As we have seen in previous chapters, both techniques were charged with neglecting all-important aspects of decision-making; for example, the major question was whether reputedly or ostensibly powerful men were *actually* involved *decisively* in *vital* political matters. Such questions can only be resolved by paying close attention to decisions: "How can one tell, after all, whether or not an actor is powerful unless some sequence or event, competently observed, attests to his power?"[9]

Having decided to study decisions, the New Haven investigators conducted an "extensive observation of the community." This included attending political meetings and public events, observing activity in the offices of several city officials, reading local newspapers, and establishing contacts with knowledgeable members of the community.[10] There was also a formal interviewing process, wherein "nearly fifty persons who had participated in one or more important decisions" were questioned.[11] As we shall see, all of this "extensive observation," coupled with the pluralist understanding of the dual nature of power, supported the view that New Haven was democratic.

It is worth noting even more exactly the true distinction between the pluralist, decision-making method practiced in New Haven by political scientists and the reputational or positional methods more fashionable among sociologists. The *manner* in which data were gathered for the New Haven study did not really differ markedly from the *manner* in which Hunter and Mills collected their facts. All students of community power interview notable people, read relevant newspapers, consult pertinent archives, establish formal and informal contacts with individual members of the community they intend to study, and keep an eye on public meetings and an ear to public utterances of significance. And surely all scholars, pluralist or otherwise, carefully assess the information they accumulate and deliberately make judgments concerning the reliability and validity of testimony they receive from informants. Therefore even though pluralist theorists complained of Hunter using reputational panels and Mills using Social Registry data, it seems likely that their own sources of information—newspapers, interviews, informants, and observation—were no less fallible. In reality, the critical difference between the New Haven study and earlier studies lay in *what* was selected for investigation. Dahl and his associates sought to avoid studying men and their resources from afar. They attempted, instead, to observe men close up, men engaged in action, men making decisions, men currently shaping events.

As Dahl defined the *what,* the *essence* of his subject, students of community power must engage in a *"careful examination of a series of concrete decisions."*[12] But this approach raised a difficult procedural problem. The number of decisions available for study is infinite, so we must of necessity study only a few. But which ones? Which decisions taken in the community reflect on the overriding issue of democracy? Which decisions must be studied before it can be said with confidence that the political system is or is not democratic? Some categorizing is easy; decisions about where to place fire hydrants are not to be classed with neighborhood-shattering decisions about locating a new innercity expressway. And the award of a contract for hauling trash from City Hall will not measurably bear on the degree of freedom found in the community, whereas awards for the construction of schools in black ghetto areas might well be viewed as crucial racial decisions. It is in the gray area between the obvious and the extremes that the problem of selection arises.

The men who studied New Haven were well aware of the importance of properly selecting decisions for study, and they wrote often of the need to investigate "key political decisions," "important decisions," and "significant issues."[13] Polsby even explained in some detail the technique used to select the decisions studied in New Haven. He listed four criteria for ranking certain matters quite important in the life of any community: How many people are affected? What kinds of benefits result? How widely are such benefits distributed? To what extent is the community's existing pattern of resource distribution—wealth, ease, status, education, and so forth—affected?[14] He argued that these criteria justified selecting three particular areas of decision-making in New Haven for investigation: areas pertaining to public education, urban renewal, and party nominations. In all three, a great many people were affected, large sums of money were at stake, and important policy decisions with lasting consequences were taken.

There was a fifth, all-encompassing criterion for choosing which decisions to study in New Haven, but this one must have seemed so self-evident to Dahl and the others that they mentioned it only in passing. It is a noteworthy fact, nonetheless, that all the decisions analyzed in *Who Governs?* were associated with governmental activity. For the scholars of the New Haven project, "community power" was to be defined with reference to political conduct, "since the political arena is the sector of community life in which large groups in the community make demands upon one another and collectively determine policy outcomes."[15] Or, as Dahl put it, the major question was who dominated *"public* governments"[16]—rather than private hierarchies—and he proposed to answer it by examining matters of public education, urban renewal, and party nominations. This principle of selection further set the pluralists apart from both Hunter and Mills. As the very title of Dahl's book *Who Governs?* indicates, the men who studied New Haven offered a more limited, more narrowly *political* view of power than that advanced in *Community Power Structure* and *The Power Elite,* which together considered social, military, economic, *and* political aspects of community power.

DAHL'S CONCEPTUAL FRAMEWORK

To restate briefly the pluralist fundamentals described thus far, *Who Governs?* relied on at least three basic concepts: first, the distinction between actual and potential power; second, the method of focusing on decisions; and third, the presumption that among criteria for selecting decisions for study, the political is paramount. With these three fundamental notions in mind, Dahl observed the city, questioned political actors, accumulated a mass of relevant information, sifted it carefully and thoughtfully, and then constructed a comprehensive explanation of political life in New Haven. Many of the elements of this explanation warrant our attention, especially those relating to the range of elite powers, the nature of noncumulative political resources, the characteristics of the political and the apolitical strata of citizenry, the role of "slack" political influence, and the maintenance of the rules of the democratic game. When his observations on these matters are collected and considered together with the axiomatic outlook already described, they mark the boundaries of the pluralistic model of a democratic community.

THE SCOPE OF POWER

Dahl assumed that in New Haven, as in any other community, only a few men would actually make important decisions; this reality he conceded to Hunter and Mills. What he sought to discover was the extent, or the range, or, in pluralist terms, the *scope* of power exercised by those few.[17] If their scope of power were limited, it could very well mean that the small number of decision-makers were responsive to the people below them in order to acquire more power or merely retain that which they enjoyed. If Dahl could prove such a situation to exist, it would demonstrate competitive politics, a choice of policies, responsible leadership, and therefore the practice of democracy in New Haven.

A lengthy procedure was used for learning about the men who made New Haven's decisions in public education, urban renewal, and party nominations. First the researchers drew up lists, which they called "leadership pools," of "all persons formally connected with decision-making" in those realms of activity. Many of the people on the lists were then interviewed in order to ascertain which specific decisions they thought were crucial. Those decisions were subsequently analyzed in considerable detail, using all available verbal and documentary information. And finally judgments were made as to precisely who had exercised the greatest power over the decisions studied.[18]

In the end the persons who were identified as predominantly powerful in making community decisions were clearly the political elite of New Haven.[19] On two broad grounds, however, Dahl concluded that those men bore little resemblance to the elites found by Hunter or Mills. For one reason, they were not, as a group, identical with or even significantly related to the highest social and economic circles of the city; the scope of their power was predominantly public. Moreover, their public power did not overlap from one area of decision-making to another; rather, the scope of their power remained quite narrow. These two conclusions about the scope of elite influence were elaborated at length in *Who Governs?*

The first conclusion rested upon a comparison of the political elite with New Haven's economic and social elites. Dahl called the latter groups Economic and Social Notables, and defined the first in terms of great wealth and the second in terms of attendance at prestigious events or inclusion in high society's esteemed registries.[20] From the leadership pools and from interview data, he discovered that relatively few of the Notables of New Haven were directly involved in making community decisions. Social Notables held only 2 out of 500 party offices; they held only 2 out of 131 offices in public education; and they comprised only 24 out of 435 citizens dominant in urban renewal.[21] Furthermore, Economic Notables were represented by only 48 men in the urban renewal leadership group, 6 in the offices of the parties, and none at all in the field of public education.[22] On the basis of these figures, the political and the nonpolitical elites of New Haven seemed to have different areas of activities and different scopes of power. It could be argued, therefore, that the powers available to political elites were largely public and subject to various forms of democratic restraint.

Not only were members of the political elite fairly distinct from the highest ranks of wealth and prestige, but their individual scopes of influence were primarily narrow and limited. Polsby noted that 1,029 persons were active in the three issue areas combined, but only 32 were active in more than one area.[23] And Dahl observed that of the 50 persons who seemed to have the most influence of all, only 3 were influential in all three issue areas, while 27 had influence in only one area.[24] A situation in which decision-makers enjoyed only such narrow ranges of influence suggested, prima facie, that leaders had to strike compromises and bargains in order to run the city smoothly. But the necessity for such compromises and bargains probably afforded alert and energetic citizens frequent opportunities for advancing their interests in return for their political support, and therefore it could be assumed that political elites who lacked certain kinds of durable power were likely to be receptive to the needs of the electorate.

NONCUMULATIVE RESOURCES

Dahl also observed that the character of political resources provided a handy explanation of the limited scopes of power exercised by New Haven's political leaders. His fundamental position in this regard was that the resources comprising the stuff of power were by their nature noncumulative. As this was so, they did not collect in the hands of a few and therefore did not accord those few irresistible power over all community affairs.

The importance of understanding the nature of resources was emphasized as early as the first sentence of *Who Governs?*, where New Haven was described as "a political system where nearly every adult may vote but where knowledge, wealth, social position, access to officials, and other resources are unequally distributed."[25] Some observers, like Hunter and Mills, claimed that the inevitable result of an uneven distribution of resources leaves most of them controlled by a few persons, and that therefore in any community those persons are ultimately powerful. Dahl disputed this view, and contended that there is in fact no necessary relationship between resources, that they will not necessarily accumulate to the benefit of a few. This contention is worth analyzing.

According to Dahl's findings in New Haven, political resources in general are marked by five characteristics. They exist in a great many forms; they are unequally distributed; usually a person who enjoys much of one has little of another; no single resource dominates all the others; and no one person is altogether lacking in each and every resource.[26] These characteristics reveal their collective importance when they are considered in terms of the many specific resources discovered in New Haven politics. As resources, Dahl and Polsby listed money and credit, control of jobs, control of information and the mass media, social standing, knowledge and expertise, popularity, esteem and charisma, legal status and rights, constitutionality and officiality, ethnic solidarity, the vote, certain skills, energy, education, and native intelligence.[27]

Dahl traced the impact of these resources through many pages of *Who Governs?*, relating them to complex decisions involving diverse conditions and numerous decision-makers.[28] Rather than attempting to follow here the details of his analysis, a quick appreciation of the role and nature of such resources may best be acquired via a hypothetical, caricatured case. James Wellington Smythe, III, for example, born to considerable wealth and there-fore enjoying the comforts that wealth accords, nonetheless lacks the proper ethnic identity necessary for election to many offices in New Haven, which has strong Italian and black voting blocks. Smythe may attend an Ivy League college and study Romance languages to the point of multiple fluency; his linguistic skill will not qualify him to understand the sewage problems of the city, though, and he will be ineffective if appointed to a city planning commission. He may be inherently intelligent and perspicacious, of course, and fully capable of acquiring the information neces-sary to enter the political arena; but he may prefer, as a matter of personal predilection and gratification, to spend most of his time and energy collecting works of art or rare stamps, in which case he will have little spare time to acquire the knowledge needed for political affairs. He may occasionally try to use his wealth to satisfy an eccentric desire such as building a home of radically modern design; but his neighbors may object and sue successfully in court for a zoning injunction to forbid such an eyesore among their no-nonsense "contemporary" dwellings.

In a highly exaggerated way, Smythe's case illustrates Dahl's contention that political resources are not cumulative: there are many kinds of resources; they do not attach to the same person; not all of them can be used in every event; and there is no one of them that dominates the rest. In sum, there are inequalities in the distribution of any single resource—for example, Smythe has *more money* than most men—but when the total of all re-sources is considered, a pattern of "dispersed inequalities"[29] may be seen. Smythe in fact has *less* of some resources than many other men. Even while they lack his money, others are better equipped to win elections, serve on city boards, devote time to politics, and win cases in court.

If resources are truly noncumulative, it is because they may usually be used alternatively—that is, no one resource is indis-pensable and dominates the others.[30] Thus the Economic and Social Notables of New Haven could employ their money and social prestige in political affairs if they chose; more ordinary men, however, while lacking both wealth and extraordinary pedigrees, could draw upon alternative sources of power such as rhetorical skills, ethnic solidarity, intelligence, energy, and charisma in order to oppose money and prestige in political battle. In the long run, competition was assured in New Haven because resources effectively challenged each other in this fashion. An enterprising man could advance his interests in the political realm even if he failed to enjoy exactly the same resources as did his opponents.

FOUR KEY TERMS

The noncumulative nature of resources cannot be fully understood solely in terms of their objective failure to blend and reinforce one another, in terms of a sort of perpetual mixing of political oil and water. Dahl also commented on a subjective factor—men's use of their resources—which further assured that resources would remain dispersed and noncumulative. In other words, *how* people choose to exercise their rights, wealth, energy, and more is a matter of great importance in the making of community decisions. To explain this matter, Dahl coined four phrases: *homo civicus, homo politicus,* the apolitical stratum, and the political stratum.

From his observation of politics in New Haven, Dahl concluded that most citizens were not interested in political affairs. They went their private ways and were usually content to be simply members of the community—*homo civicus.*[31] There were also a relatively few men who, for reasons not entirely clear to themselves or to scholars, developed an abiding interest in political matters. They therefore discussed politics frequently, read newspapers closely, and perhaps joined political clubs, attended meetings, and even campaigned actively. Such men were not merely passive members of the community; rather, they were alert, participating men of public affairs—*homo politicus.*[32]

In keeping with his belief in two kinds of political men, Dahl argued that New Haven should properly be viewed as a community divided into two citizenship strata.[33] The lower and greater in size was the apolitical stratum, comprised of the men Dahl called *homo civicus*. The members of this stratum had little interest in day-to-day political matters and rarely participated directly in the making of great community decisions. The upper aggregate, rather small in number, was the political stratum, in which every *homo politicus* was grouped. Its personnel staffed the political parties, pressure groups, civic associations, neighborhood improvement committees, and other political and civic activities.

Strongly indicative of a real democracy was the fact that the political stratum proved to be a wide-open circle of men.[34] No entrance requirements existed beyond an interest in politics and a willingness to exert some effort. Anyone could join either major party and work on its behalf. Anyone could join together with like-minded men, organize pressure groups, and advance the interests of those groups. Politically-minded persons who aspired to leadership and decision-making power had every right to solicit their fellow members of the political stratum and seek support on election day. Those who succeeded in gaining sufficient support could hold political power for a time, but they were always subject to challenge by other politicos who would ask for backing among the disaffected. The stratum of politically alert men therefore continually resembled a whirling cyclone of men and groups, some rising and some falling, some entering and some leaving.

The net effect of the constant, intense activity within the political stratum assured access for all community interests to the decision-making process, despite the fact that at any given moment the process itself was dominated by only a few men. As Dahl put it: "The independence, penetrability, and heterogeneity of the various segments of the political stratum all but guarantee that any dissatisfied group will find spokesmen in the political stratum."[35] What he meant was that the political stratum was so fluid and volatile—with Republicans, Democrats, conservatives, radicals, do-gooders, and maybe even a few flat-Earthers—that there would always be an ambitious political broker ready to champion the cause of any group promising the means for political victory.

A case in point was the issue of urban renewal in New Haven.

Mayor Richard Lee, then the most successful leader in the political stratum, appointed a great many persons to advise him on urban renewal; in fact, more than five hundred were selected for various commissions and committees.[36] Dahl closely examined these five hundred men and women and concluded that they actually represented the broad spectrum of interests present in the political stratum as a whole.[37] No doubt it was to the mayor's advantage to deliberately appoint and frequently consult with such a representative group in order to garner widespread support for his successive and successful efforts at re-election.

SLACK POWER AND INDIRECT INFLUENCE

Although most of the visible signs of democracy—competition, pressure groups, meetings, campaigning, and so forth—appeared at the level of the political stratum, Dahl was convinced that the apolitical stratum also constituted a key democratic element in the political life of New Haven. Here were the people who did not ordinarily make use of their resources, but it was a fact that their resources were always available to be employed if necessary.[38] It was this "slack," or potential power, that ultimately kept the city on a balanced political course, since it assured that no temporary accumulation of power, no momentarily successful politicking, no currently entrenched leaders, could permanently endure.[39] It assured that leaders would rise and fall regardless of their immediate access to wealth, prestige, status, or other resources, because the ultimate and decisive basis for their continuing reign would always be the extent to which they satisfied the needs of the community at large. Very simply, the existence of large amounts of slack power among the ordinarily passive citizens of New Haven constantly threatened to overthrow the established rulers of the city. The city's officials were therefore compelled to design their policies so as to keep the great majority of citizens satisfied; to protect their own careers, they ran the city in a way that would never encourage slack power to be exercised in a politically disruptive way.

Because *homo civicus* was usually politically inactive, Dahl observed that members of the apolitical stratum did not wield much *direct influence* over the few men who at any particular time made community decisions. In light of the concept of slack power, however, he argued that men in the apolitical stratum collectively exercised a great deal of *indirect influence* in the process of community decision-making.[40] Men in the political stratum—candidates for city offices, party officials, members of civic organizations, or those who sought to form ad hoc committees for any reason—constantly sought to anticipate in advance the needs of politically lethargic citizens, either in order to stimulate them to emerge from political quiescence and lend their support, or to keep them content and to discourage them from using any of their potential and possibly disruptive power.

In regard to indirect influence, an election day is clearly analogous to the Judgment Day; *vox populi, vox Dei*. So long as its coming is clearly foreseen, there will always be those who, in and out of power, seek to please the great majority of others who comprise the electorate. Dahl gave examples of this political wooing in New Haven, such as efforts by candidates and parties to shape policies designed to win decisive support for party nominees, urban renewal, and programs of public education.[41] More recently, and in a wider context, the same phenomenon of anticipating the needs of the predominantly passive appeared in candidate Richard Nixon's appeal to the "silent majority." In the 1968 Presidential campaign he asked, in effect, for the active support of a great many Americans who were ordinarily disinterested in political affairs, who would usually concentrate their attention and their efforts on private concerns of family, friends, church, and work.[42]

THE DEMOCRATIC CREED

The slack element in New Haven's political system was attributable to individual personality traits, cultural attitudes toward politics, and simple human inertia. Because it was a manifestation of what pluralists broadly referred to as potential power, it was to be found in both the political and the apolitical strata. As

Dahl pointed out, however, *homo politicus* used his resources frequently and there was therefore special significance to the presence of slack power in the apolitical stratum, where so few resources were ordinarily utilized that many were always available for mobilization.

The political temper of New Haven, where slack power helped to assure the framing of representative policies by political leaders, was summed up by Dahl's use of the phrase "democratic creed."[43] This creed, endorsing customary civility, the right to dissent, bargaining, varying degrees of good faith and trust, laws of electoral conduct, and the like, was generally upheld by all men of the city. It was of considerable importance if only because a nondemocratic society, lacking such a creed, cannot easily permit the expression of slack power. Indeed, in a society lacking the creed and its companion Liberal electoral practices, revolution and violence may be the only means by which slack power can advance urgent needs.

New Haven's creed was supported by all its citizens, but especially by the political stratum. Under most circumstances men in that stratum relied on the creed as a very practical guide in the execution of day-to-day politicking and decision-making. They did not necessarily, although they might, entertain a strong ideological faith in the unblemished excellence of democracy; rather, they almost always found the existing practices dependable, predictable, and eminently useful.[44] If men in the political stratum on occasion failed to agree as to exactly how the creed should be followed or interpreted, charges of dishonesty, unfairness, corruption, and perhaps even treason might fly back and forth at election time. The public, imbued with a deep ideological commitment to American democracy, would then resolve the conflict at the polls according to its values.[45] New Haven was therefore blessed with two pillars of support for its democratic procedures: the common sense self-interest of the political stratum, and the occasionally evoked convictions of the majority of its common citizens. Thus it could be said that the guardians of the city watched each other, and the city watched the guardians.

LOGIC AND IDEOLOGY

Potential and actual power, the decision-making focus, the scope of elite powers, noncumulative resources, *homo civicus* and *homo politicus*, the political and the apolitical strata, slack power, direct and indirect influence, and the democratic creed: these were the fundamental elements of the pluralist theory of how to study and comprehend power in American communities.[46] Together they constituted a detailed response to the challenges that Hunter and Mills raised against Liberal politics as practiced in the United States. Each step of this response seemed logical enough, but the sum total was *ideological,* and an extensive unraveling of Dahl's portrait of power is required before the magnitude of this ideological accomplishment can be fully appreciated.

NOTES

1/ Robert A. Dahl, *Who Governs? Democracy and Power in an American City* (New Haven: Yale University Press, 1961) ; Nelson W. Polsby, *Community Power and Political Theory* (New Haven: Yale University Press, 1963) .

2/ Robert A. Dahl, "A Critique of the Ruling Elite Model," *American Political Science Review* (June 1958) , pp. 463–469; "Further Reflections on 'The Elitist Theory of Democracy,'" *American Political Science Review* (June 1966) , pp. 296–305; "Reply to Thomas Anton's 'Power, Pluralism and Local Politics,'" *Administrative Science Quarterly* (March 1963) , pp. 250–256; "The Concept of Power," *Behavioral Science* (July 1957) , pp. 201–215. Nelson W. Polsby, "Community Power: Some Reflections on the Recent Literature," *American Sociological Review* (December 1962) , pp. 838–841; "How to Study Community Power: The Pluralist Alternative," *Journal of Politics* (August 1960) , pp. 474–484; "Power in Middletown: Fact and Value in Community Research," *Canadian Journal of Economics and Political Science* (November 1960) , pp. 592–603; "The Sociology of

Community Power: A Reassessment," *Social Forces* (March 1959), pp. 232–236; "Three Problems in the Analysis of Community Power," *American Sociological Review* (December 1959), pp. 796–803. Raymond E. Wolfinger, "A Plea for a Decent Burial," *American Sociological Review* (December 1962), pp. 841–847; and "Reputation and Reality in the Study of Community Power," *American Sociological Review* (October 1960), pp. 636–644.

3/ Robert A. Dahl, *Modern Political Analysis* (Englewood Cliffs, N.J.: Prentice-Hall, 1963), pp. 47–49.

4/ Dahl, "Critique of the Ruling Elite Model," p. 465.

5/ Dahl, *Modern Political Analysis,* pp. 47–48.

6/ Polsby, *Community Power and Political Theory,* pp. 108–109, belittles his nonpluralist colleagues for ascribing great significance to indices of potential power, which he refers to as "the *capacity* to realize one's will."

7/ Polsby, "How to Study Community Power," p. 476: "The first, and perhaps the most basic presupposition of the pluralist approach, is that nothing categorical can be assumed about power in any community."

8/ *Ibid.*

9/ Polsby, *Community Power and Political Theory,* p. 60.

10/ Polsby, "Three Problems," p. 799.

11/ Dahl, *Who Governs?,* p. vi.

12/ Dahl, "Critique of the Ruling Elite Model," p. 466.

13/ *Ibid.,* p. 464 ff; Polsby, "How to Study Community Power," p. 477, and *Community Power and Political Theory,* p. 96.

14/ Polsby, *Community Power and Political Theory,* pp. 95–96.

15/ *Ibid.,* pp. 4–5.

16/ Dahl, "Reply to Thomas Anton," p. 254.

17/ See Wolfinger, "Reputation and Reality," pp. 638–640, on the meaning and significance of "scope" of power.

18/ Polsby, "Three Problems," p. 798.

19/ It should be pointed out that in *Who Governs?,* Dahl did not use the term "elite" to refer to these men. It is used in the text however, since it is appropriate and will assist the reader in comparing the work of Dahl and other community power researchers. Very probably, the reason Dahl refrained from using the term "elite" was polemical; that is, he sought not to help his readers draw elitist inferences from his findings.

20/ Dahl, *Who Governs?*, pp. 63–64, 67–68.

21/ *Ibid.*, p. 64.

22/ *Ibid.*, p. 69.

23/ Polsby, "Three Problems," p. 799.

24/ Dahl, *Who Governs?*, pp. 180–183.

25/ *Ibid.*, p. 1.

26/ *Ibid.*, p. 228.

27/ *Ibid.*, p. 226; Polsby, *Community Power and Political Theory*, pp. 119–120, and "How to Study Community Power," p. 483.

28/ For example, see *Who Governs?*, pp. 63–86.

29/ The phrase is Dahl's, *ibid.*, p. 85–86.

30/ Robert A. Dahl, "Equality and Power in American Society," in William V. D'Antonio and Howard J. Ehrlich (eds.), *Power and Democracy in America* (South Bend, Ind.: Notre Dame University Press, 1961), p. 83.

31/ Dahl, *Who Governs?*, pp. 223–225.

32/ *Ibid.*, pp. 225–226.

33/ *Ibid.*, pp. 90–100.

34/ *Ibid.*, pp. 91 ff.

35/ *Ibid.*, p. 93.

36/ *Ibid.*, pp. 122–123.

37/ *Ibid.*, p. 137.

38/ *Ibid.*, pp. 224–225.

39/ *Ibid.*, pp. 305, 308–310.

40/ On direct and indirect influence, see *ibid.*, pp. 163–165.

41/ For example, see *ibid.*, pp. 105–106, 139–140, 159–162.

42/ *The New York Times,* November 4, 1969, p. 16.

43/ Dahl, *Who Governs?*, pp. 311–325.

44/ *Ibid.*, pp. 319–321.

45/ *Ibid.*, pp. 321–324.

46/ Because the pluralists denied what they believed was an overly simplistic view of politics expounded by nonpluralists, Dahl's assessment of the facts of community power was more complex than the analyses found in the works of Hunter and Mills. As a result of this complexity, it is much more difficult to summarize Dahl's ideas accurately. In the text, therefore, two intentional liberties have been taken with his enormously sophisticated and carefully qualified discussion of New Haven. First, as pointed out in note 19, the term "elite" was assigned to political leaders; Dahl himself did not so use the term. Second, a one-to-one relationship has been assumed between the apolitical strata and *homo civicus,* and also between the political strata and *homo politicus.* Dahl himself did not use these terms interchangeably, perhaps because on unusual occasions *homo civicus* could go beyond his ordinary and largely reflexive voting habits and become politically alert and active when his interests were directly threatened. At any rate, in both cases the liberties were taken in order to simplify Dahl's work without distorting its meaning. The benefits of this simplification will accrue in the next several chapters.

✪ 8 ✪

The Short Reign of Confidence:
Pluralist Theory as Neo-Liberalism

Understanding of the deepest significance of the pluralist theory of democracy must begin with an appreciation of the fact that although the theory was initially expounded in terms of the situation found to exist in New Haven, it actually pertained to both national and local communities in the United States. Dahl asserted it as a general theory of community politics embracing and explaining the broad features of all American politics, and as such it was widely accepted by his political science colleagues.

It is difficult to document this fact conclusively because, paradoxically, there is too much relevant evidence rather than too little, because scattered passages in academic writings conflict with each other as often as do those in the Bible. Thus early in *Who Governs?* Dahl stated that the main reason he chose to study New Haven was that it "is in many respects typical of other cities in the United States."[1] On the very next page, however, he stated that "explanations presented in this study are tested only against the evidence furnished in the political system of New Haven."[2] His collaborator Nelson Polsby then hedged the entire pluralist critique of nonpluralist studies by contending that the significance of pluralist findings was quite limited. "[W]hat can we infer from them [the findings] about other cities? Strictly speaking, the answer is little or nothing."[3] Nonetheless, Dahl had earlier published a short article based on some of the major results of the New Haven study, and he had entitled it "Equality and Power in American Society." There he said: "I shall lean heavily upon New Haven for information on the distribution and patterns of influence, but I do so in the belief that New Haven is similar to many other communities and strikingly similar in many ways to the United States as a whole."[4] The impression to be gained by such textual snippets is confusing, inconclusive, and hardly worth pursuing.

Additional evidence very strongly suggests, though, that the theory was taken to convey general implications extending beyond New Haven. For one thing, Dahl himself wrote *Modern Political Analysis* (1963), and in it recommended many of the fundamental concepts of *Who Governs?* as part of what he believed to be the most useful framework of analysis for the study of any political system.[5] And later he wrote *Pluralist Democracy in the United States: Conflict and Consent* (1967),[6] an introductory textbook in American government, whose very title revealed his claim of a far-flung purview for the pluralist theory. Moreover, Dahl received honors indicative of extraordinary esteem and admiration for the pluralist theory, to a degree exceeding that due a theory were it judged parochial and relevant only to the unique political affairs of a rather small city in a rather small state. *Who Governs?* was awarded the Woodrow Wilson Foundation Award in 1962,[7] and the honoring citation read, in part, that Dahl had "illuminated a central question in political science, the problem of how men can govern themselves in complex societies. . . . *Who Governs?* will become a classic reference for those seeking an understanding of political behavior in modern urban environments under democratic regimes."[8] Following this award, Dahl was elected President of the American Political Science Association (1966–1967), a distinction presumably conferred upon him because of the acknowledged brilliance of his scholarly work, mainly in the fields of community power and democratic theory.

As indicated by Dahl's own writings, therefore, and judging by the high regard shown him and his work, we can seek to understand the pluralist theory as an intellectual construct of wide significance. Appraisal on so broad a scale will no more than support the contention advanced early in Chapter 4 and applicable to the works of Truman, Hunter, Mills, and Dahl: the logic of political analysis binds together all community power studies. Whether a study is conducted at the national or at the local level of politics, the techniques, concepts, and standards for weighing and evaluating the revealed facts are all ultimately related. We must therefore begin to unravel pluralism with the stipulation that it concerns a great deal more than New Haven and must be viewed accordingly.

THE BACKGROUND OF PLURALIST THEORY

The accomplishments of the pluralist theory can best be judged in the context of intellectual history, a background outlined earlier in this book. A number of relevant and significant facts may be recalled. (1) Middle-class Liberalism has long been the orthodox American ideology. (2) In consequence of fortunate circumstances and the intentions of our founders, it became the prescription for and the justification of American political institutions. (3) During the late eighteenth and entire nineteenth centuries, Liberalism steadily strengthened its hold over our thinking. (4) At least since the late nineteenth century and continuing into the twentieth, social science findings have severely challenged the three basic tenets of Liberalism—rational men, unremarkable groups, and responsible political institutions. (5) In light of these findings and faced with the political events of recent generations, Liberals have come to doubt the value of their polities. And (6) those doubts are now particularly acute because seemingly objective facts about individual men, groups, and elites support the contentions of both the Right and the Left that Liberalism of the Center cannot be true to its tenets.

The logical response of Liberals was essentially to revise the theory of Liberalism in order to explain more accurately than before how their political institutions were constituted and what these could be expected to accomplish. The process theory of democracy came into being almost spontaneously, emphasizing competition and choice, and thereby reconciling the disturbing facts revealed by social science with the continued practices of

Liberal politics—free speech, frequent elections, multiple political parties, a widespread franchise, and more. In regard to this new theory, Schumpeter was an instructive figure; after him came Truman, whose analysis of groups was clearly a process theory, explaining how Liberal politics in America flowed from group activity and usually produced satisfactory results.

Although Truman's group theory successfully assimilated many of the ever visible and obviously important realities of organized group politicking in the United States, he failed to account persuasively for the politics of elites. Those few men were the subject of intensive investigations by Hunter, Mills, and their disciples, with the result that Truman's view of the governmental process and democracy was questioned empirically and ideologically—that is, both his grasp of the facts and his estimation of their worth were denied. Perhaps not all the accusations were warranted—in debate on politics this is usually the case—but there were enough solid charges raised against the group theory to give many thoughtful scholars pause. In effect, the stage was thus set for the appearance of another, more sophisticated process theory of democracy, one that would assist Liberals to shrug off the findings of studies such as *Community Power Structure* and *The Power Elite*.

Viewed in this historical perspective, *Who Governs?* appeared as the awaited process theory, a post-Trumanesque work of scholarship dealing with groups *and* elites and handling both with such ingenuity and subtlety that the unhappy facts of social science were affirmed while at the same time Liberals with lofty hopes for a good society were reassured. The pluralist theory of democracy was, without exaggeration, an intellectual and ideological masterpiece, and if it were substantially correct then all the acclaim Dahl received was appropriate recompense.

THE ACCEPTANCE OF REALITY

Openly, and without notable objection, the pluralist theory accepted the major postulates of social science which contradicted the tenets of Liberalism. It was conceded that men in New

Haven were by and large irrational, prejudiced, politically un-sophisticated, and ignorant of most community affairs—hardly the stuff of Liberal citizenship. Most men in the city were *homo civicus* and apolitical, and sought their satisfactions in the round of ordinary and private affairs which lay beyond politics. Comparing the bulk of New Haven's citizenry with the lesser number of men in the city's political stratum, Dahl observed that "in the apolitical strata, people are notably less calculating; their political choices are more strongly influenced by inertia, habit, unexamined loyalties, personal attachments, emotions, and transient impulses. . . . political orientations are disorganized, disconnected, and unideological. . . . the apolitical strata are poorly informed. . . . in the apolitical strata citizens rarely go beyond voting and many do not even vote."[9] We see here a judicious avoidance of blunt terms, but *homo civicus* was obviously something of a political dolt, and in the aggregate the apolitical stratum was hardly superior.

The second and third issues raised by social scientists concerned the unforeseen nature of groups and elites. In analyzing the powerful influence of both these sets of political actors, the pluralist theory resorted to a complicated structure of ideas we shall consider in a moment. What must be recognized at this point is simply that Dahl *did* deal at length with both groups *and* elites. He therefore seemed to account for the sum total of social science, as opposed to Truman, whose concentrated attention on groups left him exposed to the charge that he overlooked certain persistent and antidemocratic propensities of elites.

The pluralist theory deserved a sort of intellectual gold star for openly conceding many of the facts that ostensibly negated original Liberal tenets concerning men, groups, and democratic government. It deserved at least five more gold stars for what it further asserted, because the theory then proceeded via a magnificent conceptual tour de force to reaffirm all the expectations and aspirations conveyed by those Liberal tenets. In particular, while conceding the existence of individual human irrationality and the inevitability of elites, it simultaneously proclaimed the salutary existence of politically rational actors and the effectiveness of democratic controls over those elites. Figuratively spiking the guns of its potential critics in advance by boldly accepting reality, the theory went on to interpret and explain our political circumstances in reassuring, even laudatory, terms.

HOMO POLITICUS AS A RATIONAL MAN

The ideological serviceability of pluralism may be said to have begun logically with the concept of *homo politicus*. Relatively speaking, there were never very many who could be called *homo politicus*, and Dahl remarked that their metamorphosis out of the "apolitical clay" of *homo civicus* was still inexplicable.[10] Nonetheless, they were on the political stage and they strongly resembled the rational man envisioned by Liberals in the nineteenth century. As Dahl described them: "Political man, unlike civic man, deliberately allocates a very sizable share of his resources to the process of gaining and maintaining control over the policies of government. . . . political man usually allocates an important share of his resources to the process of gaining and maintaining influence over voters."[11]

Almost by definition, *homo politicus* in the aggregate constituted the political stratum, that constantly self-regenerating body of men with political interests and the determination to advance them. Here were the pressure groups, the professional associations, the ad hoc committees, the party clubs, the Chamber of Commerce, the Lions, the Kiwanis, the Rotary, and more. And how did Dahl portray this conglomeration of politically relevant forces? "In the political stratum, individuals tend to be rather calculating in their choice of strategies; members of the political stratum are, in a sense, relatively rational political beings. . . . In the political stratum, information about politics and the issues of the day is extensive."[12] Here men were "involved," and this entailed interest, concern, information, and activity.[13] In short, the political stratum was in fact a reasonable component of the body politic. Generally speaking, *homo politicus* might easily be viewed as a twentieth-century conceptual substitute for the early Liberal image of political groups, that is, collections of rational men united by deliberate purpose.

THE POLITICAL STRATUM AND RESTRAINTS ON ELITES

Because the political stratum embraced "relatively rational political beings," it had to be judged the pivotal factor assuring democratic and reasonable government in pluralist systems. Most importantly, it accounted at least in part for all the restraints laid upon elites. Dahl had of course conceded the existence of elites—of Economic and Social Notables, and political leaders. His findings in New Haven indicated, however, that although only a few men fulfill the roles of decision-making in a highly organized society, à la Michels, those few are constantly hampered and limited in their power and therefore deserve to be known as responsible leaders. Five pluralist concepts referred to this continual pressure on elites: noncumulative resources, scopes of influence, slack power, indirect influence, and the democratic creed. If those concepts accurately reflected reality, the political stratum was clearly the pluralist mainstay of Liberal hopes and expectations about American government.

If political resources are indeed as noncumulative as Dahl claimed, political elites cannot acquire enough resources to dominate a community's affairs. If the few in New Haven had money, they may not have taken an interest in politics; if they took such an interest, they may not have enjoyed popularity; if they enjoyed popularity, they may not have created an effective strategy for gaining their ends; and so forth. In all of this, the political stratum played a key role. Its members possessed and exercised certain resources—including energy, interest, dedication, intelligence, affability, and persistence—all of which were dispersed and therefore noncumulative. And because such resources were inherently attached to different individuals separately, they could not be monopolized by anyone. As long as these diversified sources of power were wielded effectively by many people in the political stratum, the city's political elites could *never* be all-powerful.

The reality of noncumulative resources in New Haven explained why elites were usually confined to narrow areas of influence. Within these limited scopes of power, New Haven's leaders operated in only one or two areas of broad community concern. Their power was thus securely checked, since they were compelled to draw on elements of the political stratum if they wished to build coalitions of compromise and unite realms of elite power in order to bring about general, overlapping policies for the entire city. Figuratively, the city's elites resided on separate mountains of power, but if they were to implement coordinated policies for their community, they had to go down among the valley dwellers—the bulk of the political stratum—to achieve effective communication between one peak and another.

The political stratum itself gave birth to the political elite who constituted, as it were, the most successful of all *homo politicus.* But it must be remembered that there were always still other alert men within the political stratum who also sought success, who aspired to office, who attempted to replace those at the top. Such men were continually and shrewdly calculating strategies to propel themselves into power at future elections. Their plans, and the actions they took to fulfill those plans, generated a constant ferment within the political stratum as a whole, a force exerting multiple restraint on the political elite.

This ferment in the political stratum provided endless opportunities for the exercise of slack political power, the potential power usually not employed by disinterested people of the apolitical stratum. Ambitious politicos constantly circulated among the majority of voters in search of support in return for promises to implement policies favorable to the electorate. But the existing leadership, anxious for its survival and fearful of the possibility of electoral defeat, sought to forestall the exercise of slack power by itself serving the needs of the electorate. The net result of maneuvering by those both in and out of power was to accord the apolitical stratum a good deal of indirect influence and thus narrow the parameters of elite action.

Finally the constant challenging of established leaders focused attention on election day. It thereby encouraged candidates to frame issues in terms of the democratic creed. Here was the ultimate device for circumscribing the freedom of political leaders, a constraint on them to conform at least ostensibly to the community's widest standards of decency and fair play. The political stratum could be relied upon to speak of the creed and to make it a part of every election campaign because, as Dahl noted, the political stratum was itself collectively concerned that the creed be enforced wherever possible.

PLURALIST THEORY AS NEO-LIBERALISM

There can be no doubt that the pluralist theory was a process theory *par excellence*. As such, it provided a neo-Liberal explanation of Liberalism in action. Its rationale was new, yet it succeeded in justifying and even extolling the politics that an earlier Liberalism had already established.

The logic of the new theory of Liberal democracy should be noted. From the outset of *Who Governs?*, Dahl accepted conditions in New Haven as actually democratic. "In everyday language, New Haven is a democratic political community. Most of its adult residents are legally entitled to vote. . . . Elections are free from violence and . . . free from fraud. Two political parties contest elections, [and] offer rival slates of candidates."[14] Thus the pattern of politics in a Liberal community was accorded the same honorific title that Liberals themselves were accustomed to conferring upon it. This title could no longer be justified in terms of its original rationale, since that intellectual and ideological construct had been challenged by social science research. Nonetheless, in Dahl's opinion the cardinal point was that Liberal democracy worked: "New Haven is a republic of unequal citizens—but for all that a republic."[15] In the mid-twentieth century, such a statement is laudatory if only because of its implication that what we enjoy is unquestionably superior to a *non*republic, such as the Soviet Union.

The question was, how did it work, this republic? this democracy? It certainly did *not* depend on the active, informed political participation of many citizens; on this point Dahl and social science were agreed. But his assessment of reality was not pessimistic, for "what we call 'democracy' . . . does seem to operate with a relatively low level of citizen participation. Hence it is inaccurate to say that one of the necessary conditions for 'democracy' is extensive citizen participation. It would be more reasonable simply to insist that some minimal participation is required."[16] How much? In fact, "for such control as we exert over our political leaders in democratic organizations, we must rely heavily on the competitiveness of leaders, that is, on their constant and unending rivalry in satisfying the demands of *relatively small groups*."[17] [Emphasis added.] "Minimal participation," "competitiveness of leaders," "relatively small groups": these are the essence of democracy according to the pluralists.

From such passages, and in light of the elaborate explanation of community politics offered by the pluralist theory's collected concepts, Dahl's view of democracy must be judged equivalent to Schumpeter's classic definition: "the democratic method is that institutional arrangement for arriving at political decisions in which individuals acquire the power to decide by means of a competitive struggle for the people's vote."[18] But the pluralist theory enjoyed a much wider reception than Schumpeter's succinct phrases, and if we seek the key to the theory's success we should probably identify it with the concept of the political stratum.

THE KEY ELEMENT OF LIBERAL POLITICS

As defined by Dahl, the political stratum was the essential feature of democracy, the *sine qua non* of Liberal politics. *It* served as the arena for the minimal citizen participation required in a democracy. *It* provided from within itself the competition of both elites and groups. *It* preserved and enforced, at least on a day-to-day basis, the very creed by which democratic people managed to conduct their affairs moderately and tolerably.

And in the final analysis, the political stratum constituted the polemical key to the pluralist theory as the last of a series of great community power theories. The members of the stratum included both powerful elites and powerful groups, and therefore provided a more complete and persuasive basis for democracy than Truman's groups. Indeed, the political stratum effectively replaced Truman's notion of a distinctively group-oriented political process, and while doing so greatly weakened the arguments of Truman's critics. Broadly speaking, Dahl's understanding of the political stratum explained the activity of both Atlanta's elite and what Hunter called Atlanta's "political understructure." It also explained the interplay of what Mills called the national "power elite" and the "middle level" of power. By logically and analytically embracing both the political understructure and the middle level of power within his description of the political stratum, Dahl contended that the visible pluralism of American life—the associations, pressure groups, lobbyists, ad hoc committees, party clubs, and so forth—was at once a sign and a vital element of Liberal democracy. Whereas Hunter and Mills had derogated the apparent freedom of this pluralism, Dahl evoked it as the lynchpin of his complicated understanding of a democracy of unequal citizens. If what he claimed for the political stratum were true, then what the reputational and positional theories of elitism had concluded was demonstrably false.

THE SUBJECTIVE FEATURES OF *WHO GOVERNS?*

Like most other forceful and persuasive lines of political argument, the pluralist theory made a great impression because it was at least partly subjective, because it did not quite "tell it like it is." No social science researcher, of course, can ever be certain that as a human being he is capable of complete objectivity. For this reason, it is worthwhile seeking out the subjective elements of *Who Governs?*, for although they were obscured by customary claims to straightforward reporting of the facts,[19] they were nevertheless present and enormously significant.

The truth of the matter is that the pluralist theory consisted of a delicate balance of assertions buttressed by a careful selection of supporting evidence chosen from the totality of available facts. A well-rounded understanding of Dahl's accomplishment must therefore take into account this balancing act: inclusion of certain concepts and exclusion of others, acceptance of some data as relevant and rejection of other data as irrelevant, emphasis on particular community affairs and disregard of others. Dahl himself, of course, did not assign labels to such matters, but they may be summed up as the Significant Sidestep, the Conceptual Backtrack, the Great Separation, the Pluralist Hero, and the Prophylactic Perspective. These terms are not designed to be facetious;

rather, they are intended to draw the reader's attention forcefully to the important phenomena they describe.

The Significant Sidestep was taken when Dahl judged New Haven to be democratic and its political system quite good without applying any external and independent standards as to what is either true democracy or an acceptable political system. This course of analysis is the hallmark of any process theory; one accepts as democratic that which Liberals call democratic, and then one explicitly or implicitly conveys the judgment that such is desirable. A footnote from *Who Governs?* indicates the logic that was necessary for the pluralist theory on this point. "Here as elsewhere [in *Who Governs?*] terms such as benefit and reward are intended to refer to subjective, psychological appraisals by the recipients [citizens], rather than appraisals by other observers [Dahl, Polsby, or Wolfinger]. An action can be said to confer benefits on an individual, in this sense, if he *believes* he has benefited, even though, from the point of view of observers, his belief is false or ethically wrong."[20] Thus if the men Dahl and his associates interviewed in New Haven believed their politics were democratic, and if those selected persons believed they gained from their special form of political action, these beliefs were worth noting and even, perhaps, worth taking as proof of a commendable political system.

This line of reasoning conveniently bypassed a major and nagging problem in the study of community power—the fact of widespread apathy and lack of political participation. No investigator can interview *all* the citizens of any community, and Dahl interviewed only some in New Haven. But when he of necessity failed to interview most of those who were nonparticipants, there was only one way to conclude that most nonparticipants were satisfied with their political circumstances. This was to first assume, without affirmative basis, that because they had a legal right to participate, they subjectively decided that they were pleased *not* to participate. The Significant Sidestep was thus taken when Dahl and his fellow pluralist theorists concluded that the political apathy of the ordinary citizen—they called it "inertia" in their commentaries on New Haven[21]—was indeed a sign of subjective satisfaction and therefore consonant with democracy as a desirable form of government. The pluralists might have decided, on the other hand, that such apathy was not natural, not inherent in the personality of those they called *homo civicus*. Indeed, the apparent widespread indifference might as well have been caused by conditions prevalent in New Haven, and might therefore be cited as an index of deranged political practices in the city.

The Conceptual Backtrack grew out of Dahl's notion of noncumulative resources. If resources were truly as noncumulative as he claimed, real comprehension of community power required knowledge of them all—at least ten or eleven by Dahl's own count. But this requirement, if widely accepted, would in effect have subjected community power researchers to the same conceptual uncertainty that had existed in the 1920s and 1930s. There would simply be too many power factors to analyze, as Charles Merriam, Harold Lasswell, and Bertrand Russell had unwittingly demonstrated. So many presumably significant power factors would make it impossible for an investigator to *rank* any of them as more powerful than any others, and pluralists were firmly opposed to such rankings. Thus the whole thrust of the theories of Hunter and Mills would be set aside, and commentators would be left with a confusing array of political actors and forces which, after all, most Americans choose to call democratic.

Along with the Conceptual Backtrack, the Great Separation emerged as an implicit idea. Dahl contended that the study of community power properly entailed only *political* affairs, and that it was neither necessary nor advisable to study social and economic affairs as well. He argued at length that different scopes of power existed and that political leaders were not influential in social and economic affairs, or, as Polsby put it in the language of social science: "power is an empirically separable variable of social stratification."[22] But then he simply ignored the *private* scopes of power enjoyed by Economic and Social Notables as if these matters were of no concern to him, and presumably irrelevant to the issue of democracy. If this axiomatic line of separation were accepted—a matter of definition and not necessarily of fact—he would have effectively reestablished the classic Liberal distinction between politics and economics. He would therefore have bypassed some of the very fundamental charges raised by both Hunter and Mills, that in a Liberal, capitalist society where economic inequality is inevitable, the private sector may be so tightly controlled that political democracy is impossible or a farce.

Understandably, the Great Separation made possible the Pluralist Hero, the politician. If community power were really a matter of public politics alone, then the politician was without question the catalyst of democracy, the man who made the system work, the man who handled the bargaining among diverse interests in the political stratum. One may read Dahl's description of New Haven's Mayor Richard Lee in this light, for Lee was the epitome of the Pluralist Hero. Even discounting the fact that the entire New Haven study could not have been carried out without Lee's assistance, and that his future cooperation might be helpful to Dahl or other political researchers, it was still an extraordinarily complimentary sketch.[23] Indeed, the Mayor appeared as a sort of twentieth-century urban version of Henry Clay, the "Great Compromiser." This image challenged Mills' disparaging vision of corporate chieftains and other men of wealth dominating the affairs of the entire nation, men who, according to Mills, are "not so much dogmatic as they are mindless."[24] Dahl's evaluation of Lee therefore, in general, stood opposed to any findings by community power researchers tending to prove that community affairs are controlled by men of entrenched and long-lived economic power independent of the day-to-day hurly-burly of politics.

And finally, in order to be ideologically persuasive, *Who Governs?* had to talk about how democracy actually worked in New Haven. It would have been pointless to concentrate attention on how democracy did *not* work very well, hence the Prophylactic Perspective: Dahl repeatedly emphasized stability and the sharing of certain political benefits. He did not stress, as he might have, other aspects of the total culture that were inseparable parts of the seamless web of democratic New Haven—the rising crime rate, the increasing air and water pollution, the growing incidence of divorce, the soaring sales of tranquilizers, the terrible discrimination against blacks that led to racial riots in New Haven only a few years after publication of *Who Governs?*, and many other local signs of a nation-wide breakdown in the quality of life in urban areas.

In effect, the Prophylactic Perspective constituted something of a closet around a number of skeletons created by Liberalism. But it provided a reassuring view of the condition of Liberal politics and, to the extent it did, we can understand why the Woodrow Wilson Foundation Award cited *Who Governs?* for telling us "how men can govern themselves in complex societies." To most readers, *Who Governs?* undoubtedly conveyed the impression that Dahl had also explained "how men can govern themselves" *well.*

THE CONCOMITANTS OF LIBERALISM

The pluralist theory was an outstanding intellectual and ideological achievement. Its conceptualization was brilliant, conceding the obvious discrepancies between reality and original Liberal beliefs about the nature of man and politics. Its net result was to construct a new rationale for Liberalism, to fashion a neo-Liberalism. It was a comforting view of American politics, at least to most political scientists. For its analytical ingenuity and its support of traditional American beliefs, it fully deserved the honors it received.

As the history of all art demonstrates, however, even the reputation of masterpieces may fluctuate suddenly. Doubts about the theory's worth soon arose as the result of a deepening general awareness that Liberalism was in serious trouble, that it was a concomitant of racism, domestic violence, ecological imbalance, the urban crisis, and other problems. Of course Dahl did not recommend that Liberal democracy produce such results, but perhaps they ensued because political affairs in American communities no longer, or never had, fit his description. Here was a possibility that stimulated considerable commentary.

NOTES

1/ Robert A. Dahl, *Who Governs?* (New Haven: Yale University Press, 1961), p. v.

2/ *Ibid.,* p. vi.

3/ Nelson W. Polsby, *Community Power and Political Theory* (New Haven: Yale University Press, 1963), p. 97.

4/ Robert A. Dahl, "Equality and Power in American Society," in William V. D'Antonio and Howard J. Ehrlich (eds.), *Power and Democracy in America* (South Bend, Ind.: Notre Dame University Press, 1961), p. 78.

5/ In Robert A. Dahl, *Modern Political Analysis* (Englewood Cliffs, N.J.: Prentice-Hall, 1963), see esp. pp. 15–17, 32–35, 64 (noncumulative resources), pp. 45–46 (scopes of influence), pp. 47–49 (potential and actual power), pp. 56–58, 63–68 (the political stratum), and pp. 58–63 (the apolitical stratum).

6/ Robert A. Dahl, *Pluralist Democracy in the United States: Conflict and Consent* (Chicago: Rand McNally, 1967).

7/ The prestigious Woodrow Wilson Foundation Award is presented annually by the Woodrow Wilson Foundation "for the best book written within the year on Government and Democracy."

8/ These phrases appear on the back cover of the paperback edition of *Who Governs?*.

9/ Dahl, *Who Governs?,* pp. 90–91.

10/ *Ibid.,* p. 225.

11/ *Ibid.*

12/ *Ibid.,* pp. 90–91.

13/ Dahl, *Modern Political Analysis,* pp. 56–58.

14/ Dahl, *Who Governs?,* p. 3.

15/ *Ibid.,* p. 220.

16/ Robert A. Dahl, "Hierarchy, Democracy, and Bargaining in Politics and Economics," in Heinz Eulau, Samuel J. Eldersveld, and Morris Janowitz (eds.), *Political Behavior* (Glencoe, Ill.: Free Press, 1956), p. 87.

17/ *Ibid.*

18/ Joseph Schumpeter, *Capitalism, Socialism and Democracy*, 3rd ed. (orig., 1942; New York: Harper & Row, 1962), p. 269.

19/ Dahl, *Who Governs?*, pp. 335–336.

20/ *Ibid.*, p. 52, footnote 1.

21/ For example, see Polsby, *Community Power and Political Theory*, pp. 116–117.

22/ *Ibid.*, p. 104.

23/ Dahl, *Who Governs?*, pp. 118–119.

24/ C. Wright Mills, *The Power Elite* (New York: Galaxy, 1959), p. 356.

Pluralism Opposed:
The Critique of Method

As the pluralist theory was essentially an important variant of the process theory of democracy, its weak points may be divided along the lines already suggested by close analysis of Schumpeter's work (see pp. 52–56). On the one hand, critics said that the New Haven study and the theory it developed did not identify the true holders of community power and therefore could not supply the last word on the issue of whether or not any community is free, open, competitive, and democratic: this was the methodological critique. On the other hand, critics charged that there were a host of pressing political, social, and economic problems in American life that were inherently bound up with politics as practiced. So long as these remained unresolved, perhaps pluralist theory too easily embraced conditions and events that denied or even subverted our traditional, Liberal hopes for a good society; this was the critique of tolerance.

FOUR METHODOLOGICAL PROBLEMS IN PLURALIST RESEARCH

The methodological critique was advanced in numerous books and professional journals beginning in the early 1960s. The elements of this critique do not fall into a neat and consistent pattern, since they were expounded either by different persons or for different purposes. But to appreciate its major outlines we can focus on four broad areas of concern. (1) Did the theory select the proper political issues for study? (2) Are power resources actually noncumulative? (3) Did Dahl and his associates satisfactorily account for the various phenomena of political manipulation, including subtle effects of potential power and indirect influence? (4) Can decision-making research deal with quietly resolved matters, matters never openly debated and resolved in public forums, matters involving a power factor critics called *non*decision-making? These questions collectively challenged the pluralist theory on the grounds that it failed to identify accurately the most important holders of community power.

HOW TO SELECT ISSUES FOR STUDY

We have already noted that Polsby himself conceded the difficulty of fairly selecting specific political matters for study from among the great number of presumably relevant political events that occurred in New Haven. One pluralist critic who commented on the difficulty described it this way: unlike some scholars such as Hunter and Mills who held a priori opinions about enduring institutions, the pluralists insisted on making no presumptions whatsoever about the location of community power. Lacking a starting point, or points presumably warranting investigation, logic therefore obliged them to investigate each and every person in the community, if only to discover whether he did or did not enjoy some power. But as this logical requirement created an obvious procedural impossibility, pluralists were compelled by circumstances to choose for their study only a few decisions, a few issue areas, a few political matters.[1]

The way Dahl eventually chose issues in New Haven was faulted for several reasons. Critics very strongly objected, for example, to his insistence on selecting for analysis only issues where conflict was overt and therefore observable. In a theoretical essay, Dahl argued that powerful persons can only be identified as such in relation to political decisions where differences of opinion are present—as in a hotly contested fluoridation dispute. Otherwise, uniformity of opinion makes it impossible to ascertain who originated the policy in question, whose interests it best serves, and whether some people who approve it do so with a more effective voice than others, and therefore possess more power.[2] But when this approach to community power was applied in New Haven, it seemed unreliable in two respects, one particular and one general.

In particular, two of the three major issues studied in New Haven, public education and party nominations, were by Dahl's own admission quite unimportant to the Economic and Social Notables of the city.[3] Most of those people lived in suburban towns, sent their children to exclusive private schools, and could neither vote nor hold public office in New Haven. The apparent disinterest of so many Notables was significant because it raised the analytical problem of *salience*.[4] If the economic and social elites of New Haven were by and large unconcerned with public education and party nominations—that is to say, if those matters were not salient in their minds and among their affairs—then Dahl's findings of elite impotence in the city were not entirely persuasive. Critics charged that his research failed to establish conclusively that Economic and Social Notables wielded merely ordinary influence; *Who Governs?* only demonstrated that they were not interested in these particular issues, and perhaps this proved no more than that they permitted other men to make decisions on matters of little importance to themselves.[5]

A more instructive way of choosing issues for study might be to select intentionally an issue that is not only visibly contested but *also* widely salient, an issue that convulses an entire community—enactment of right-to-work legislation, establishment of a civilian police review board, or enforcement of school integration and equal employment opportunity—and then gauge the power of every citizen who acts on that issue.[6] A controversy of great salience to everyone is more likely to reveal those who hold significant power than issues of little salience to men who enjoy imposing wealth and status.

The criterion of visible conflict in selecting decisions for research was also criticized because, in general, analysis of most decisions chosen on that ground seemed to lead only to democratic conclusions.[7] If we study matters where conflict flares openly, competing interests and competing power holders will probably be present, and we are therefore likely to conclude that power is dispersed. But this choice of subject matter excludes from consideration many matters where conflict is not evident, where there do not seem to be competing interests and power holders, and where one might therefore conclude that power is not dispersed, but is instead so concentrated as to be unopposed.

As a case in point, consider the enormous stockpiling of atomic weapons in the United States since World War II, bombs enough to kill the entire population of the world many times over. If we were to study the political process whereby money for these weapons was authorized, we might conclude that concentrated political power has long been exercised with little regard for urgent social needs, and we might consequently conclude that a substantial portion of the national budget has been undemocratically controlled for the benefit of a few—the military and certain elements of the industrial and scientific community.[8] On the surface, one might argue that little opposition was voiced, that a broad consensus reigned, and that in fact overkill in nuclear bombs was approved by all. But one might also and persuasively claim that potential opposition was hoodwinked, bought off, or stifled, and this would raise perplexing questions concerning the nature of political manipulation. It is enough to note here that because of political manipulation, which we shall discuss below, decisions that are apparently uncontested may be vitally important in understanding the exercise of community power.

The pluralist preference for studying only openly contested decisions was related to another criterion of selectivity that disturbed critics. Dahl proceeded as if the terms "community" and "community power" referred only to public decision-making. And it was this that led him to concentrate his attention on government officials and their affairs. But in consequence, his inquiry and commentary left large and important private areas of New Haven's life unexamined. Using a common and widely accepted scholarly definition of politics we can see what was at stake in his narrow view. Political scientist David Easton has defined politics as "the authoritative allocation of values for society."[9] But if Easton's terms are accurate it could reasonably be argued that great realms of *private* as well as *public* power are involved in allocating broad community values, especially in the private economy where most of us must work, live, seek recreation, and find most of whatever satisfactions life affords.

In light of Easton's definition, Dahl's opponents demanded that the study of community power embrace the entire range of institutions in any community, since, as one commentator observed, "there is a basic similarity between . . . [General Motors and the United States Government]: they both authoritatively allocate values for society."[10] The two are analogous because we are inevitably affected by the decisions they both make, decisions of great consequence such as whether to permit automobiles to continue to pollute the air or to take steps to stop it.

The powerful impact of what we call private decisions is strong indication that institutions such as the modern corporate giants are "enclaves that are private in name only,"[11] and it suggests that political power may best be defined as the means "to make and enforce decisions with regard to matters of major social importance."[12] Such a nonpluralist definition of power opens wide the question of whether or not political power applies only to government and politics narrowly defined. It permits every community power researcher to discuss the nongovernmental matters he deems vital to the community, such as job discrimination, shoddy consumer goods, and organized crime, all of which Dahl substantially ignored in *Who Governs?*.

Dissatisfaction with pluralist concentration on governmental decision-making proceeded apace with doubts about the significance of contested political decisions, since critics again believed that the pluralist approach predetermined the ideologically soothing conclusion that power in our communities is exercised democratically. After all, finding democracy was assured when one excluded from consideration precisely those private areas where one would expect to find rigid hierarchies and a chain of command. It was easy to label New Haven, or any other community, democratic, if Dahl first set aside from his inquiry religious institutions, industry, commerce, and the realm of pedigreed society, and then proceeded to ignore the impact they made on the city.

ARE RESOURCES REALLY NONCUMULATIVE?

Pluralist theorists justified their selections of subject matter and issues by their professed objectivity and their analytical concept of political inertia. As we saw above, Dahl adopted the Significant Sidestep; he argued that researchers must not impose their standards on the community, that they must, instead, accept at face value what seems to be subjective satisfaction by a community's citizens with the existing state of affairs. This Significant Sidestep was closely linked to the pluralist presumption that all politically relevant behavior involves a measure of inertia, a stability flowing from satisfaction with the status quo. In theory at least, government is constitutionally supreme and it can, if it chooses, regulate the private economy and most private institutions; the law is so written. And it is a fact that citizens who are seemingly uninterested in politics and who do not actively participate in political affairs do enjoy legal rights to vote, to speak, to campaign, and to contribute. If they do not use these rights in a way that firmly instructs the government on election day to reorder the private worlds of hierarchical and undemocratic power, according to the Significant Sidestep, we can conclude only that the great majority of citizens are satisfied with the results of concentrated private power, wherever it may reside, and are happy in their jobs, their housing, their automobiles, their churches, and so forth. We must presume that they choose to remain politically dormant, seeking no great social and economic changes through the exercise of their political rights and resources.[13]

The pluralist position at this point—that inertia implies political satisfaction and obviates any need to study uncontested decisions or private power—depended upon the pluralist assessment of the nature of political resources. Inertia indicates satisfaction only if citizens in reality enjoy resources that they *can* use if they *are* dissatisfied. Such resources are surely dispersed unequally, but according to pluralist theory they are noncumulative; everyone has some and can, if he chooses, turn them from potential into actual power and contribute toward upsetting an undesirable status quo. The trouble with this notion of noncumulative resources is simply that it is not true, the critics charged; yet if it is false, then visions of an open society, a competitive polity, and a fundamentally democratic community are difficult to sustain.

Information today about highly cumulative resources has become so commonplace that theoretical reliance on the concept of noncumulative resources seems almost absurd, comforting only to those of us determined to be ideologically content. Consider the government itself, for example, which Truman perceived as a power factor but which *Who Governs?* ignored. A resource such as luck may be randomly distributed, but access to government certainly is not. Some private political groups control specific public agencies, and they use this control to ensure the exclusion of competing interests from serious consideration by government officials. The Federal Trade Commission, the Federal Communications Commission, the Interstate Commerce Commission, and like regulating agencies are particularly dominated by the very people they are supposed to regulate, and federal departments such as the Department of Agriculture may be so partial to farmers' interest groups that, like the regulatory agencies, they rarely put the public interest first. These situations constitute what Lowi called "interest group liberalism" (see pp. 79–80), and they certainly entail a cumulative resource—access to government and its power—because large bureaucracies are so glacial in nature that governmental agencies are rarely abolished or radically revamped.

Information is another highly cumulative resource, and it generates great power in the extraordinarily complex society in which we live;[14] indeed, without information we are less than free. Men may passively accept their condition in life without understanding that better circumstances may be arranged, but such men cannot properly be called free if they are in fact restrained by their own ignorance.[15] Yet the majority of us do lack information in a bewildering, bureaucratic environment. A common bond of ignorance unites Kafka's anxious and harried characters in *The Trial* and *The Castle*[16] with a poor black or poor white man confronted by the tortuous labyrinth of procedures established by American urban renewal agencies. Both the fictional characters and the real men know too little about their surroundings to control their destinies. Similarly, many ordinary citizens who file their yearly income tax forms without expert accounting advice pay the price of ignorance.

Information is plainly cumulative when it can be purchased in large amounts as needed. Education, leisure time to spend at a library, legal advice, income tax assistance, every kind of expertise: all can be obtained for an appropriate sum, and those who can afford to pay will do so and benefit. The necessity of such payments raises the question of the nature of another power resource mentioned by pluralists: legality. Every citizen presumably enjoys some fundamental rights that are his by birth—rights, for example, to vote, to speak freely, to receive a trial by jury. But it is an obvious reality of the American legal system today that enjoyment of many legal rights is largely dependent on our capacity for hiring a competent lawyer. Aside from those few extraordinary cases in which poor men are defended by prestigious law firms for reasons of social conscience and professional ethics,[17] the outcome of the legal process ordinarily turns upon adversary proceedings. If the lawyer is clever and well paid, his client will usually benefit. It is widely understood, therefore, that wealthy clients enjoy a much more rewarding relationship with our laws and government than do poor men.[18]

Since information and legality are linked to financial resources, it is worth considering a factor inherent in much American wealth: tenure. Although pluralists did not discuss the tenure of wealth, its significance should not be overlooked, for in an economy where money begets money, those who enjoy it in large amounts will probably continue to do so. "From shirt sleeves to shirt sleeves in three generations" may still be a popular aphorism, but in a stable capitalistic society such as the United States, a man's money can be managed by hired agents and passed to his heirs intact or even increased—*vide* the Mellons, the Rockefellers, the Vanderbilts, the Kennedys, and the Du Ponts.

Wealth is therefore doubly powerful, not only for what it can purchase now but for what it can buy in the future. In this double sense wealth negates, or at least frustrates, other more fleeting power factors that unquestionably *are* dispersed—ethnic popularity, ingenuity, luck, and others. Men of wealth can afford to wait, to bide their time while maintaining continual pressure on behalf of their interests. The politician who builds his career on other factors cannot risk greatly offending the interests of propertied people; the tenure of their power, either singly or collectively, is long and compels a large measure of deference from him. His resources may be short-lived; for example, if he is Italian-American and popular in Brooklyn, the population of his neighborhood may change in ethnic composition and Puerto Rican–Americans may become more popular as candidates. Most politicians must therefore compromise with the interests of wealth, its legal talents, its diverse experts, its campaign contributions, and the many other forms of community power that wealth can constantly bring to bear against them.

If we were to summarize the foregoing discussion of resources and abstract from it an antipluralist point of view, the following contention would emerge: some resources are quite cumulative, and money, the prime example, although not absolutely powerful in our society, must be ranked more powerful than many other power factors. The pluralist theorists, of course, refused to assign relative ratings to power factors, since rankings clearly imply that some interests in society will be served first and more fully than others. Yet we may conclude that there is no necessity for Americans as Liberals to be quite so opposed to ranking, or to be totally dismayed if some political resources are in fact cumulative and many even a reflection of the degree of wealth each man possesses. True, we live in a pecuniary society which often prides itself on assigning a price to everything, and this means that every man on occasion has his price. A realist with historical hindsight might argue, however, that such a system confers great benefits daily. He might argue that the pecuniary aspect of Liberalism arose at least partly in opposition to the nonfinancial morals of a pre-Liberal society, in a rejection of the uncompromising standards of piety and pedigree largely responsible for the theologically inspired horrors of the wars of the Reformation and the rigid caste system of feudalism. Piety and pedigree were once even more cumulative and less dispersed than money, and individual men had less opportunity to make progress against either.

THE NATURE OF POLITICAL MANIPULATION

Closely related to scholarly disagreement over the nature of political resources was additional disagreement on how such resources are actually exercised, how political manipulation in its various forms is accomplished. On this score the concept of potential power, a concept that Dahl explicitly criticized, became enormously important. Potential power is a factor in political decisions because of what political scientists call "the rule of anticipated reactions."[19] The rule states that politicians anticipate the needs and responses of other men and act so as to fulfill those needs, gain supportive political responses, and in the end remain in office. Dahl himself conceded such anticipation on the part of governmental officials in New Haven, but he did not suggest that the indirect influence it mirrored should be described as a kind of potential power.

Potential power must be judged significant to an understanding of community power because it "may provide a situational framework that conditions greatly the exercise of overt power."[20] Indeed, "the sheer fact of the possession of a power-potential or resources may . . . [be] sufficient to determine the actions of others. . . . There is thus no reason for those who hold a power-potential to exercise their power, unless, and only unless, their domains are directly challenged."[21] In other words, if researchers focus their attention upon observable behavior associated with concrete decisions, as the pluralists urged, they may fail to discover every kind of political manipulation that bears upon those decisions. This point requires some explanation.

If one man firmly controls a vast family estate worth hundreds of millions of dollars, he can wield great influence over many politicians without having to participate directly in their decisions. They will automatically defer to what they conceive his interest to be, for they will sense the implicit threat that if their actions substantially offend him, he can punish them by heavy contributions and support for their opponents in the next election. But the degree of influence such a wealthy figure exercises cannot be ascertained by the pluralist decision-making approach since he does not usually appear on the scene unless his interest is *not* served.[22] It is this kind of behind the scenes influence that gives rise to what has been called the "leg man" problem in community power research.[23] Ostensibly powerful officials in some communities may be no more than functionaries running errands on behalf of other men, as Hunter contended in Atlanta. The reputational method may therefore be necessary for separating "leg men" from actual power holders, even if it relies to some extent on what a pluralist theorist would judge unreliable evidence at best and simple gossip at worst.

The possibility that the New Haven study overlooked a "leg man" situation was raised in connection with the urban renewal program studied there. Polsby wrote that the city's redevelopment plan originated in the offices of Mayor Richard Lee and his appointee Redevelopment Director Edward Logue, and that it was subsequently approved both by elected officials and by the Citizens Action Commission (CAC), which the Mayor himself appointed.[24] But Dahl conceded that the Mayor was careful to formulate only proposals that he thought the CAC would approve,[25] and critics charged that the Mayor's caution was evidence of a necessary deference to the desires of the numerous Economic and Social Notables who sat on the CAC.[26] If the charges were well founded, the possibility arose that the CAC controlled the Mayor rather than vice versa. Such a situation would be undemocratic, since it would flatly contradict Dahl's evidence of separate scopes of power for the political, the economic, and the social elites of the city. It would suggest, in fact, that the Mayor might willingly or unwillingly be a leg man for various private interests operating through him covertly and using his public power to assure satisfaction of their own ends.

In all likelihood, of course, the mayor of a city as large as New Haven is never completely dominated by any single interest or group of interests. But the very possibility that he might be subservient to some who are not dependent upon open and measurable electoral success presents a difficult problem of analysis. Political power is often exercised in what may technically be called a "closed-loop system," where "the variables within the system are related in such a way that one can trace a chain of relationships from a given variable through other variables and back to the original starting point without retracing one's steps."[27] In more common terms, suppose the Notables enjoy some influence over the Mayor and he in turn influences them to some degree. The process of influence is subtle and implicit; it may operate through a great many proverbial winks and nods. It is difficult to grasp empirically; we know only that there is a circular flow of power—a closed loop—from one point to another and back. But who, in the chain, exercises *more* power? Who *dominates* the relationship? No method has yet been devised, including the pluralist technique of analyzing specific decisions, for precisely ascertaining the measure of power wielded by all elements of a closed-loop power system.

Dahl confidently concluded that the Mayor, as a duly elected government official, held dominant political power in the area of urban renewal, but the problem of analyzing relationships of mutual influence detracted from the persuasiveness of his observations. The closed-loop problem also undermined his reassuring conclusion that ordinarily passive citizens knowingly or unknowingly enjoyed indirect influence over the Mayor and other politicians because of anticipated reactions in the hopes of gaining or maintaining electoral support. If it may be said, on the basis of apparent acquiescence, that the masses exert power over politicians in this way, it seems logical to add that politicians seek constantly to influence the masses and to shape their opinions to their own advantage. As Andrew Hacker has succinctly remarked, "the chief aim of public relations is to throw sand in the public's eyes."[28] Yet American politicians practice public relations with a passion—holding press conferences, sending newsletters to their constituents, distributing press releases, delivering patriotic speeches, denouncing taxes, praising the police, lambasting the international Socialist menace, and doing a great many other things to confuse unwitting voters.[29] Of course, such voters may believe themselves to be satisfactorily served by their leaders; collectively, the citizenry may think that this is the best of all possible political systems, and its leaders either the boldest or the most cautious of men, depending on the era and the fashion. When such satisfaction prevails, the Significant Sidestep allows pluralist theorists to judge the situation satisfactory, free, and democratic. It even permits them to conclude that the political elite has anticipated the needs of the voters. But if it is the politicians who actually induce the voters to desire certain ends, who exercises power over whom? Most probably, politicians never exercise absolute control in their reciprocal relations with the electorate, but this likelihood tells us only that it is unwarranted optimism to stress the indirect influence of the masses and to slight the impact of the political elite's attempts at indirect manipulation.

Then too, once the possibly circular nature of indirect influence is recognized, the possibility of indirect influence by the nonpassive and the politically alert becomes apparent. As one severe critic of Dahl has argued, the notion of indirect influence from the apathetic might quite logically be extended to "top leaders of other institutions in society, such as the business community," since such men enjoy "great potential power."[30] But to suggest that the business community may indirectly control the government is to strike at the foundation of pluralist analysis, for if economic elites control political elites, the pluralist strategy of choosing government decisions for study is invalid. Government affairs cannot be equated with community affairs if government is in reality not supreme, if it is not free from domination by other institutions. Yet Dahl could not be certain that government is *not* so dominated, because he concentrated on the Mayor's planning for renewal and ignored the strategies of "downtown merchants and bankers."[31]

And finally, the pluralist theory was faulted because it could not account for political manipulation which takes place privately, in confidence, in forums not exposed to study by social scientists. Polsby remarked at one point that "if a man's major life work is banking, the pluralist presumes he will spend his time at the bank, and not in manipulating community decisions."[32] The example could hardly be more poorly chosen, for it suggests a clear distinction between private and public scopes of power where none may in fact exist. Consider David Rockefeller, for example, President of the Chase Manhattan Bank, a man of enormous wealth and influence in the private community, with great oil properties and foreign investments. Late in 1969, Rockefeller met with President Nixon at the White House to advise him concerning American policy in the Middle East, in the Arab-Israeli dispute.[33] The advice offered was presumably based on Rockefeller's private and commercial knowledge of that region, yet it constituted a factor of considerable influence in the formulation of a national policy. That his private and public scopes of influence are not clearly separable appears in his relationship to local community politics as well. The money lending practices of the Chase Manhattan Bank must surely be a factor in New York City's housing situation, and thus Rockefeller's nominally private decisions as a banker are closely linked to the public realms of rent control policy and urban renewal. On both the national and local levels, therefore, Polsby's distinction between private occupations and public decision-making is untenable.

Even more difficult to analyze and measure than the influence of a single man, however rich, is another matter that the pluralist theory ignores entirely, and that is deliberate secrecy and subterfuge in political manipulation. No ordinary method of inquiry can weigh and assess such factors precisely, but that is not reason enough for overlooking them. For example, in the spring af 1967 certain facts concerning operations of the Central Intelligence Agency (CIA) were publicized, and it was learned that the CIA had extended its activities to philanthropic foundations, banks, law firms, university faculties, student groups, and a host of other ostensibly private groups, using them and their members to conduct government business under private auspices.[34] Most of the CIA's domestic activities remained unrevealed, but even that relatively small portion of its affairs that came to light suggested strongly that researchers must not draw too strict a pluralist line between the private and public realms of power.

The Rockefeller case and the CIA revelations carry significant implications concerning the role of the public in what we commonly call public policy. When behind the scenes manipulations of power exist, how much influence can the public be said to exert in matters concerning the Middle East and the foreign policies advanced by the CIA? The point is not that power indices in such matters can easily be devised, but only that the positional method of power recommended by Mills may very well draw our attention to truly important political actors while the pluralist approach to decision-making may ignore people whom common sense and all available evidence tells us are powerful.

NONDECISION-MAKING

A final realm of political manipulation that has received great critical attention is now called *non*decision-making. As one sociologist has remarked, "community analysts must look behind overt decisions and ask how it is that certain issues are never brought up."[35] In this realm of nondecisions, of matters which do not overtly occur, of gentlemen's agreements and legal fictions, of affairs which lie beyond observed behavior, at least three phenomena are significant: negative decisions, mobilization of bias, and latent interests.

Peter Bachrach and Morton Baratz, who first drew attention to the realm of nondecision-making, referred to the negative side of decision-making as the act of "deciding not to act or deciding not to decide."[36] Such a shadowy corner of the political process does not encourage systematic analysis, because, unlike the "concrete decisions" Dahl urged researchers to study, negative decisions constitute a way of *not* doing something, a process of *not* deciding. Negative decisions are nevertheless important because they collectively help to shape the agenda of public controversy and public decision-making. Negative decisions, usually taken quietly, in large part determine what shall *not* be discussed, what shall *not* be acted upon, and what shall *not* be considered for a concrete decision.[37] Thus the agenda of public politics is cast, subsequently to be televised, editorialized, speechified, lobbied, and otherwise acted upon by interested parties.

Negative decisions are taken in the light of what Bachrach and Baratz called the "mobilization of bias," the sum total of community views and practices that set the boundaries of legitimate politics, "the dominant values and the political myths, rituals, and institutions which tend to favor the vested interests of one or more groups, relative to others."[38] In all of our communities, the two argued, politicians and other powerful political actors seek to work with the prevailing bias, and seek to limit "the scope of actual decision-making to 'safe' issues,"[39] issues that will permit them to maintain their desirable positions within the status quo.

A background of community bias is directly relevant to the constant issue of democracy which pervades community power studies. If certain biases dominate the on-going process of politics, it follows that some groups and their particular needs will not receive adequate consideration from the entire body politic; in fact, some groups and their respective claims may not even be considered legitimate by the rest of society. Regardless, therefore, of formal rights to organize, to speak, to campaign, and to make known our views, there may be an entrenched power factor in community politics that prevents some interests from being taken seriously, and certain minorities may remain permanently neglected, their needs ignored. It would seem the essence of democracy, however, that a community enjoy considerable political flexibility, at least enough so that all interests are taken into account at some point by decision-makers. Representation and balancing of all interests was presumably the function of the political stratum in New Haven, but if that stratum as a whole were actually subordinate to a particular mobilization of bias, it would be inherently predisposed in favor of some people and against others despite the variety of groups and individuals it embraced.

Matters involving community bias are commonplace. A notable example appeared in 1970 in a speech by Vice President Spiro Agnew. In a widely publicized address to the Missouri Republican party, he criticized those who oppose the Vietnam war in the following words: "as for these deserters, malcontents, radicals, incendiaries, the civil and the uncivil disobedients among our young, SDS [Students for a Democratic Society], PLP [Progressive Labor Party], Weatherman I and Weatherman II, the Revolutionary Action Movement, the Yippies, hippies, Yahoos, Black Panthers, lions and tigers alike—I would swap the whole damn zoo for a single platoon of the kind of young Americans I saw in Vietnam."[40] By invoking reflexive symbols of patriotism, the Vice President intentionally cast automatic disrepute upon the ideas, the programs, and the proposals of all the people he grouped together in such language. The audience of course applauded enthusiastically and undoubtedly felt no urge to seriously consider any dissenting views on such an exhilarating occasion. Within the framework of such a mobilization of bias, however, politics as "the art of the possible" excludes certain possibilities—such as total troop withdrawal from Vietnam—for they cannot be discussed on their merits alone, apart from fervent emotions and implicit or explicit allegations of treason.

On certain issues, community bias may be so powerful as to suppress expressions of dissatisfaction entirely. Such issues have been called latent;[41] they are rooted in grievances that cannot be debated and eased in the prevailing climate of opinion but which nonetheless reflect unequal burdens and harmful practices. An obvious example in the past was racial discrimination. For almost one hundred years after the Civil War, the white majority in the United States convinced itself that black Americans were by and large satisfied and content; the whites even created Amos and Andy style stereotypes of happy and singing "darkies." For generations, therefore, racial discrimination was a latent issue in American politics, and it only became a live controversy after World War II. The dearth of prewar public debate on this matter, however, should not have been taken to indicate that a latent racial issue did not exist, that all racial needs were adequately met. In the late 1960s, many Americans gradually became aware of other latent issues that had long been ignored, some of which we shall examine in the next chapter.

Bachrach and Baratz held that the realm of nondecision-making is enormously significant, that students of community power should carefully assess the mobilization of bias and decide who benefits from it, that researchers should then investigate the extent to which beneficiaries of the bias perpetuate it from positions in community institutions, governmental and otherwise, and that only after attaining full knowledge of the bias and its supporters should the behavior of men making concrete decisions be studied.[42] The point here is that only when political decisions are viewed against the nondecision-making background of bias can it be said that they are important or not, that they demonstrate who wields significant power in the community, that they account for latent issues and submerged needs, that they bear or do not bear upon the fundamental configuration of benefits, rewards, advantages, and disadvantages that constitute the substance of a community of human beings. In short, without an understanding of community bias it is not possible to assess accurately the real degree of freedom, competition, and democracy that exist in American politics.

The pluralist response to this suggested approach relied on the Significant Sidestep. Studying nondecision-making is equivalent to analyzing nonevents, events that are significant precisely because they do not occur, decisions that are crucial because they are never made. But who is to say, of the infinity of events that do not happen, which are important? As Polsby put it, an independent and objective observer is not qualified to say that some nonevents are important if the community itself fails to voice some expression of their worth.[43] And it is a fact that when pluralist researchers inquired in New Haven, their respondents agreed that the decisions chosen for study by the pluralists were the most important issues in the city at that time.

By positing a realm of nondecision-making Bachrach and Baratz in effect recommended analysis of the realm of political consensus, the field of usually uncontested decisions, the behavior of omission as well as commission. They therefore clearly raised, in special terminology, the problem of properly selecting subject matter for a community power study, a problem we have already examined. They conceded that their suggestions involved power factors that are extremely difficult to measure empirically, forces such as ideology, prejudices, stereotypes, patriotism, habits, traditions, and anticipations. In a sense, then, the concept of a realm of nondecision-making is as methodologically weak as David Truman's concept of a potential group, or the pluralist notion of indirect influence. All these are concerned with real power factors, but they reintroduce into the fabric of democratic theory the "soul stuff" which Bentley had explicitly ruled out as impossible to grasp or assess (see pp. 41–42). Whereas Truman and Dahl did not inquire very closely into the effects of their versions of "soul stuff," and merely cited the existence of potential groups and indirect influence as proof of democracy in action, students of nondecision-making argue that in the intangible realm of politics are exactly the subjects that must be studied most intensively. In these realms forces must be examined with great care, and rankings must be devised to reveal who enjoys dominant power and great benefits. Indeed, in these realms where analysis is exceedingly difficult we must make no comfortable presumptions that our political system is working well when it may, in reality, be operating on behalf of certain interests and against others.

SUMMARY

In sum, the various charges that comprised the methodological critique of pluralist theory cast doubt on most of the significant elements, explicit and implicit, of that theory. The pluralist manner of selecting issues was faulted, and in the process the presumed objectivity of the Significant Sidestep was derogated. The pluralist belief in noncumulative resources was challenged, and therefore power factors were ranked and the confusing Conceptual Backtrack was rejected. Indirect influence as a concept was extended in various directions and to various people, to the point where the Great Separation of politics from the economic world became untenable. And a realm of nondecision-making was posited, a realm so all-embracing that the politician, the Pluralist Hero, was downgraded to the status of being only one among many different significant actors and forces. Of course, the scholars who complained separately of the pluralist theory's inadequacies were not aware that their collected criticisms might be cast in the pattern we have used here. In light of that pattern, however, we can see that it remained only to highlight the shortcomings of the Prophylactic Perspective, and this was accomplished by what we shall refer to as the critique of tolerance.

NOTES

1/ Thomas J. Anton, "Power, Pluralism and Local Politics," *Administrative Science Quarterly* (March 1963), pp. 449–451 ff.

2/ Robert A. Dahl, "A Critique of the Ruling Elite Model," *American Political Science Review* (June 1958), pp. 466–469.

3/ Robert A. Dahl, *Who Governs?* (New Haven: Yale University Press, 1961), pp. 69–71.

4/ M. Herbert Danzger, "Community Power Structure: Problems and Continuities," *American Sociological Review* (October 1964), pp. 714–716, discusses the concept of salience.

5/ Peter Bachrach and Morton S. Baratz, "Two Faces of Power," *American Political Science Review* (December 1962), pp. 950–951.

6/ See Delbert C. Miller's discussion of selecting issues in William V. D'Antonio and Howard J. Ehrlich (eds.), *Power and Democracy in America* (South Bend, Ind.: Notre Dame University Press, 1961), pp. 105–107.

7/ Bachrach and Baratz, "Two Faces of Power," pp. 949–950.

8/ On the politics of post-World War II military spending in general, see Richard J. Barnet, *The Economy of Death* (New York: Atheneum, 1969).

9/ David Easton, *The Political System* (New York: Knopf, 1953), p. 129.

10/ Peter Bachrach, *The Theory of Democratic Elitism* (Boston: Little, Brown, 1967), p. 102. See also Anton, "Power, Pluralism and Local Politics," pp. 452–453.

11/ Henry S. Kariel, *The Promise of Politics* (Englewood Cliffs, N.J.: Prentice-Hall, 1966), p. 39.

12/ Robert Paul Wolff, *The Poverty of Liberalism* (Boston: Beacon, 1968), p. 93.

13/ Nelson W. Polsby, "How to Study Community Power: The Pluralist Alternative," *Journal of Politics* (August 1960), pp. 479–481. See also Anton, "Power, Pluralism, and Local Politics," p. 446.

14/ John Kenneth Galbraith argues that information is the key to power in modern society. See his *The New Industrial State* (Boston: Houghton Mifflin, 1967), pp. 46–71.

15/ William V. D'Antonio and Howard J. Ehrlich, "Democracy in America: Retrospect and Prospect," in D'Antonio and Ehrlich, *Power and Democracy in America,* p. 144.

16/ Franz Kafka, *The Trial* (New York: Knopf, 1937), and *The Castle* (New York: Knopf, 1954).

17/ Anthony Lewis, *Gideon's Trumpet* (New York: Vintage, 1964).

18/ Jacobus tenBroek and the Editors of *California Law Review* (eds.), *The Law of the Poor* (San Francisco: Chandler, 1966); and R. H. Smith, *Justice and the Poor* (Montclair, N.J.: Smith, Patterson, 1970).

19/ Carl Friedrich, *Constitutional Government and Democracy* (Boston: Little, Brown, 1941), pp. 589–591.

20/ Robert Presthus, *Men at the Top* (New York: Oxford University Press, 1964), p. 61.

21/ Howard J. Ehrlich, "Power and Democracy: A Critical Discussion," in D'Antonio and Ehrlich, *Power and Democracy in America,* p. 92.

22/ The case of a man controlling such wealth and power is not hypothetical. See Robert Sherrill, *Gothic Politics in the Deep South* (New York: Grossman, 1968), pp. 141–146.

23/ Presthus, *Men at the Top,* pp. 116–121.

24/ Nelson W. Polsby, *Community Power and Political Theory* (New Haven: Yale University Press, 1963), p. 73.

25/ Dahl, *Who Governs?,* p. 137.

26/ Bachrach and Baratz, "Two Faces of Power," pp. 951–952.

27/ James G. March, "An Introduction to the Theory and Measurement of Influence," *American Political Science Review* (June 1955), p. 433, footnote 6.

28/ Andrew Hacker, "Liberal Democracy and Social Control," *American Political Science Review* (December 1957), p. 1022.

29/ On the practice of political public relations, see Daniel J. Boorstin, *The Image: A Guide to Pseudo-Events in America* (New York: Colophon, 1964), esp. pp. 7–44.

30/ Jack Walker, "A Critique of the Elitist Theory of Democracy," *American Political Science Review* (June 1966), p. 292.

31/ Thomas J. Anton, letter to the editor, *Administrative Science Quarterly* (September 1963), pp. 264–266.

32/ Polsby, "How to Study Community Power," p. 480.

33/ *The New York Times,* December 22, 1969, pp. 1, 16.

34/ For a variety of views on the CIA, see Young Hum Kim (ed.) , *The Central Intelligence Agency: Problems of Secrecy in a Democracy* (Lexington, Mass.: Heath and Co., 1968) .

35/ Richard L. Simpson, "Comment by a Sociologist," *Southwest Social Science Quarterly* (December 1967) , p. 287.

36/ Peter Bachrach and Morton S. Baratz, "Decisions and Non-decisions: An Analytical Framework," *American Political Science Review* (September 1963) , p. 461.

37/ Commenting on the unwillingness of Congress to change its oligarchical rules of procedure, Senator Joseph Clark of Pennsylvania remarked that "the durability of these devices [rules] is . . . a tribute to the curious notion that to do nothing does not constitute a decision." See his *Congress: The Sapless Branch* (New York: Harper & Row, 1964) , p. 147.

38/ Bachrach and Baratz, "Two Faces of Power," p. 950.

39/ Bachrach and Baratz, "Decisions and Nondecisions," p. 632.

40/ Speech by Vice President Spiro Agnew to a fund raising dinner of the Missouri Republican party in St. Louis, Mo., February 10, 1970. See *The Washington Post,* February 12, 1970, p. 18.

41/ Bachrach and Baratz, "Decisions and Nondecisions," p. 641–642.

42/ Bachrach and Baratz, "Two Faces of Power," p. 952.

43/ Polsby, *Community Power and Political Theory,* pp. 96–97.

☻ **10** ☻

Pluralism Opposed:
The Critique of Tolerance

Even if Robert Dahl and other pluralists might have harbored some private doubts about various aspects of American life, there seemed to be a pattern of reassurance in *Who Governs?* and in related works. Certain facts were presented and emphasized; others were slighted and ignored; and from this selectivity, the Prophylactic Perspective emerged. Pluralist theory highlighted the most desirable qualities of American politics, with the result that the paucity of protests about the distribution and exercise of power in *Who Governs?* and other pluralist writings conveyed a very definite impression of substantial confidence in the American political system.

This confidence became suspect when viewed in the light of explicit and implicit criticism from three quarters: scholarly commentators who rejected pluralism as an uninspiring theory of democracy; all writers—scholarly or otherwise—who were dissatisfied with the quality of the results of community power in practice; and Americans in every walk of life who, with increasing frequency, complained about the effects of politics-as-usual. There is no need to draw hard and fast lines between these various sources of criticism, since all three reached similar conclusions; indeed, they should be viewed as mutually reinforcing component parts of a growing and widespread awareness that the

American condition commonly known as democracy suffers a number of extremely serious shortcomings.

TOLERANCE OF WHAT?

Collectively, the hostility to pluralism in theory and in practice may be seen as constituting a critique of tolerance. As one critic observed from an analytical point of view, tolerance of diverse interests is "the virtue of the modern pluralist democracy which has emerged in America."[1] Yet, as another critic charged with regard to the effects of this pluralist democracy, "tolerance is extended to policies, conditions, and modes of behavior which should not be tolerated because they are impeding, if not destroying, the chances for creating an existence without fear and misery."[2] Opposition to pluralism as the theory and practice of tolerance, then, might be rooted in a conviction that present circumstances are just too disastrous to bear with equanimity.

Unfortunately, it is extremely difficult to abstract a pattern, to systematically analyze the critique of tolerance, because its sources and elements are too disparate. Let us first discuss some of the expressed dissatisfaction with pluralism in practice, and then proceed to show how this dissatisfaction was translated by scholarly commentators on democracy into an ideological critique of pluralist theory for failing to deal with grave social problems. This seems to be the most useful course of analysis, since it was a rising general dissatisfaction with existing politics that lent weight to scholarly criticism of pluralist theory, that challenged the reassuring support the theory gave to established democratic institutions.

Even this approach to the critique of tolerance, however, cannot do it justice. Recent commentators have publicized so many ills affecting American society that we can hardly discuss them all here. Consider, for example, some of the urgent problems: racial discrimination, air and water pollution, violence, crime, suppression of political dissent, urban decay, inequitable tax structures, the deterioration of mass transportation, the widespread use of drugs, the plight of American Indians, the Vietnam atrocities, the condition of the poor, consumer fraud, planned obsolescence, the inferior status of women, and more. (See Appendix B, pp. 228–232.) The list alone severely indicts the Prophylactic Perspective.

Given the context of this book and the limitations of space, we may most profitably examine three broad areas of concern: limited political participation, the problem of permanent minorities, and economic imbalance. These matters affect most of us and are therefore typical of the nation's ills. Moreover, they may all be viewed in similar terms of social costs, an index of political activity that the pluralist theory did not stress. It appears that we enjoy an equilibrium of political forces, and thus we enjoy a measure of general stability and ordinarily peaceful change. But as Mills would have asked, who are the victims of this equilibrium? (See p. 116.) What appears on the debit side of the pluralist ledger? What are the costs of tolerating all that the equilibrium embraces? When it became clear in the 1960s that some of these costs were enormously high, the confidence of pluralist theory was questioned and scholarly commentators began to contend that the theory itself must be rejected because it commended to us a democracy that actually denied our common expectations for a good society.

LIMITED POLITICAL PARTICIPATION

The costs of limited political participation are essentially what Robert Pranger has called "the eclipse of citizenship."[3] In modern democracies, and especially in American politics as described by Dahl,[4] the truth of the matter is that most people have little or nothing to do with making the great decisions that affect their communities and thus the course of their lives. The most frequent kind of political participation is voting, and yet as few as half of all adults ordinarily vote in national elections, and far fewer vote in state and local contests. As for political activity more complex and time-consuming than casting ballots, only a minute fraction of the total citizenry ever campaigns, holds office, lobbies, or is otherwise intimately involved in the political decision-making process.

Pranger observed that democracy as practiced is mainly an affair for elites, activists, and those whom social scientists call "influentials."[5] For this reason, he referred to ordinary democratic politics as the *politics of power* and contended that we lack a *politics of participation*. In the realm of democratic power politics, most men are " 'in' the world of power but not 'of' it." The law assures many rights to act, but politics is so vast and requires so many resources most men do not possess that in effect they are excluded from the circle of those who wield decisive power. In short, the great majority of us are citizens in the sense that we are members of a political state, with all the rights and privileges membership confers; we are not true citizens, however, in the classic sense of participating in community affairs and sharing the power that determines the community's destiny.

In the pluralist theory, the inactivity of most men was explained by the concept of *homo civicus,* the citizen whose natural inclination is to shun politics and seek the easier satisfaction of a private life. But Pranger claimed that "slothful citizenship is only a feedback response from a prevailing culture, a response which in turn reinforces that culture."[6] The legal rights of every citizen may be meaningless vis-à-vis community decisions, devoid of practical effect; and he may know it. For example, voting was the participatory act crucial to Dahl's concept of indirect influence, the act whereby the masses have some restraining effect on elites. Yet if indirect influence exists, it is so intangible that its effects cannot be precisely measured, and Pranger contended that most Americans are actually convinced that voting bears no necessary relationship to many policies formulated in the people's name and affecting everyone. Referenda are conducted before raising taxes to build new schools, but none are conducted to ascertain our collective opinions on ultimate matters of life and death, on matters of war and peace.[7] Thus, when 250 thousand antiwar demonstrators traveled to Washington, D.C., on November 15, 1969, the President informed them in advance that he would not be influenced by their views. Then, while they exercised their constitutional rights of free speech, assembly, and petition in the largest peaceful rally in American history, he belittled their efforts by indicating that he would watch a college football game on television.[8] From Pranger's point of view, a realist might validly conclude that our rights permit us to speak, but they do not oblige our leaders to pay attention. Great decisions seem to be made by only a few, perhaps even in secret, and Pranger argued that when citizens realize this they may minimize their sense of helplessness and frustration by becoming disinterested and passive. Limited participation may therefore be the sign of a widely adopted psychological defense mechanism.[9]

It should be noted that Pranger and Dahl could probably agree to a stipulated set of facts concerning who *may* participate, who *does* participate, and who *actually makes* political decisions; they would differ only in their interpretation of the significance of those facts. The general public, however, clearly sides more with Pranger than with Dahl, and that is itself a significant fact. In the late 1960s, both American conservatives and American radicals—not necessarily to be equated with historical Conservatives and Socialists—concurred in their condemnation of American politics as overly centralized and bureaucratized. Both called for a return of power from Washington to the state capitals, from the state capitals to the cities, and from city halls to the neighborhoods of America.[10] These sentiments came from various organized groups, such as the John Birch Society, the Minutemen, the Young Americans for Freedom, the Coalition for Peace, the Students for a Democratic Society, the Black Panthers, and from many ad hoc local organizations, and represented the feelings of great numbers of corporation executives, small businessmen, professionals, many of the middle class, the lower middle class, poor whites, poor blacks, hippies, and those whom Vice President Agnew has labeled "effete snobs." When people at opposite ends of a political spectrum agree like this on a single issue, we can be certain that a real grievance exists and is widely suffered.

Low rates of participation are a mark of great social costs. Despite formal freedom to exercise many democratic rights and privileges, most citizens feel powerless, avoid involvement in their communities, become alienated from their neighbors, and in general fail to fulfill their potential as creative and psychologically secure social beings. In a complex twentieth-century society of 200 million people, it may be obvious that we cannot return to the sense of solidarity once characteristic of New England town meetings; but we should not therefore mislead ourselves about the costs of sheer size by using soothing labels like "pluralism." We should more accurately call our political system a "presidium of elites,"[11] a comfortless phrase that draws attention forcefully to the harsh reality of limited participation. Indeed, we might speak of limited participation as a manifestation of the failure of traditional American expectations that Liberal political devices can assure an ideal political life for all, a point to which we shall return shortly.

PERMANENT MINORITIES

The matter of permanent minorities is perhaps the most intractable problem of American politics-as-usual, and it may prove to be the most costly because America's largest permanent minority consists of more than 20 million black men and women who are becoming increasingly militant about their continued exclusion from many of the benefits of their own society. Other apparently permanent, or at least semipermanent, minorities exist—for example, Mexican-Americans, American Indians, and migrant farm workers. But their condition is not as well known and therefore not as instructive here as a few of the most basic facts concerning the black community.

Permanent minorities share a common plight since they are in most circumstances unassimilable among the political majority because of discrimination, and they cannot easily avoid that discrimination by changing their names, language, or dress. It is the essence of democracy, however, that the majority rules, or at least its legitimate representatives rule. And therefore if prejudice prevents a permanent minority from entering the ranks of the majority, that minority will derive few benefits from majoritarian politics; indeed, as a permanent outsider, so to speak, such a minority cannot work through the political system to overcome the inferior economic and social conditions that private prejudice forces upon it.

Pluralist theory proceeded as if all citizens are at least politically equal; Dahl asserted that the black men in New Haven were disadvantaged socially and economically but gaining in political benefits as they became more and more active politically.[12] In its overall thrust, therefore, pluralist theory was optimistic because it portrayed the reality of American politics as a vast arena full of competing races, ethnic blocks, religious sects, pressure groups, associations, and institutions, all ultimately reduceable to disparate but interchangeable citizens who hold equal voting power and whose various interests will therefore be served by members of the political stratum who are eager to amass electoral support. But a permanent minority is permanent precisely because its members are *not* deemed interchangeable with all other men. In both the South and the North, refusal to accept black men as most others is so commonplace that black unemployment is much higher than white unemployment, housing for blacks is often wretchedly poor in quality and available mainly in segregated ghettos, and the average income of non-white Americans is from one half to two thirds that of whites. Many white politicians are pleased to accept black votes and some even work on behalf of black causes, but the larger picture is dismal. Black men are *not* solicited politically as are most other segments of the American body politic; in fact, they usually find themselves excluded from the political bargaining process, confronting a solid majority of white Americans who are either actively hostile to blacks or indifferent to their collective fate. Tension has increased so markedly that President Nixon has widely been reported to have adopted a "Southern strategy,"[13] a course of delay and inactivity designed to deemphasize the hardships and needs of black citizens, and simultaneously to appeal to the prejudices of the white majority which, if united behind a single Presidential candidate, could elect that man to the White House in 1972.

Pluralism in America cannot solve the problem of permanent minorities unless society as a whole chooses to pursue any or all of three courses: (1) minorities may be accepted socially and through marriage they will eventually disappear; (2) they may be accepted morally in principle and therefore treated impartially in fact; or (3) they may be granted political independence as a separate national entity. Intermarriage depends on moral acceptance, and national liberation presumes a failure to adopt either of these two. None of the three seems likely to be pursued in the near future, and unless there is a violent revolution, blacks working within the existing political system can only attempt to consolidate "black power," to "close ranks" and operate as a single, immensely powerful pressure group.[14] Even by closing ranks, though, American blacks will continue to constitute only a fraction of the larger community, and they may by their solidarity so anger and frighten many whites as to find themselves just as effectively excluded from the national majority as they are today. And if blacks should come to constitute local majorities here and there, in this city or that, their white neighbors may emerge as new permanent minorities.

The cost of tolerating permanent minorities in our political system is clear to the oppressed, and a resulting breakdown in social order may bring some of their suffering home to the majority as well; indeed, a rising crime rate seems already to have begun to apportion the burden more equitably. What is analytically significant about the current racial polarization is that within the pluralist theory, and within the prevailing sentiment that is perhaps mirrored in that theory, the problem of permanent minorities cannot be solved. What we require is a widespread willingness to ignore race, to abolish status, to treat men as truly equal. We must cease to infuse our political system with outworn prejudices and biases, with simple power, competition, and the vectors of narrowly interested political forces. We must deliberately create a new and public sense of social responsibility and decency to guide our political behavior. These are extraordinarily difficult imperatives, of course, and there are no clear indications that the nation will do what it must. What *is* clear, however, is that a new public standard appears nowhere in *Who Governs?*, which after all does not purport to expound moral theory.

Once again, as in the case of limited participation, a failure of Liberal expectations is revealed, a failure to construct a policy that assures a healthy political life for every member of the community. The forms of democracy—our rights and our frequent elections—may be satisfactory while the substance somehow is not.

ECONOMIC IMBALANCE

The problem of economic imbalance is today widely discussed in terms of ecology.[15] It seems that everyone—Republicans and Democrats, collectivists and capitalists, rich and poor, black and white—is on record favoring sound ecology; everyone advocates an intelligent use of national resources, a restoration of the natural environment, and the creation of a viable human one. But when so many different people seek political gains under the aegis of a single issue, they tend to overwork it, to confuse it with partisan appeals, to dull men's critical senses with analytically useless platitudes. Writings about ecology may tell us *what* is wrong, but economist John Kenneth Galbraith's *The Affluent Society* (1958)[16] discusses *why* we suffer imbalance. Galbraith defined the problem of economic imbalance in terms of public goods, which we lack, and private goods, which threaten to inundate us and destroy the quality of life.

As noted in Chapter 4, public goods are characteristically shared by a great many men, yet are difficult to finance because most people refuse to pay voluntarily their fair share of the cost of providing such goods. Public goods include clean air, clean water, wilderness areas, mass transportation, playgrounds, parks, safety on the streets, and more. Government ordinarily makes sure we get some of these goods, but it can do so only by compelling us to pay taxes. Even though each of us may understand that he will benefit from an adequate supply of public goods, we are all so irresponsible that we must be forced to pay for our own welfare.

As Galbraith observed, our economy as it presently operates results in a perpetual shortage of public goods; he explained this in a "theory of social balance," which analyzed imbalance.[17] We are so committed to the consumption of private and apparently profitable goods—washing machines, automobiles, movie cameras, radios, clothing—that we tend always to underallocate the nation's resources to the production of public ones. In the search for more and more private pleasures, we have long ignored their side effects and by-products: the pollution of our atmosphere, the poisoning of our lakes and streams, the despoliation of our countryside, and the overcrowding of our cities. We enjoy large families but do not build enough schools; we pay for a great many air conditioners and too few public power stations; we drive enormous numbers of cars and permit public transportation to deteriorate; we spend too much on pleasure craft and not enough on marine biological research.

There are many reasons for the imbalance between private and public goods, but chief among them is our habitual underestimation of government's ability to produce public benefits. This traditional misunderstanding is perpetuated by the pervasive influence of private advertising, which constantly and persuasively tells us that beer, underarm deodorants, hair sprays, color televisions, soft drinks, and a great many other privately consumed items are the essence of youth, vitality, prosperity, and the American Way of Life.[18] The result of this unrelenting pressure to consume private goods is a collective and compulsive fixation on the benefits of nongovernmental production and a disbelief that public goods are vitally important.

Therefore it may be true, strictly speaking, that we are constitutionally free to vote and authorize our governments to collect and spend more money on public goods to maintain social balance, to restore our environment to a healthy condition, and to beautify our surroundings, but as free men we usually choose to spend our money on well-advertised private goods and afterward complain that we are so limited in means that we cannot "afford" to increase taxes and provide for sufficient public goods. The problem of imbalance, then, is that the private and immediately profitable side of our economy is in virtually uncontrolled ascendency. The nation seeks a constantly expanding Gross National Product while ignoring public needs that if unmet will make a mockery of all our private comforts. As with other matters entailing great social costs, pluralist practice and theory both fail to comprehend the problem. In practice, our social norms are seriously askew; in theory, under the assumption that nominally private power is not "community power," Dahl's reluctance to examine private structures of power in New Haven ignored the reality that private power is translated into public policy by shaping our minds so decisively that we permit an imbalance of private and public goods to endure. Once more, as with regard to limited participation and permanent minorities, American society seems to lack incentives for men to seek the reasonable amenities of a healthy communal existence. Here is yet another example of substantive failure of Liberal expectations in a country enjoying at least a framework of Liberal institutions and practices.

THE COMMON DENOMINATOR OF SOCIAL COSTS

All three problems share a common denominator of social cost; limited participation, permanent minorities, and economic imbalance are all apparently normal adjuncts of pluralist democracy in action, and all stand together on the debit side of the ledger that sums up what the community derives from the present distribution and exercise of community power. What remains to be seen is how this common denominator of social cost may be taken to bespeak a common theoretical dissatisfaction with the pluralist theory and the reality it embraces. The answer to *why* our society must suffer these costs seems to be that even though the political system guarantees many freedoms and rights, and is in many important senses competitive, it does not encourage people to behave reasonably and responsibly. We simply do not act as wisely and as rationally as Liberals once hoped citizens of a Liberal society would individually and collectively act. We have created some of the political devices that Liberal thinkers told us to create, and that much is commendable. But the expected results have not all materialized.

This unreasonableness that apparently produces great social costs is the key to ideological rejection of the Prophylactic Perspective. The critique of pluralist tolerance may be reduced to an all-encompassing theoretical charge: pluralist theory as a kind of neo-Liberalism praises Liberal political devices but implicitly accepts certain conditions that classical Liberals would have opposed vigorously. This charge underlies critical scholarly observations such as the following: "The reality of irrational mass emotion, self-interest, group egoism, and the prevalence of oligarchic and hierarchical social and economic organizations need no longer be denied [by researchers such as Dahl] in the name of democratic values."[19] Or, "what may now be called 'democracies' [by researchers such as Dahl] may function with little rationality, interest, or participation on the part of the majority of citizens."[20]

Such statements are actually part of a larger view, for theoretical dissatisfaction with the results of pluralism goes further than charging the political system with embracing great faults. The critics even go so far as to claim that our political system is part and parcel of a way of life that makes such faults inevitable. On this score, that which Dahl chose to call democracy is said to be inherently unsound because its political and economic realms together cause us to lack rationality. This is a point that merits our closest attention.

SUBSTANTIAL OR FUNCTIONAL RATIONALITY

In modern social science, rationality is frequently defined in two broad senses suggested by the German sociologist Karl Mannheim. According to Mannheim, rationality should be viewed as either "substantial" or "functional." Substantial rationality he described as a capacity for independent judgment, while functional rationality is a logical capacity for achieving a "defined goal."[21] As a later commentator on American politics repeated the distinction, a man can be rational in the sense of being "the author of [his] . . . actions, to act rather than to be acted upon," or he may instead be efficient in respect to "given" ends.[22]

Mannheim originally differentiated substantial from functional rationality in order to observe that in modern societies, characterized by large-scale organization in industry, government, commerce, and every other field of endeavor, men act in accordance with complicated circumstances. This requires a great deal of functional rationality, of efficiency with respect to goals set by large groups, of proficiency in gaining ends made possible and indeed necessary by technology and bureaucracy. Paradoxically, however, in modern societies functional rationality has increased while substantial rationality has declined.[23] Functional rationality has become extraordinarily refined, so that corporations like General Motors can produce millions of devilishly complex cars and trucks on assembly lines that are miracles of efficiency and precision; yet substantial rationality has become more and more difficult to attain, for most of us understand less and less of the world that surrounds us. Our freedom of action is in important respects more limited and circumscribed than when organizations were small and our lives correspondingly simple. We are in command of ourselves and the situation when we kick a mule to get him moving, but ignorance makes most of us helpless, and thus we cannot get a stalled car to move by kicking it during an emergency.

Mannheim's remarks on the paradox of rationality in modern societies has been echoed by the critics of American pluralism, even if they do not use precisely his terms. From every field of inquiry, critics agree that the technological, commercial, and political framework of our national community is so massive and complicated that ordinary men can barely understand it, much less resist its imposition of conformity on their lives. Erich Fromm, a psychologist, has remarked that the "normal" man in our society may well be considered insane because his society is inhuman, because he is caught up in a frenzy of economic consumption, because he is alienated from everyday artifacts whose intricacies he cannot fathom, and because he is made constantly anxious by his inability to do more than react defensively to his circumstances.[24] Herbert Marcuse, a philosopher, has defined our dilemma in terms of a one-dimensional existence, where the prevailing wisdom of science and technology so dominates us that we cannot even conceive of a second dimension of reality, a second kind of life we might prefer to live, a more relaxing and less hectic society we might choose to create.[25] And Jules Henry, an anthropologist, has observed that our culture is "against us": it is committed to technology, innovation, change, and planned obsolescence; as individuals we are unable to concentrate on the needs of the self; instead we sublimate psychic requirements in an orgy of endless consumption dictated by an economy that produces so many commodities that they must be consumed somehow.[26]

From different perspectives, then, and in different terms of reference, critics of contemporary American society agree that it is enormously difficult for any of us to stop and take stock of his situation, to think for himself, to calculate a goal in life different from that laid down in popular stereotypes, to break out of the accepted patterns of behavior. In short, it is almost impossible for us to be substantially rational, independent human beings, deliberately and freely deciding important matters according to our own values. In the end, most of us do what we must in order to survive, and we leave substantial rationality as a subject for church services and commencement exercises.

When the distinction between substantial and functional rationality is applied to the three areas of concern discussed above, it becomes apparent that social costs and functional rationality are intimately related. The aggregate of functionally rational behavior by individuals adds up to a situation in which most of us are compelled to lead lives lacking in substantive rationality, lives of frenzy, anxiety, or fear—lives that are distorted because it is impossible to fulfill our innate capacities as neighborly and communal beings. In these terms, limited participation is simply a functionally rational response to a complex political system. As it requires a great deal of effort for most of us to make even the slightest impact on political decisions, most men stay home, passive and inert. Dahl himself argued that *homo civicus* prefers the satisfactions of private life to the bother of political participation, and this would be perfectly in accord with the notion of functional rationality. The problem of permanent minorities is also at least partly a result of functional rationality. Indifference or outright hostility to the needs of others may be caused by the need to get along as best one can under immutable circumstances. Unfortunately, it *is* functionally rational for a white family to flee the central city of a metropolitan area in order to place its children in an excellent suburban public school. After all, how can one white family afford *not* to move, to be morally sensitive, to remain behind in the central city if it is not assured that other whites will also remain, that racial tensions will ease, and that central city schools will be safe and efficient? The result of such individual functional rationality, of course, is de facto segregation, increased racial tension, and thus fewer opportunities for substantial rationality in the lives of either blacks or whites. And finally, the imbalance between private and public goods is also very much a matter of functional rationality. The economic system in its ceaseless search for profits turns us into avid consumers and perpetuates the imbalance by derogating government as an instrument of economic productivity. All our standards are adjusted to the acquisition of private goods, and individual men are persuaded to assess themselves in terms of their neighbors' pecuniary accomplishments. One look out the window in a major American city quickly reveals that this is figuratively *and* literally a shortsighted system of individually functional rationality; indeed, if the smog is heavy, you may not even be able to see the length of a city block.

In the abstract, then, it can be argued that the social problems we have examined, and others that we did not examine but that are similarly expensive to society, are a consequence of men behaving in a functionally rational way, getting along by going along, or, as the British say, muddling through.´ The fundamental flaw in leading such an unexamined national existence, the critics complain, is that we pay too much attention to our fleeting *desires* and not enough to our basic needs.[27] But our desires are induced and reinforced by advertising and by the complicated technological society in which we live, while our needs and requirements as human beings may be left unexpressed, even undefined. Under the circumstances it is not very helpful to argue, as the pluralist theory did, that the process of American politics is quite free, open, and competitive. As one commentator remarked about this point of view, it may be descriptively accurate insofar as it goes, but "it does not allow us to come to terms with our ideals."[28]

THE PROBLEM OF APATHY

To critics of pluralist tolerance it seems as though pluralist theory was so intent on praising Liberal political devices, such as voting and other statutory legal rights, that it ignored the obvious and tolerated the intolerable. But to leave the matter on such a note would be unfair to the men who expounded pluralist theory; the critics, after all, do not possess a monopoly on idealism and compassion, and they do not see the world so clearly as to perceive social costs and injustices to which Dahl and other pluralists are blind.

What is the crucial difference separating the pluralist theorists from those who explicitly rejected the encouraging selectivity of the Prophylactic Perspective? Although generalizations are hazardous in dealing with the opinions of a great many commentators, nevertheless, some scholars have argued that the fundamental difference between pluralists and antipluralists may be found in their respective judgments concerning limited political participation or, in a word, apathy. Apathy surely *exists,* but what does it *imply?* The critics of pluralist tolerance by and large hold that apathy is inherently undesirable for several reasons: it stands as evidence of an underdeveloped civic personality; it is a sign of alienation and frustration; and it may be linked to such enormous problems as de facto segregation and the mounting dangers of economic imbalance. The critics call for a society of nonapathetic, fully participating citizens,[29] a society of "mature individuals"[30] who presumably will think reasonable thoughts and lead substantively rational lives. In the end, it is hoped, such a society will function without great social costs. The Prophylactic Perspective is charged with comfortably accepting apathy while failing to elaborate on the benefits that would flow from overcoming it.

But was the pluralist view simply misleading, or did it instead concentrate attention on another concept of social costs and benefits, the value of the political system as a whole? Some critics complain that pluralist theory concerned itself with the health of the entire body politic rather than that of the individual citizen,[31] but this may be precisely the reason why pluralist theory accepted apathy. Briefly, Dahl and his pluralist associates stood in a tradition of post-World War II orthodoxy among American political scientists and that orthodoxy actually approves of the systemic virtues of limited participation and apathy. Writing in a century plagued by totalitarianism, and speaking in the shadow of the Cold War, many political scientists have noted that apathy may contribute to national political stability, and that without that stability even such benefits as do flow from the existing political system would be denied us. In other words, stability may be viewed as a cardinal political benefit, an asset so valuable that on balance some social costs are not intolerable.

In this view of apathy,[32] it is observed that where the great majority of men are ideologically impassioned, where they have definite opinions on every conceivable aspect of public policy, and where they insist on an affirmative voice in the formulation of that policy, compromise becomes difficult if not impossible. Governments then become either fickle or rigid, mobs appear in the streets, social order collapses, and dictatorship may ensue. In *Who Governs?*, Dahl refined this point of view with his concept of slack power. Slack power was deemed a vital control over the activities of elites, yet it only exists because most men are apathetic and therefore ordinarily leave their potential power unused. Where slack power is present, then, dictatorship is impossible, but so long as the functional requirement of slack power is a considerable measure of apathy, it appears that apathy itself is a functional requirement of democracy and a bulwark against totalitarianism.

From this point a democratic political system can be convincingly characterized as a balanced division of political labor.[33] Some men lead and others follow, and those who lead are sensibly restrained by their awareness of the ultimate control that may be exercised by those who follow. Stability—or "equilibrium" in David Truman's vocabulary—is the happy result of such democratic politics and once it is assured a society can get on with the business of dealing with its social problems.

It was on this notion of a division of political labor that pluralists and the critics of pluralist tolerance parted company.[34] Dahl would contend that such a division is acceptable because it not only produces stability but may help to reduce social costs. After all, every citizen in America possesses some rights and some resources, and if his private life becomes intolerable Dahl assumed he will overcome his apathy—or "inertia," as the pluralists preferred to call it—and join his neighbors in instructing government to solve urgent problems. But those who found apathy intolerable argued that it does not flow from subjective choice, that the political and economic systems impose it,[35] that it cannot be shed quickly to deal with social problems, and that widespread apathy may in fact cause or perpetuate such problems. For Dahl's critics, then, an enduring division of political labor is per se a sign of nondemocratic politics, of politics that deny men freedom to make an independent and objective political choice.

As a typical critic of apathy, Peter Bachrach conceded that in the long run it is administratively impossible to enable many men to participate in political decision-making at high levels of government. But he argued that we can compensate for such limited opportunities by instituting reforms permitting more participation in the private realms of power that exist in the corporate world.[36] As a result of more participatory activity in decision-making on the job, so to speak, most men will presumably grow more mature and responsible, gain incentive and experience, become substantially rational, develop competence as both leaders *and* followers, and eventually go on to create a better society. Such an optimistic assessment of the potential abilities of men is no more than a modern reiteration of classical Liberal aspirations, fully in accord with the predominant Liberal ideology in America, with the rhetoric of Fourth of July speeches, Veterans' Day eulogies, and State of the Union messages.

In a society so thoroughly committed to Liberal ideology, the critics of pluralist tolerance may seem to some to be on the side of angels, and pluralists somewhere else. But when intelligent men differ, it is the better part of wisdom to give serious consideration to their alternative views. Perhaps there is more than a grain of truth in the pluralist view of apathy. No doubt apathy is more deep seated and more difficult to overcome than the pluralist theory suggests, and to this extent the critics are persuasive; but just as surely there is danger in the possible effects of very widespread political participation. Even Robert Pranger remarked that the politics of participation that he recommended "may be inimical to order, for sobriety is not necessarily a cardinal citizen virtue."[37] Radicals may wish to recall this when they deplore the effects of mobilizing a great many ordinary citizens in support of George Wallace's Presidential campaign in 1968, while the "silent majority" may also pause to consider what they believe to be the extremely dangerous effects of grass roots phenomena such as antiwar demonstrations, student sit-ins on college campuses, and the various militant black movements.

There is, of course, no definitive answer to the question of whether apathy is desirable or not, for our assessment of apathy must depend on the circumstances of the times, the kind of stability that is being preserved, the price that that stability costs us separately and collectively. All we need to note is that pluralist theory highlighted those qualities of the American political system that are unquestionably Liberal, and slid smoothly over limited political participation and all it entails, the most glaringly non-Liberal aspect of our politics. But when stability began to dissolve in the late 1960s under the pressure of racial tensions, the Vietnam war, crime, poverty, and other seemingly intractable difficulties, both scholars and ordinary people began to ask searching questions about apathy and indifference to government, neighbors, and public needs. From all this, the pluralist theory became less than convincing as an adequate explanation of community power and democracy. We have reached a point at which further discussion of these two subjects must concentrate on matters the reassuring selectivity of *Who Governs?* did not.

NOTES

1/ Robert Paul Wolff, "Beyond Tolerance," in Wolff, Barrington Moore, Jr., and Herbert Marcuse, *A Critique of Pure Tolerance* (Boston: Beacon, 1965), p. 4.

2/ Herbert Marcuse, "Repressive Tolerance," in *ibid.,* p. 82.

3/ Robert Pranger, *The Eclipse of Citizenship: Power and Participation in Contemporary Politics* (New York: Holt, Rinehart and Winston, 1968).

4/ Pranger specifically cites Dahl's writings as typical of the views of political scientists on modern democracies, *ibid.,* p. 3.

5/ *Ibid.,* pp. 2–5.

6/ *Ibid.,* p. 52.

7/ *Ibid.,* pp. 52–53.

8/ *The New York Times,* November 16, 1969, p. 61.

9/ Pranger, *The Eclipse of Citizenship,* pp. 27–28. For an empirical study of the degree to which elected officials actually respond to voter preferences, see Kenneth Prewitt, "Political Ambitions, Volunteerism, and Electoral Accountability," *American Political Science Review* (March 1970), pp. 5–17.

10/ Columnist James Reston analyzed Richard Nixon's strategy of appealing to all elements of the political spectrum during the 1968 Presidential campaign. See *The New York Times,* August 10, 1968, p. 12.

11/ The phrase "presidium of elites" is from Robert Presthus, *Men at the Top* (New York: Oxford University Press, 1964), p. 31.

12/ Robert A. Dahl, *Who Governs?* (New Haven: Yale University Press, 1961), pp. 293–294.

13/ The "Southern strategy" is outlined in Kevin Phillips, *The Emerging Republican Majority* (New Rochelle, N.Y.: Arlington House, 1969).

14/ See Stokely Carmichael and Charles V. Hamilton, *Black Power: The Politics of Liberation in America* (New York: Vintage, 1967), *passim.*

15/ For example, see Garrett de Bell (ed.), *The Environmental Handbook: Prepared for the First National Environment Teach-In* (New York: Ballantine, 1970); and Robert and Leona Train Rienow, *Moment in the Sun: A Report on the Deteriorating Quality of the American Environment* (New York: Ballantine, 1967).

16/ John Kenneth Galbraith, *The Affluent Society* (Boston: Houghton Mifflin, 1958).

17/ *Ibid.,* p. 251–269.

18/ *Ibid.,* p. 260–261; see also pp. 152–160.

19/ Lane Davis, "The Cost of Realism: Contemporary Restatements of Democracy," *Western Political Quarterly* (March 1964), p. 39.

20/ Graeme Duncan and Steven Lukes, "The New Democracy," *Political Studies* (June 1963), p. 163.

21/ Karl Mannheim, *Man and Society in an Age of Reconstruction* (London: Routledge and Kegan Paul, 1940), pp. 51–58.

22/ Robert Paul Wolff, *The Poverty of Liberalism* (Boston: Beacon, 1968), p. 90.

23/ Mannheim, *Man and Society,* pp. 58–60.

24/ Erich Fromm, *The Sane Society* (New York: Holt, Rinehart and Winston, 1955).

25/ Herbert Marcuse, *One Dimensional Man* (Boston: Beacon, 1964).

26/ Jules Henry, *Culture Against Man* (New York: Vintage, 1963).

27/ This is the basic theme in Galbraith, *The Affluent Society;* Fromm, *The Sane Society;* Marcuse, *One Dimensional Man;* and Henry, *Culture Against Man.*

28/ Henry S. Kariel, *The Promise of Politics* (Englewood Cliffs, N.J.: Prentice-Hall, 1966), p. 19.

29/ This is the basic theme of all the works cited in notes 1, 9, 20, 21, 25, 26 and 29 of this chapter.

30/ Kariel, *The Promise of Politics,* p. 83.

31/ See Davis, "The Cost of Realism," p. 42; and Duncan and Lukes, "The New Democracy," p. 169.

32/ For examples of this view, see Bernard Berelson, Paul Lazarfeld, and William McPhee, *Voting* (Chicago: University of Chicago Press, 1954), pp. 305–323; William Kornhauser, *The Politics of Mass Society* (Glencoe, Ill.: Free Press, 1959); Gabriel A. Almond and Sidney Verba, *The Civic Culture* (Boston: Little, Brown, 1965), pp. 337–374; Lester Milbrath, *Political Participation* (Chicago: Rand McNally, 1965), pp. 142–154; and W. H. Morris Jones, "In Defense of Apathy: Some Doubts on the Duty to Vote," *Political Studies* (February 1954), pp. 25–37.

33/ Milbrath, *ibid.,* p. 143 ff.

34/ Peter Bachrach, *The Theory of Democratic Elitism* (Boston: Little, Brown, 1967), p. 95.

35/ For a brief and incisive analytical argument along these lines, see Morris Rosenberg, "Some Determinants of Political Apathy," *Public Opinion Quarterly* (Winter 1954), pp. 349–366.

36/ Bachrach, *The Theory of Democratic Elitism,* pp. 86–88, 95–98, and 102–105.

37/ Pranger, *The Eclipse of Citizenship,* p. 92.

◦ **11** ◦

The Present Scholarly Impasse

Since the academic controversy caused by the New Haven study, no comprehensive new theories have been introduced into the debate over community power and democracy. Scholarship continues, but for the most part it either proceeds along theoretical lines already laid down by earlier research, or it is so narrow in scope and technical in nature that it does not advance our understanding of the complex issue of democracy. In short, the challenge and response of polemical confrontation in the field of community power studies has come to an impasse; ferment is sustained, but no progress is made. Scholars who have fixed views criticize each other with much confidence and little charity, but hardly anything original is being said. As a case in point, in 1967 G. William Domhoff produced an up-to-date positional study of national power, *Who Rules America?*, and Nelson Polsby promptly called it "amateur sociology," shedding "no light whatever on how anything works."[1]

The impasse exists—that much is certain—but it is difficult to pinpoint precisely the terms of the stand-off. Roughly speaking, scholars seem to have divided into two camps, each holding firm to a different view of what we have called the process theory of democracy. On the one hand, there are those who rely on group theory and pluralist theory, and use these either separately or in combination to describe the American political system as a flourishing democracy, give or take a few structural flaws such as the seniority system in Congress. All these men may be referred to as *pluralists*,[2] because in essence those who formulated what we have specifically called the pluralist theory of democracy simply agreed with earlier commentators such as Truman that power in America is widely dispersed; Dahl's nominally pluralist theory in this sense only superseded and refined but did not reject Truman's work. On the other hand, there are the scholars who hold to the logic and findings of the reputational and positional theories of elitism; relying on these alone, or in combination with later charges against the theory and practice of pluralism, they insist that something is seriously wrong with the American political process, that we deceive ourselves into unwarranted complacency when we label our politics substantially democratic. All these men we shall call *antipluralists*,[3] assuming that even though the critics of pluralist theory per se added to the concepts earlier employed by Hunter and Mills, they were in full agreement with such scholarly predecessors in the critical conviction that power attaches to public and private institutions, habits, the economy, and other enduring social phenomena. This second group does not reject the idea that a democracy can be defined in terms of workable processes, but its members assert, albeit without perfect agreement among themselves, that certain current practices must be eliminated and others quickly established so that the revised process will be *truly* democratic.

On its surface, the impasse seems easy to explain. For each great theory of community power there has been a counter-theory; for every element of each theory there has been a plausible criticism; and for every criticism there has been a not-unreasonable rejoinder. The impasse might be defined, then, in terms of a large number of scholars committed to theoretical and methodological views that can always be challenged on the ground that they are apparently no more valid than patently contradictory views. For some reason or another, each scholar takes a position in the debate, and he is invariably confronted by another scholar who has taken an opposing position. Since all the people involved in this picking and choosing are confident of the wisdom embodied in their methods and the ultimate truth revealed by their research, the result is an impasse.

But to explain the impasse as a result of equally convincing logical and analytical rationales is to fail to explain why some persons choose the positions they do in fact take. "For some reason or another" each scholar takes a stance that, as we have repeatedly seen, actually seems to predetermine the findings of any research he will conduct; and thus "for some reason or another" he takes a position that will foreseeably lead him to either favorable or unfavorable commentary on our political system. Whatever these reasons are, we can be certain that they are singularly important, because they must represent and reflect the force of an ideological factor that bears on the issue of democracy. Beneath the surface of the impasse, there must be a very fundamental force at work that tends to create the stalemate, that tends to direct some scholars to the pluralist camp and other scholars to the antipluralist camp.

Unfortunately, it is extremely difficult to comprehend this force directly, because most contemporary social scientists do not make their normative biases explicit. Nonetheless, in a roundabout way, we can gain some appreciation of their preferences; we can assume that it is possible to know what the social scientists of either school of thought accomplish with their research, even if it is often virtually impossible to know *why* they set out to accomplish it. Such an assumption does no violence to the argument of this book thus far, for we have already examined the accomplishments of four community power theories without inquiring very closely into the normative convictions of their chief proponents. If this mode of analysis is extended to ascertain the accomplishments on both sides of the community power study impasse, it will not be necessary to make speculative and perhaps unfounded assertions about why certain scholars *choose* one side or another of the impasse; we need only advance an hypothesis as to why, in light of their accomplishments, they *remain* unreconstructed and uncompromising. Without attempting to deal with the very tricky problem of the *origins* of the impasse, then, we can shed some light on why it *persists*. In this manner, we can even predict that the impasse will not soon be broken.

THE LOGIC OF POLEMICAL DISPUTATION

Let us begin to explore the persistence of the impasse by high-lighting a peculiar fact found in the discussion in the last chapter. On the issue of apathy, critics of Dahl's complimentary vision of American politics were grouped with those Americans who maintain idealistic Liberal hopes and expectations for democracy and a good society. But how could Dahl's critics be classified as Liberal, if Dahl and Truman were persuasive precisely because they were *Liberal*, because their theories were ideologically reassuring and comfortable? If both pluralists and antipluralists actually stand together within the Liberal tradition, why the impasse at all? If, so to speak, Dahl and Pranger are ideologically capable of delivering a Fourth of July speech liberally—and Liberally—sprinkled with expressions such as "liberty," "opportunity," "freedom of expression," "frequent elections," "choices of policy," and so forth, what is it that separates the two men?

To appreciate the implication of the paradox here we must set it against the sweep of intellectual history. Briefly speaking, America developed as a society marked by Liberal institutions and a strongly Liberal outlook, yet for more than a century this same society has been challenged by Conservatism on the Right and Socialism on the Left. In fact, the challenge from both sides was very keenly felt, because America was *too* Liberal; that is, without an historical background of feudalism and class-based institutions, and therefore without great and home-grown internal diversity of opinion as in France, Italy, or England, the prevailing orthodoxy of Liberalism in America viewed any ideological deviation as foreign, perverse, and perhaps even dangerous. Our dominant beliefs and our dominant institutions were deemed natural and good;[4] and that was that.

But America's sensitivity to divergent views has always been a source of great trouble for dissenters in our solidly Liberal society. If one does not espouse Liberal tenets concerning the nature of men, the characteristics of groups, and the possibilities for responsible democratic government, one may look suspiciously like either a Conservative or a Socialist. Such has been the unwelcome fate of many who have deviated from the Liberal mainstream. Early in the life of our Republic the Federalists were accused of being Conservatives, of wanting to make George Washington a king; and more recently those we usually call "liberal" are sometimes also called Socialists, for various reasons and by various opponents. Yet it must be remembered, and this is a point of enormous consequence, that originally the ideological tenets of Liberals, Conservatives, and Socialists were formulated in logical opposition to one another. Therefore regardless of an American dissenter's formal affiliations or what he chooses to call himself, if he disagrees with the orthodox outlook, *the logic of polemical disputation* dictates that he will assume a position that can be branded heretically Conservative or Socialist.

The relation of all this to the impasse in community power studies is not obvious at first glance, but we are actually repeating the tri-partite pattern of ideological confrontation, with new actors playing old roles. The scenario is very complicated and involves a great many actors, but the plot may be simplified and likened to an interplay of several roles in the style of the Japanese drama *Rashomon*.[5] In that play, an occurrence is observed by several characters on stage, some actually participating in its enactment. When the activity is completed, however, it is discovered that each character has formed his own impressions of what happened and what he and the others did. The same is true of the scholars locked into the community power studies impasse; the two schools opposing each other have their own respective views of what they and the other side have accomplished, so there are four roles in the impasse, all differentially perceived: (1) the antipluralists believe themselves to be heirs of the Liberal tradition because they espouse classical Liberal hopes and expectations for every man in a democratic society; (2) the pluralists view themselves as modern-day Liberals because they support Liberal political institutions and practices; but (3) the antipluralists act as if pluralists are really Conservatives in disguise; and (4) the pluralists seem to suspect that antipluralists are expounding Socialist principles. The pattern of accomplishments that each side sees for itself and its opponents thus leads directly to a deadlock even though, as we have observed, both parties to the impasse in fact claim to occupy the Center and serve its Liberalism.

THE ANTIPLURALIST POSITION

Again briefly, the role that antipluralists perceive themselves playing is characterized by the political goal of substantial rationality for all men. As Henry Kariel put it, "the only publicly defensible good . . . [is] a society of individuals in command of themselves."[6] John Stuart Mill, the greatest of nineteenth-century English Liberals, outlined this objective for classical Liberalism when he asserted that "the worth of a State . . . is the worth of the individuals composing it; and a State which postpones the interests of their mental expansion and elevation" will find that it has failed to provide for the replenishment of its own vital life force.[7]

The ideological peculiarity of the Liberal quest for a society of reasonable men is that such a quest has also been pursued by Socialists, and by Marxists in particular. We have already noted the similarity of Liberal and Marxist expectations (see pp. 23–24), and although their terminology differs, substantial rationality is very much a part of the Marxian concept of man as a *species-being,* as an animal uniquely endowed with a potential for reason and a capacity to mature as a thinking creature. It has always been clear, of course, that many men do *not* think properly, and Marxists explained this by arguing that the fault lies with society; it is society that creates false consciousness, a compulsive kind of thinking that is forced on men by their circumstances and that leads them away from their objective interests. Given Marxian hopes, it was entirely logical to blame the shortage of reasonable men on society, and when confronted by the unreasonableness of many men in America, antipluralists have similarly blamed society.

It is thus a major contention of antipluralist scholars that we cannot accept the present behavior of men as final proof that they are capable of no better; apathy, on this score, is *not* an indication that limited participation is all men can collectively achieve. To accept only the observable facts virtually predetermines the conclusion that what is, ought to be, or, as Peter Bachrach put the same proposition in social science language, reliance on "explanatory theory" alone would lead us "to accept as unalterable the configuration of society as shaped by impersonal forces."[8] On this point, a great many critics of conditions as they exist in America today agree. C. Wright Mills, Erich Fromm, John Kenneth Galbraith, Herbert Marcuse, Jules Henry, Henry Kariel, Peter Bachrach, Graeme Duncan, Steven Lukes, Lane Davis, Robert Pranger: each of these men argues in his own way that society, through the family, the economy, and the polity, shapes men in limited patterns. We must therefore go beyond the evidence such patterns present in order to plan in terms of what men *ought* to do, *ought* to want, *ought* to receive, *ought* to pay for. Like it or not, this point of view may be said to resemble Marxism.

As Polsby has remarked, this rejection of the facts as inconclusive does not conform to pluralist research standards. If we cannot accept the facts of human behavior as evidence of both our capacities and our limitations, we are led to a situation where each researcher must decide for himself what the real interests of all men are.[9] Polsby did not add, although he might have, that antipluralist reasoning along these lines can make for intense ideological confrontation, with various and perhaps antagonistic groups claiming to speak on behalf of the *real* interests of workers, students, the poor, blacks, American Indians, consumers, and others. The pluralists pride themselves on their tough-minded sensibility, their allegedly dispassionate analysis of the world as it really is. To them, antipluralist logic probably partakes of the confusing notion that one should not let the facts stand in the way of the truth, or, as Marcuse put it more elegantly, "the telos of tolerance is truth."[10]

Moreover, if we recall the insistence of antipluralists, from Hunter to Mills to Kariel to Bachrach, that unequal distribution of economic resources makes an inevitable and unjust impact on our political rights and their exercise—that the rulers of the economic realm cannot be ignored when we consider power in the political realm—it is quite plausible to conclude that what the antipluralists have actually accomplished is a Marxian style analysis of American society, with or without a commitment to Marxism itself. We cannot be sure that all pluralists believe this to be the case, but we can be fairly certain that for so long as the categories of antipluralist thought remain unchanged, pluralists will feel that somehow those categories are uncomfortable and unreliable. Antipluralist notions will thus continue to be unacceptable to pluralists who, after all, think that *they* are the bearers of the Liberal tradition.

THE PLURALIST POSITION

Pluralists do in fact seem to believe that they stand alone in the role of true modern-day Liberals, a belief that is implicit in Dahl's response to his critic, Jack Walker, who called for more political participation. Dahl correctly pointed out that "classical" democratic theorists—including Liberals such as John Stuart Mill—disagreed on how much political participation is desirable or even humanly possible;[11] indeed, the only common ground among democratic theorists has always been an insistence on a free and open method for electing leaders. Given the historical disagreement and the solitary point of unquestionable agreement, we may assume that the pluralists, whether they emphasize Dahl's concepts or Truman's or both, think of themselves as fundamentally democratic and Liberal. Certainly they do endorse the basic, undisputed lynchpin of Liberalism, the everyday democratic belief that we must guarantee frequent elections and inviolable civil rights in order that we may choose our leaders and make them responsible.

Acceptance of Liberal democratic practices is matched by the pluralists' rejection of an important Socialist charge—that Liberal politics is ultimately a matter of competing class interests. As we have observed in regard to Truman's view of groups, and as the conclusions of the New Haven study concerning the political stratum also demonstrate, pluralists say that Liberal politics in fact consist of *factional strife* rather than *class conflict*.[12] Groups are seen as collectivities that extend vertically through class strata in American society, and so long as they are free to organize or disband, policy choices are assured for every segment of every American community. Relying on this conceptualization of our politics, pluralists offer their research as proof that the economy and the polity are not inextricably linked. They may therefore tend to view themselves as Liberals of the Center, and to classify antipluralists who disagree with them as somewhere on the Left.

Pluralists perceive their accomplishment as distinctively Liberal, but their opponents see pluralist scholarship as intentionally or unconsciously Conservative.[13] Pluralists are committed to empirical research, or, as Truman put it, "inquiry into how men *ought* to act is not a concern of research in political behavior."[14] The danger with purely empirical research, as many critics have pointed out, is that it tends to suggest a level of human competence equal only to existing circumstances, and therefore it gives us no incentive to *change* those circumstances. Conservatives, of course, historically sought *no* change, and their emphasis on empirical facts may be likened to Truman's. Edmund Burke, for example, insinuated that commoners in France had no right to govern because they had no experience at governing;[15] it could be argued, however, that the Third Estate had no experience at governing only because it had never been *permitted* to govern before the French Revolution. Similarly, Dahl concluded that most men in New Haven should be called *homo civicus* because they are *naturally* indifferent to politics and do little participating; but many critics reply that our political system *forces* men into apathy, and that a truly Liberal concept of man must be prescriptive, not merely descriptive, of this oppressive reality.[16]

The pluralist emphasis on facts instead of ideals had led to a second emphasis, which we noted in Chapter 10 and which may also be construed as Conservative. Democracy is now defined by pluralists as a political system rooted in a balanced division of political labor. But in the logic of confrontation among Liberalism, Conservatism, and Socialism, a division of political labor is exactly analogous to the Conservative conception of political groups. Some men should govern, and others should follow; all men have their places and their responsibilities in the community; and when all men make their appropriate contributions, a stable and decent society will be established and maintained. In the reality of American politics, which pluralists have by and large endorsed, more and more of a division of labor appears, with numerous oligarchical structures of power: labor unions, corporations, universities, government bureaucracies, and more. Yet as Kariel pointed out, "in preserving a wildly complicated, interlaced federalism, we have actually accepted the ground for a community structure which in many revealing ways resembles that of previous, seemingly remote societies, notably the Western European society of the *Ancien Regime*,"[17] the French monarchy that Burke made it his business to justify.

SUMMARY

The foregoing analysis must be judged partly speculative, for it has impressed on community power research a series of generalizations that may not be acceptable to all researchers who are a party to the impasse. Nevertheless, it does not seem unreasonable to argue (1) that pluralists and antipluralists see themselves respectively as the true heirs of Liberalism; and (2) that both schools of thought find their own presumptions, methods, and conclusions comfortable and persuasive. Yet, (3) the two parties to the impasse certainly see their opponents' work as analytically incompatible with their own; and (4) since the logic of their respective positions is so contrarily symmetrical and comparable to other historical schools of thought, the two parties probably see each other's work as ideologically distasteful. Under these circumstances the impasse continues, with both pluralists and antipluralists secure and confident in their self-styled roles as theorists of the Center—theorists of moderation, balance, decency, and reason.

From all this we can conclude that the impasse will persist, at least for some time. In order to break it, an imaginative scholar must come forward with a new theory of community power that avoids any resemblance to the three great historical ideologies, that discovers a fourth position of analysis and prescription. Yet there is much in the logic of polemical disputation to suggest that most of our arguments about power *must* fall into one or another of the already existing categories of thought and therefore only reinforce the impasse. Consequently, for so long as we

lack the necessary new theory, we can expect at best only
scholarly refinement of the old ones.

NOTES

1/ G. William Domhoff, *Who Rules America?* (Englewood
Cliffs, N.J.: Prentice-Hall, 1967); Nelson W. Polsby, "Review of G. William Domhoff, *Who Rules America?*," *American Sociological Review* (June 1968), p. 477.

2/ The community power scholars, here called pluralists, belong to a larger group of pluralists, mostly political scientists,
who have commented on all aspects of American politics—
institutions such as Congress and the Supreme Court, as well
as whole communities—and concluded that we enjoy democracy. For discussions of pluralists in general, see Theodore J.
Lowi, *The End of Liberalism: Ideology, Policy, and the
Crisis of Public Authority* (New York: Norton, 1969), pp.
29–54; and Darryl Baskin, "American Pluralism: Theory,
Practice, and Ideology," *Journal of Politics* (February 1970),
pp. 71–95.

3/ The term "antipluralist" is not entirely satisfactory, because
it implies that the scholars it labels are opposed to diversity,
which is not true. But the term usually used to characterize
those opposed to pluralist notions is "elitist," and that is
even more unsatisfactory in this context because it implies
that those who oppose the existing situation in American
politics are in favor of rule by elites. William E. Connolly,
Political Science and Ideology (New York: Atherton, 1967),
pp. 22–24 ff. and 31–41 ff., uses the term "elitist" as opposed
to "pluralist."

4/ Daniel J. Boorstin, *The Genius of American Politics*
(Chicago: Phoenix, 1958), pp. 8–35.

5/ Fay M. Kanin and Michael Kanin, *Rashomon* (New York:
Random House, 1959).

6/ Henry S. Kariel, *The Promise of Politics* (Englewood Cliffs,
N.J.: Prentice-Hall, 1966), p. 25.

7/ John Stuart Mill, *On Liberty* (orig., 1859; New York: Library of Liberal Arts, 1956), pp. 140–141.

8/ Peter Bachrach, *The Theory of Democratic Elitism* (Boston: Little, Brown, 1967), p. 99.

9/ Nelson W. Polsby, *Community Power and Political Theory* (New Haven: Yale University Press, 1963), p. 23.

10/ Herbert Marcuse, "Repressive Tolerance," in Robert Paul Wolff, Barrington Moore, Jr., and Herbert Marcuse, *A Critique of Pure Tolerance* (Boston: Beacon, 1965), p. 90.

11/ Robert A. Dahl, "Further Reflections on 'The Elitist Theory of Democracy,'" *American Political Science Review* (June 1966), pp. 296–297, 305.

12/ Robert A. Dahl, *Who Governs?* (New Haven: Yale University Press, 1961), p. 83; and Polsby, *Community Power and Political Theory*, pp. 90–94.

13/ Henry S. Kariel, *The Decline of American Pluralism* (Stanford: Stanford University Press, 1961), pp. 113–137; and C. Wright Mills, *The Power Elite* (New York: Galaxy, 1959), pp. 325–342.

14/ David B. Truman, "The Implications of Political Behavior Research," *Items* (December 1951), p. 39.

15/ Edmund Burke, *Reflections of the Revolution in France* (orig., 1790; New York: Library of Liberal Arts, 1955), pp. 46.

16/ Graeme Duncan and Steven Lukes, "The New Democracy," *Political Studies* (June 1963), pp. 156–177; and Lane Davis, "The Cost of Realism: Contemporary Restatements of Democracy," *Western Political Quarterly* (March 1964), pp. 37–46.

17/ Kariel, *The Decline of American Pluralism*, p. 129.

° **12** °

A Proposal for Specific Inquiries

It has taken eleven chapters to trace the logic of community power analysis to the present scholarly impasse. In the Introduction, readers were warned that power and democracy are extraordinarily complex matters, and that the net effect of even the most careful scholarly thought on both is inconclusive. The impasse proves this to be the case, yet no doubt some readers are even now thinking: *Now* comes the brilliant closing stroke, the masterly suggestion that cuts the Gordian knot of ideology that grips community power research and logic, the simple but profound truth, somehow overlooked thus far, that will enable us to weigh power precisely and determine definitively whether we do or do not enjoy democracy in America.

Unfortunately, there is no such simple truth, no easy way to measure and assess power in our ideologically volatile circumstances. It may be possible, however, to circumvent the impasse and reach selectively beyond it to specific matters that are unquestionably significant and clearly merit our utmost attention. Some conclusions are in order about the possibility of an approach to community power and democracy that would be fashioned from two elements: the process theory of democracy and an emphasis on issue areas of enormous importance.

THE NEED FOR A NEW FOCUS OF INQUIRY

The process theory is useful because it offers a widely acceptable formula for judging our politics. In fact, both pluralists and antipluralists alike agree that democracy can be defined in terms of competitive processes; their dispute arises only when pluralists tend to equate *existing* processes with democracy, while antipluralists argue in favor of *new* practices and procedures. The source of contention is an implicit presumption that underlies the process theory, a presumption that may be brought to light by quoting Joseph Schumpeter's now familiar definition: "The democratic method is that institutional arrangement for arriving at political decisions in which individuals acquire the power to decide by means of a competitive struggle for the people's vote." In this theory of democracy, it is clear that the notion of "fairness" is implied and should be inserted into Schumpeter's terms as follows: the democratic method proceeds "by means of a [*fair*] competitive struggle for the people's vote."[1] Obviously, we do not wish to tolerate an armed competition for "the people's vote," which in effect takes place in a totalitarian state with one-party, *pro forma* elections. Armed competition is inherently *unfair,* and is therefore the mark of an *undemocratic* polity. In short, a state is to be judged truly democratic only if its political process is fair.

Opposing scholars have actually quarreled, then, over the degree of fair competition that they perceive in the political systems of America, at both local and national levels. This quarreling has resulted in a stalemate that focuses on methodological techniques that have an ideological foundation, but which may for convenience be reduced to a single question: *What shall we study in relation to democracy?* Groups? Reputations? Positions? Decisions? Nondecisions? What data will demonstrate conclusively that our politics are democratic or not?

Reducing the scholarly impasse to a single question provides a clue for by-passing the deadlock entirely, for when men disagree long and passionately on the answer to a question, the fault may lie in the question rather than the answers. In such cases, we may change the question rather than seek more accurate answers, and in the case of power analysis, this means that we must simply reject the temptation to comment comprehensively on the overall nature of the American political process. Instead of asking what counts for democracy *in general,* we should ask *where* do we enjoy democracy and *where* do we lack it? Instead of becoming entangled in the impasse over which selected data will tell us all about democracy, we should examine specific issues *where* the country clearly suffers great social, economic, and political problems. That is to say, we can easily select subject matters that are so widely recognized as unquestionably important that there can be no doubt they are worthy of our serious attention. Rather than study the entire province of political life in New Haven or Atlanta, for example, we might study only *racial tension* in New Haven, or *air pollution* in Atlanta. Consequently, without ever framing ideologically charged questions of grand social theory as to whether or not either city is generally democratic, we would be able to comment with some authority as to the competitive or uncompetitive nature of forces that bear on those specific issues in those particular cities. In effect, we could thereby apply the standard of the process theory to a limited part of the political process in any community.

POWER ANALYSIS FOR LAYMEN

By-passing the scholarly impasse on community power analysis in favor of applying the process theory directly to specific issues and problems will be especially attractive to the layman, the college student, the general reader, the alert citizen who worries about both community power and democracy because he is troubled by matters such as the Vietnam war, urban decay, discrimination, poverty, crime, and more. Even if he declines to take sides along the lines of ultimate ideological confrontation which constitute the impasse, even if he refuses to argue the great questions of democracy as they pertain to entire political systems, he can assimilate various elements of the logic of community power analysis into his own outlook and thereby sharpen his thinking about power and democracy.

Thus the importance of the kind of information contained in

Appendix B: Selected Readings on Contemporary American Problems. The reader may turn to the works cited in that Appendix or other works like them, acquaint himself with some of the facts of great American problems, and assess those facts in terms of the concepts discussed in this book. After all, analyzing a specific problem would be tantamount to analyzing a small-scale political equilibrium, a distinct range of forces that have achieved a balance vis-à-vis one another. In the matter of water pollution, for example, one would discover conservationists, consumers, manufacturers, miners, sanitation bureaucrats, fishermen, and many more ranged against one another. But it will be recalled that equilibrium situations were of great interest and concern to both pluralists and antipluralists, and that they together devised many concepts to grasp the reality of those situations. David Truman discussed the influence of "potential groups"; C. Wright Mills was dissatisfied with the "balance of power"; Robert Dahl was impressed with the impact of "slack power"; and Peter Bachrach and Morton Baratz paid close attention to the "mobilization of bias."

There are apparently some weaknesses in each of these concepts and others related to them; that much seems clear from previous chapters. But the layman may still benefit from an appreciation of such scholarly concepts, for surely he enjoys more strength, more analytical precision than common, popular concepts of power such as "the international Communist conspiracy," or "the Wall Street bankers," or "the merchants of death." In fact, scholarly concepts may be used undogmatically and with a grain of common sense by anyone who wishes to clarify his own thinking about this most intangible of substances: power. Accordingly, one might agree with Dahl that it is necessary to consider political *decisions* and how they are *indirectly influenced* by *slack power*. But one may also observe that Dahl himself pointed to military policy as an area where *"key decisions"* are made.[2] In the area of military affairs, clearly a vital matter worth much investigation, secrecy encompasses so much of what occurs—in the Pentagon, the Congress, and the White House, as in the C.I.A.—that it would seem only reasonable to use a *nondecision-making* approach to study military *decisions*, an approach that would embrace *reputations, positions, inertia,* and *mobilization of biases,* all of which affect military policy.

We may never attain absolute precision about power, of course, but the concepts created by scholars in the community power impasse come far closer to approximating reality than any other terms men have yet contrived. Laymen may use these concepts with a sense of balance and restraint in order to arrive at substantially realistic conclusions concerning the distribution and exercise of power relating to our great community problems. Then, in light of the "fair competition" standard implicit in the process theory, they may decide whether or not social, economic, and political reforms are required in those areas.

POWER ANALYSIS FOR SCHOLARS

Oddly enough, by-passing the impasse on power analysis may even find favor among community power scholars themselves. Making specific inquiries is often intellectually unexciting compared to formulating intricate statements or restatements of democratic theory. Nonetheless, community power scholars in recent years have conducted fewer and fewer comprehensive community power studies, perhaps neglecting this research genre in keeping with a great public sense of urgency, a widespread feeling that America is faced with so many serious problems as to warrant laying aside theoretical disputation and concentrating all our analytical energies on understanding and coping with those problems. In this regard, one should note that since 1961, when Dahl formulated the reassuring pluralist theory of *Who Governs?,* America has endured the shattering experiences of political assassinations, racial riots, university disruptions, the Vietnam war, antiwar demonstrations, conspiracy trial of the Chicago Seven, and urban bombings. With hindsight, we may conclude that the confidence of pluralist theory was a sign of confident times, a sort of New Frontier manifesto. But as the works in Appendix B in effect testify, those days are far behind the nation, and more and more scholarly attention is being demanded and devoted to specific and pressing community problems. Community power researchers can play an important role here by conducting substantive inquiries and by providing some of the information on power that the country needs in order to come to grips with the reality of its politics.[3]

NOTES

1/ Joseph Schumpeter, *Capitalism, Socialism and Democracy,* 3rd ed. (orig., 1942; New York: Harper & Row, 1962), p. 269.

2/ Robert A. Dahl, "A Critique of the Ruling Elite Model," *American Political Science Review* (June 1958), p. 469.

3/ An excellent example of what can be accomplished by a skilled community power researcher is Peter Bachrach's study of Baltimore racial relations *via* the nondecision-making approach. See Peter Bachrach, "A Power Analysis: The Shaping of Antipoverty Policy in Baltimore," *Public Policy* (Winter 1970), pp. 155–186.

Appendix A

Selected Readings on Community Power and Democracy

ANTON, THOMAS J. "Power, Pluralism and Local Politics," *Administrative Science Quarterly* (March 1963), pp. 425–457.

A thorough comparison of the sociological and the political science views of community power, citing works by Floyd Hunter, Robert Dahl, Nelson Polsby, and Raymond Wolfinger.

BACHRACH, PETER. *The Theory of Democratic Elitism: A Critique.* Boston: Little, Brown, 1967.

Criticizes Joseph Schumpeter and others for accepting the dominance of elites in what is commonly called "democracy."

BACHRACH, PETER, AND MORTON S. BARATZ. "Decisions and Nondecisions: An Analytical Framework," *American Political Science Review* (September 1963), pp. 632–642.

Argues that nondecisions, whereby some actions are not taken and certain options are not permitted, can be as important as well publicized and easily observed decisions.

BERELSON, BERNARD. "Democratic Theory and Public Opinion," *Public Opinion Quarterly* (Fall 1952), pp. 313–330.

One of the earliest statements of the view that American democracy can function with many ignorant and irrational voters, so long as the political system enjoys competition among viewpoints and possible policies.

CONNALLY, WILLIAM E. *Political Science and Ideology.* New York: Atherton, 1967.

A closely argued interpretation of the ideological character of different views of community power.

DAHL, ROBERT A. "Further Reflections on 'The Elitist Theory of Democracy,'" *American Political Science Review* (June 1966), pp. 296–305.

A reply to criticism that Dahl's work and that of some other political scientists too enthusiastically accepts the present role of elites in American politics.

———. "Reply to Thomas Anton's 'Power, Pluralism and Local Politics,'" *Administrative Science Quarterly* (March 1963), pp. 250–256.

A defense of the pluralist view of community power.

———. *Who Governs? Democracy and Power in an American City.* New Haven: Yale University Press, 1961.

See Chapters 7 and 8.

D'ANTONIO, WILLIAM V., AND HOWARD J. EHRLICH (eds.). *Power and Democracy in America.* South Bend, Ind.: Notre Dame University Press, 1961.

A symposium pitting Delbert C. Miller, a sociologist, against Robert Dahl, a political scientist, with different methods of studying community power attacked and defended.

DOMHOFF, G. WILLIAM. *Who Rules America?* Englewood Cliffs, N.J.: Prentice-Hall, 1967.

A national power study based on the positional method of locating elites.

——— AND HOYT B. BALLARD (eds.). *C. Wright Mills and The Power Elite.* Boston: Beacon, 1968.

A collection of scholarly articles and book reviews about C. Wright Mill's *The Power Elite.*

HUNTER, FLOYD. *Community Power Structure.* New York: Anchor, 1963.

See Chapter 5.

KARIEL, HENRY S. *The Decline of American Pluralism.* Palo Alto, Calif.: Stanford University Press, 1961.

A critical analysis of pluralism as it exists in American politics, and a rejection of pluralism as a theory of community power and democracy.

————. *The Promise of Politics*. Englewood Cliffs, N.J.: Prentice-Hall, 1966.
An appeal for a theory of democracy that will go beyond describing what ought to be.

KEYNES, EDWARD, AND DAVID M. RICCI (eds.). *Political Power, Community, and Democracy*. Chicago: Rand McNally, 1970.
A collection of articles on community power and democracy, plus an extensive annotated bibliography on community power.

KORNHAUSER, WILLIAM. *The Politics of Mass Society*. Glencoe, Ill.: Free Press, 1959.
Argues that democracy must encourage the formation and persistance of groups that will mediate between the masses and elites.

LOWI, THEODORE J. *The End of Liberalism: Ideology, Policy, and the Crisis of Public Authority*. New York: Norton, 1969.
Argues that interest groups control many government agencies and that democracy can only be restored by clearly defining the powers and responsibilities of those agencies.

MARCUSE, HERBERT. *One Dimensional Man*. Boston: Beacon, 1964.
A philosophical interpretation of existing diversity in American politics, with the conclusion that enforced conformity permits Americans only superficial and meaningless choices of policies and life styles.

MAYO, HENRY B. *An Introduction to Democratic Theory*. New York: Oxford University Press, 1960.
A theory of democracy based on the notion that competition of parties and leaders is both the sign and the requisite of democratic political systems.

MCCONNELL, GRANT. *Private Power and American Democracy*. New York: Knopf, 1966.
A study of how interest groups dominate certain government agencies.

MCCOY, CHARLES A., AND JOHN PLAYFORD (eds.). *Apolitical Politics: A Critique of Behavioralism*. New York: Crowell, 1967.
A collection of some of the most influential articles critical of the pluralist acceptance of elite influence in American politics. Includes articles by men such as Peter Bachrach, Morton

Baratz, Graeme Duncan, Steven Lukes, Lane Davis, Christian Bay, James Petras, and Jack Walker.

MILLS, C. WRIGHT. *The Power Elite*. New York: Galaxy, 1959.
See Chapter 6.

OLSON, MANCUR. *The Logic of Collective Action: Public Goods and the Theory of Groups*. Cambridge, Mass.: Harvard University Press, 1965.
Explains why unorganized interests in society have difficulty getting organized, and why they can therefore be slighted by political leaders who make policy.

POLSBY, NELSON W. *Community Power and Political Theory*. New Haven, Conn.: Yale University Press, 1963.
Surveys a great many community power studies from the pluralist point of view and concludes that most of them lack analytical precision.

PRANGER, ROBERT J. *The Eclipse of Citizenship: Power and Participation in Contemporary Politics*. New York: Holt, Rinehart and Winston, 1968.
Argues that most people in America are for a variety of reasons excluded from political participation, even though they enjoy formal rights to participate.

SCHATTSCHNEIDER, E. E. *The Semi-Sovereign People: A Realist's View of Democracy in America*. New York: Holt, Rinehart and Winston, 1960.
An analysis of American national politics that concludes that most effective political groups operate on behalf of business or property.

SCHUMPETER, JOSEPH. *Capitalism, Socialism and Democracy*, 3rd ed. New York: Harper & Row, 1962.
See Chapter 3.

TRUMAN, DAVID B. *The Governmental Process*. New York: Knopf, 1951.
See Chapter 4.

WOLFF, ROBERT PAUL, BARRINGTON MOORE, JR., AND HERBERT MARCUSE. *A Critique of Pure Tolerance*. Boston: Beacon, 1965.
Three essays that agree that America is now tolerating political opinions, pressures for conformity, and specific groups, all of which are inimical to an ideal society.

WOLFINGER, RAYMOND E. "Reputation and Reality in the Study

of Community Power," *American Sociological Review* (October 1960) , pp. 636–644.
A discussion from the pluralist point of view of how the reputational approach to community power fails to distinguish between actual power and potential power, between reputation and reality.

Appendix B

Selected Readings on Contemporary American Problems

The books cited here all pertain to problems that raise urgent questions concerning the exercise of community power and the democratic quality of our politics. Some of these books deal with more than one problem, but the topical headings indicate their major emphasis. The volumes marked by an asterisk are available in paperback editions.

Race Relations

*BALDWIN, JAMES. *The Fire Next Time*. New York: Dell, 1962.

*BARBOUR, FLOYD (ed.). *The Black Power Revolt*. Boston: Porter Sargent, 1968.

*CARMICHAEL, STOKELY, AND CHARLES HAMILTON. *Black Power: The Politics of Liberation in America*. New York: Vintage, 1967.

*CLEAVER, ELDRIDGE. *Soul on Ice*. New York: Delta, 1968.

*KILLIAN, LEWIS M. *The Impossible Revolution: Black Power and American Dream*. New York: Random House, 1968.

*MENDELSON, WALLACE. *Discrimination*. Englewood Cliffs, N.J.: Prentice-Hall, 1962.

*SILBERMAN, CHARLES E. *Crisis in Black and White*. New York: Vintage, 1964.

*WRIGHT, NATHAN, JR. *Black Power and Urban Unrest*. New York: Hawthorne, 1967.

Urban Affairs

*JACOBS, JANE. *The Death and Life of Great American Cities.* New York: Vintage, 1961.

*————. *The Economy of Cities.* New York: Vintage, 1970.

*JACOBS, PAUL. *Prelude to Riot: A View of Urban America from the Bottom.* New York: Vintage, 1966.

*LYFORD, JOSEPH P. *The Airtight Cage: A Study of New York's West Side.* New York: Harper Colophon, 1968.

Report of the National Advisory Commission on Civil Disorders. New York: Bantam, 1968.

The Challenge of Crime in a Free Society: A Report by the President's Commission on Law Enforcement and Administration of Justice. New York: Avon, 1968.

Ecology

*CARSON, RACHEL. *Silent Spring.* New York: Fawcett, 1962.

*DAY, LINCOLN H., AND ALICE TAYLOR DAY. *Too Many Americans.* New York: Delta, 1965.

*DE BELL, GARRETT (ed.). *The Environmental Handbook: Prepared for the First National Environmental Teach-In.* New York: Ballantine, 1970.

*EHRLICH, PAUL R. *The Population Bomb.* New York: Ballantine, 1968.

*MARX, WESLEY. *The Frail Ocean.* New York: Ballantine, 1969.

*RIENOW, ROBERT, AND LEONA TRAIN RIENOW. *Moment in the Sun: A Report on the Deteriorating Quality of the American Environment.* New York: Ballantine, 1967.

Vietnam

*CHOMSKY, NOAM. *American Power and the New Mandarins.* New York: Vintage, 1969.

*FULBRIGHT, J. WILLIAM. *The Arrogance of Power.* New York: Vintage, 1966.

*GETTLEMAN, MARVIN E. (ed.). *Vietnam: History, Documents, and Opinions on a Major World Crisis.* New York: Fawcett, 1965.

HOOPES, TOWNSEND. *The Limits of Intervention*. New York: McKay, 1969.

*MENASHE, LEWIS, AND RONALD RADOSH (eds.). *Teach-Ins: U.S.A.* New York: Praeger, 1967.

*SCHELL, JONATHAN. *The Military Half*. New York: Vintage, 1968.

*SCHLESINGER, ARTHUR, JR. *The Bitter Heritage*. New York: Fawcett, 1966.

The Military-Industrial Complex

*BARNET, RICHARD J. *The Economy of Death*. New York: Atheneum, 1969.

*COFFIN, TRISTAM. *The Armed Society: Militarism in Modern America*. Baltimore, Md.: Penguin, 1964.

*COOK, FRED J. *The Warfare State*. New York: Collier, 1964.

*GALBRAITH, JOHN KENNETH. *How to Control the Military*. New York: Signet, 1969.

*MELMAN, SEYMOUR. *Our Depleted Society*. New York: Delta, 1966.

University Unrest

*COHEN, MITCHELL, AND DENNIS HALE (eds.). *The New Student Left*. Boston: Beacon, 1967.

Crisis at Columbia: Report of the Fact-Finding Commission Appointed to Investigate the Disturbances at Columbia University in April and May 1968. New York: Vintage, 1968.

*DRAPER, HAL. *Berkeley: The New Student Revolt*. New York: Grove Press, 1965.

*KENNAN, GEORGE F. *Democracy and the Student Left*. New York: Bantam, 1968.

*KUNEN, JAMES SIMON. *The Strawberry Statement: Notes of a College Revolutionary*. New York: Avon, 1970.

*LIPSET, SEYMOUR MARTIN, AND SHELDON S. WOLIN (eds.). *The Berkeley Student Revolt: Facts and Interpretations*. New York: Anchor, 1965.

The Economy

*BAZELON, DAVID T. *The Paper Economy*. New York: Vintage, 1963.

*GALBRAITH, JOHN KENNETH. *The Affluent Society*. New York: Mentor, 1958.

MISHAN, EZRA J. *The Costs of Economic Growth*. New York: Praeger, 1967.

*PACKARD, VANCE. *The Waste Makers*. New York: Pocket Books, 1963.

*THEOBOLD, ROBERT. *The Challenge of Abundance*. New York: Mentor, 1962.

Poverty

*BAGDIKAN, BEN H. *In the Midst of Plenty: A New Report on the Poor in America*. New York: Signet, 1964.

*DONOVAN, JOHN C. *The Politics of Poverty*. New York: Pegasus, 1967.

*HARRINGTON, MICHAEL. *The Other America*. Baltimore, Md.: Penguin, 1963.

*KOLKO, GABRIEL. *Wealth and Power in America*. New York: Praeger, 1962.

*MILLER, HERMAN. *Rich Man, Poor Man*. New York: Signet, 1964.

*WAXMAN, CHAIM I. (ed.). *Poverty: Power and Politics*. New York: Grosset and Dunlap, 1968.

Consumer Affairs

COX, EDWARD F., ROBERT C. FELLMETH, AND JOHN E. SCHULZ. *"The Nader Report" on the Federal Trade Commission*. New York: Baron, 1969.

*KEFAUVER, ESTES. *In a Few Hands: Monopoly Power in America*. Baltimore, Md.: Penguin, 1965.

MAGNUSON, WARREN, AND JEAN CARPER. *The Dark Side of the Marketplace*. Englewood Cliffs, N.J.: Prentice-Hall, 1968.

METCALF, LEE, AND VIC REINEMER. *Overcharge*. New York: McKay, 1967.

*NADER, RALPH. *Unsafe at Any Speed.* New York: Pocket Books, 1966.

*PACKARD, VANCE. *The Hidden Persuaders.* New York: Pocket Books, 1958.

Corporations

BARBER, RICHARD J. *The American Corporation: Its Power, Its Money, Its Politics.* New York: Dutton, 1970.

*GALBRAITH, JOHN KENNETH. *The New Industrial State.* New York: Signet, 1968.

*HACKER, ANDREW (ed.). *The Corporation Take-Over.* New York: Anchor, 1965.

*MASON, EDWARD S. (ed.). *The Corporation in Modern Society.* Cambridge, Mass.: Harvard University Press, 1964.

*MOORE, WILBERT E. *The Conduct of the Corporation.* New York: Vintage, 1966.

*REAGAN, MICHAEL D. *The Managed Economy.* New York: Galaxy, 1967.

Miscellaneous

*GETTLEMAN, MARVIN E., AND DAVID MERMELSTEIN (eds.). *The Great Society Reader: The Failure of American Liberalism.* New York: Vintage, 1967.

*LEVINE, MARK, GEORGE C. MCNAMEE, AND DAVID GREENBERG (eds.). *The Tales of Hoffman: From the Trial of the Chicago Seven.* New York: Bantam, 1970.

**Rights in Conflict: The Walker Report to the National Commission on the Causes and Prevention of Violence.* New York: Signet, 1968.

**The Politics of Protest: The Skolnick Report to the National Commission on the Causes and Prevention of Violence.* New York: Ballantine, 1969.

Index